bad machinery

THE CASE OF
THE MISSING PIECE

AN ONI PRESS PUBLICATION

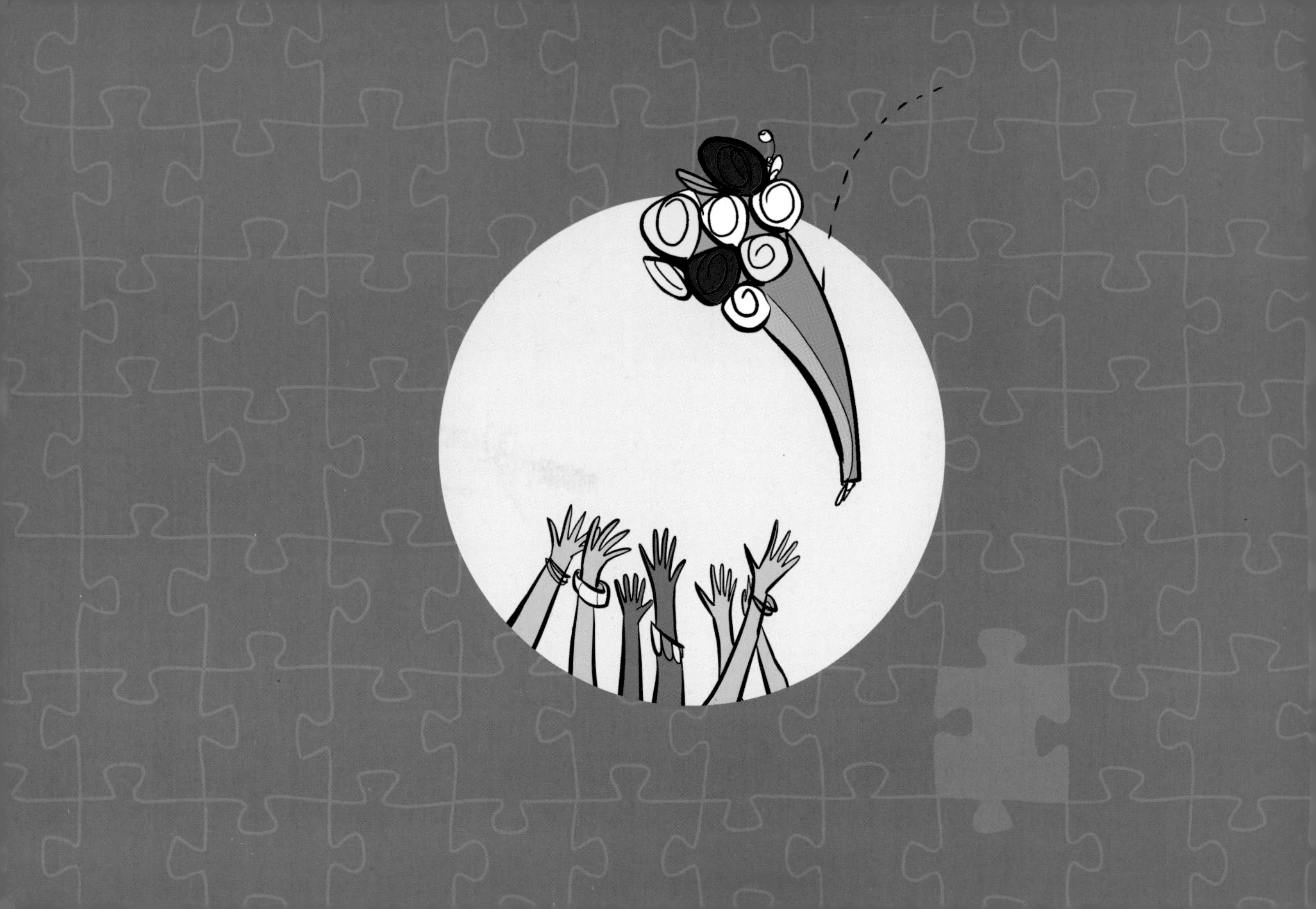

bad machinery

THE CASE OF THE MISSING PIECE

by
John Allison

Edited by
Ari Yarwood

Designed by
**Hilary Thompson
& Sonja Synak**

PUBLISHED BY ONI PRESS INC.

founder & chief financial officer **Joe Nozemack**
publisher **James Lucas Jones**
editor in chief **Sarah Gaydos**
v.p. of creative & business development **Charlie Chu**
director of operations **Brad Rooks**
director of sales **Margot Wood**
special projects manager **Amber O'Neill**
director of design & production **Troy Look**
digital prepress lead **Angie Knowles**
senior graphic designer **Kate Z. Stone**
graphic designer **Sonja Synak**
graphic designer **Hilary Thompson**
senior editor **Robin Herrera**
executive assistant **Michelle Nguyen**
logistics coordinator **Jung Lee**

onipress.com
facebook.com/onipress
twitter.com/onipress
onipress.tumblr.com
instagram.com/onipress

scarygoround.com

First Edition: January 2020

ISBN 978-1-62010-668-6
eISBN 978-1-62010-696-9

Library of Congress Control Number: 2019939959

1 2 3 4 5 6 7 8 9 10

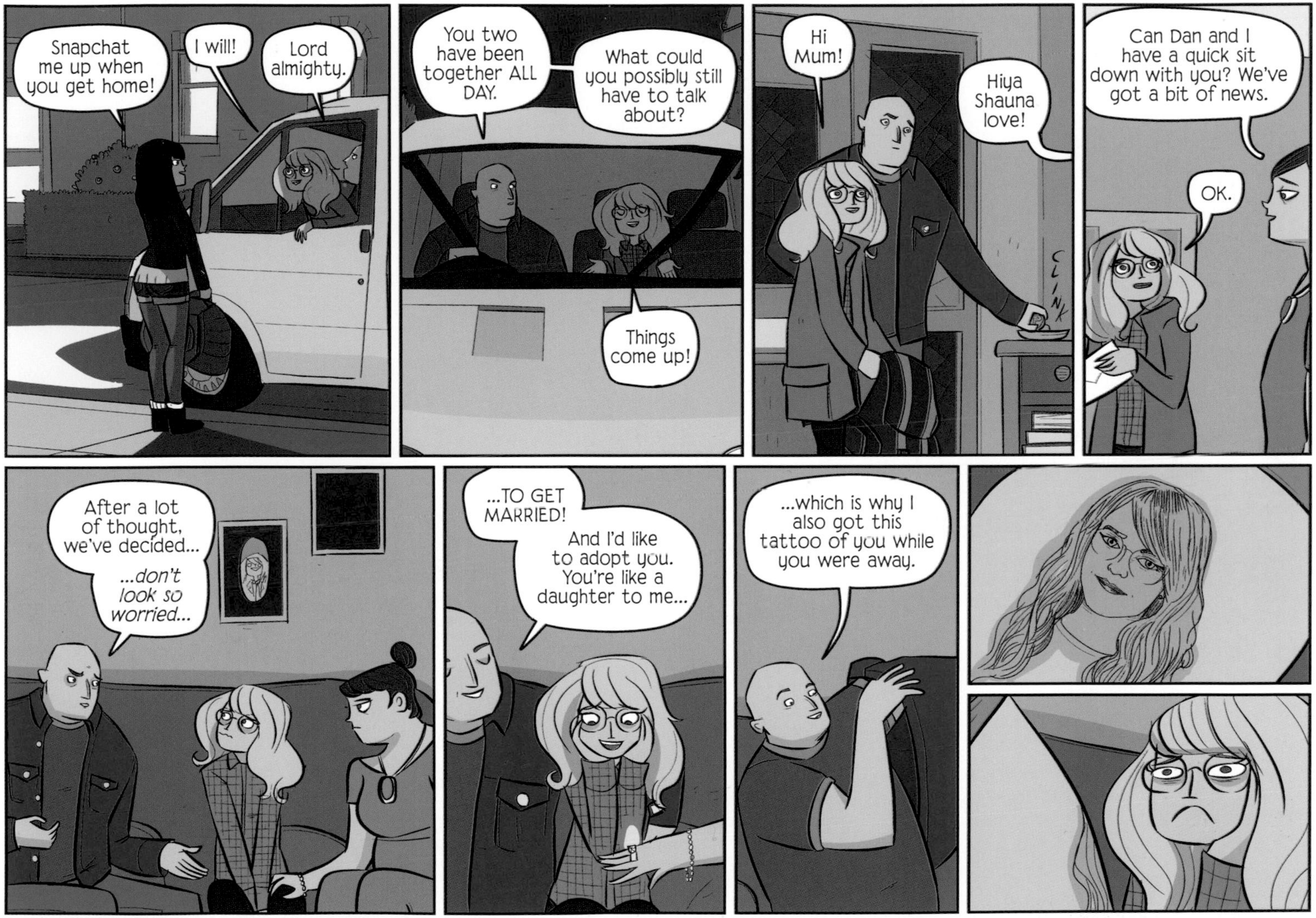
Snapchat me up when you get home!
I will!
Lord almighty.
You two have been together ALL DAY.
What could you possibly still have to talk about?
Things come up!
Hi Mum!
Hiya Shauna love!
CLINK
Can Dan and I have a quick sit down with you? We've got a bit of news.
OK.
After a lot of thought, we've decided...
...don't look so worried...
...TO GET MARRIED!
And I'd like to adopt you. You're like a daughter to me...
...which is why I also got this tattoo of you while you were away.

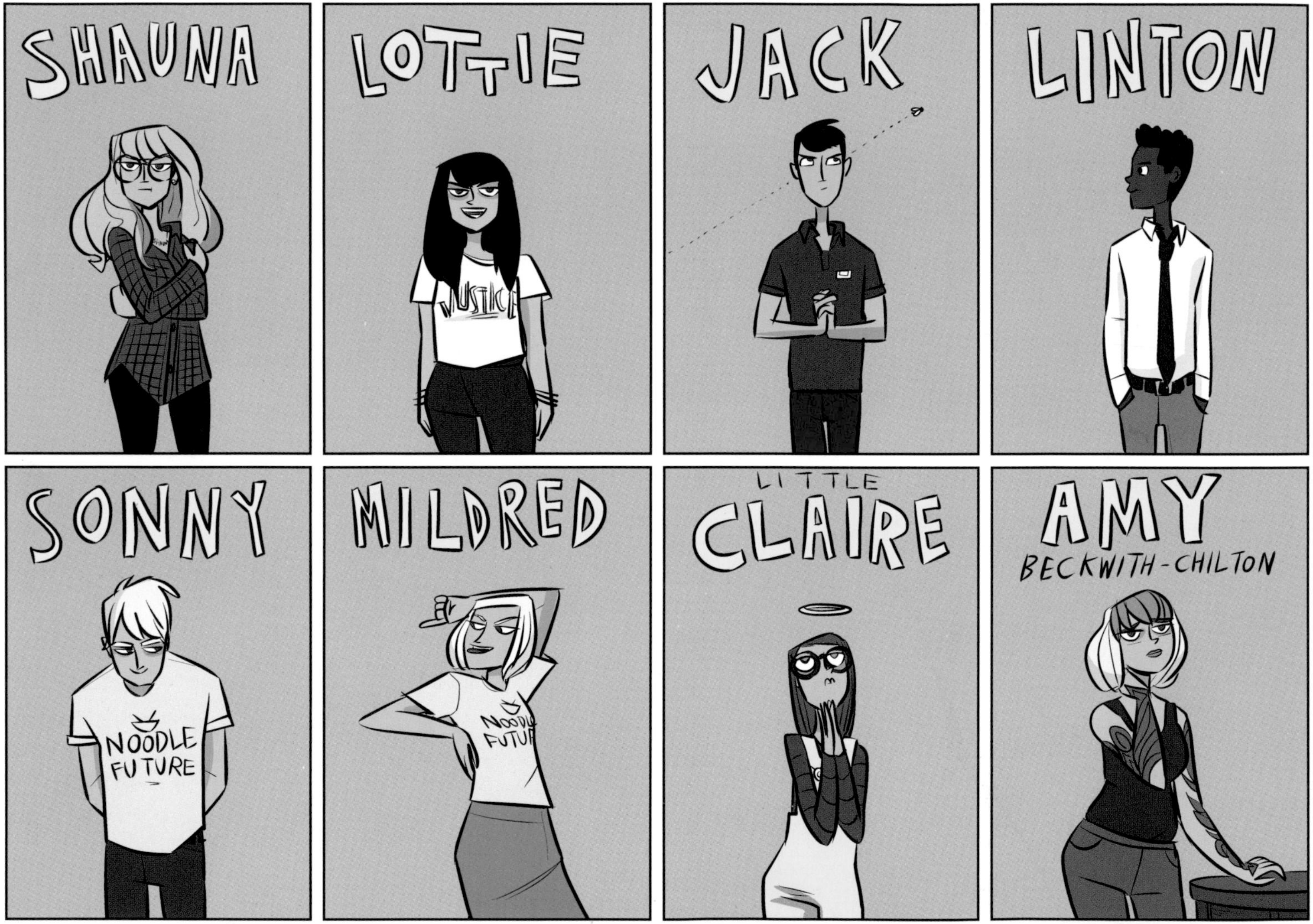
SHAUNA
LOTTIE
JUSTICE
JACK
LINTON
SONNY
NOODLE FUTURE
MILDRED
LITTLE CLAIRE
AMY BECKWITH-CHILTON

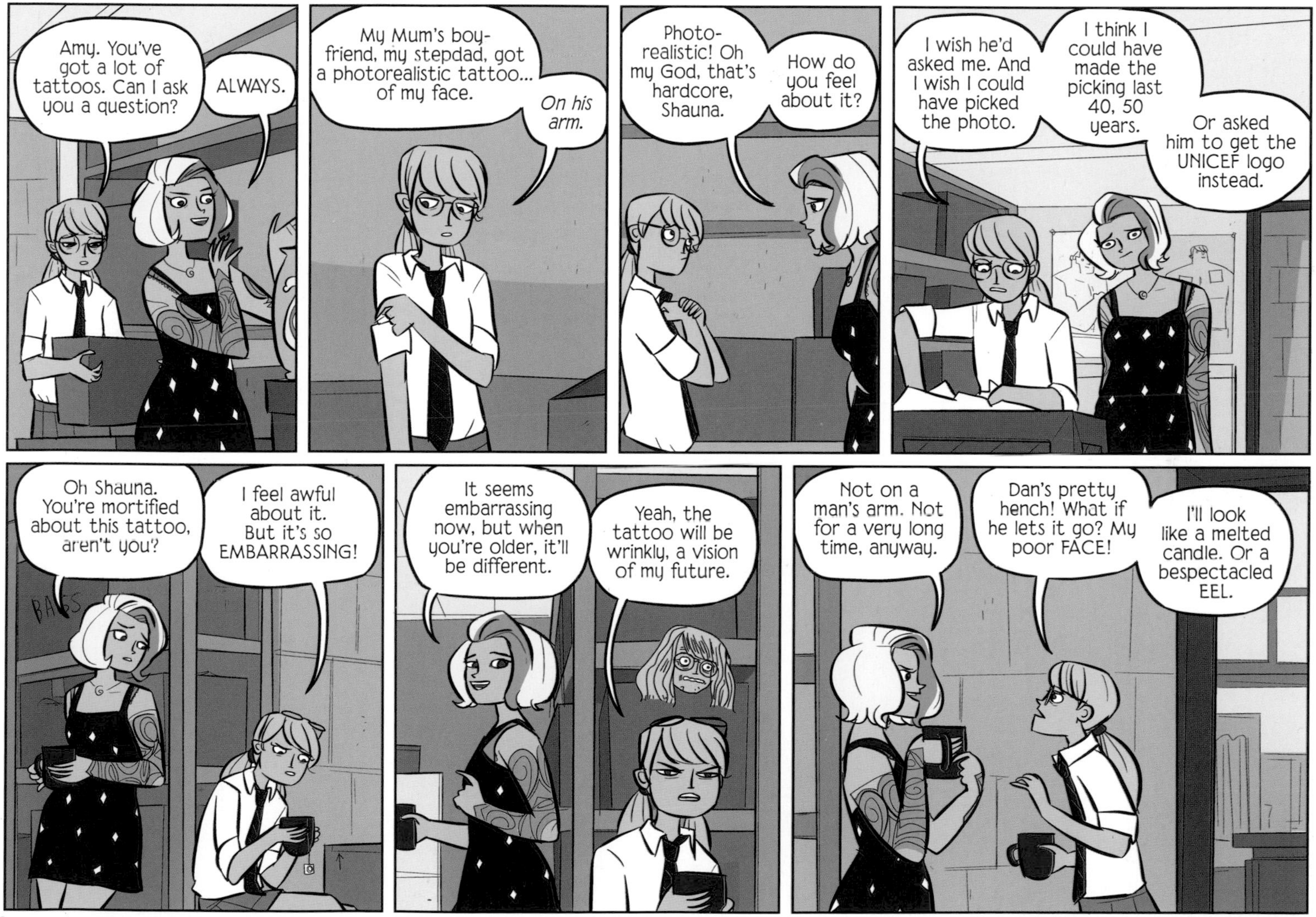
Amy. You've got a lot of tattoos. Can I ask you a question?
ALWAYS.
My Mum's boyfriend, my stepdad, got a photorealistic tattoo... of my face.
On his arm.
Photo-realistic! Oh my God, that's hardcore, Shauna.
How do you feel about it?
I wish he'd asked me. And I wish I could have picked the photo.
I think I could have made the picking last 40, 50 years.
Or asked him to get the UNICEF logo instead.
Oh Shauna. You're mortified about this tattoo, aren't you?
I feel awful about it. But it's so EMBARRASSING!
It seems embarrassing now, but when you're older, it'll be different.
Yeah, the tattoo will be wrinkly, a vision of my future.
Not on a man's arm. Not for a very long time, anyway.
Dan's pretty hench! What if he lets it go? My poor FACE!
I'll look like a melted candle. Or a bespectacled EEL.

THE CASE OF THE MISSING PIECE.

Dan and your Mum are getting married?
Actually, I thought they *were married.*
No.
Would you have to take his surname?
I suppose! He wants to adopt me. I'd be... Shauna FINSTER.
I'm SHAUNA FINSTER.
HAND MODEL. WINE EXPERT.
Shauna FInster, rear of the year. Pleased to meet you.
Shauna Finster, bounty hunter.
You're coming with me, Jack. Dead or alive.
Shauna Finster is COMPLICATED!

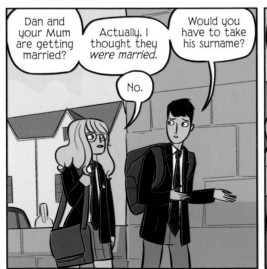

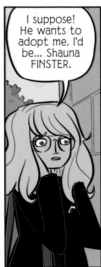

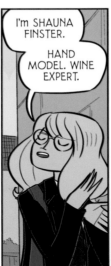

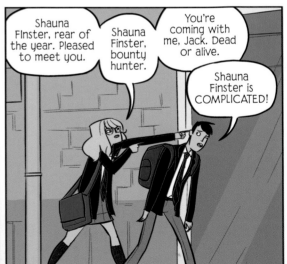

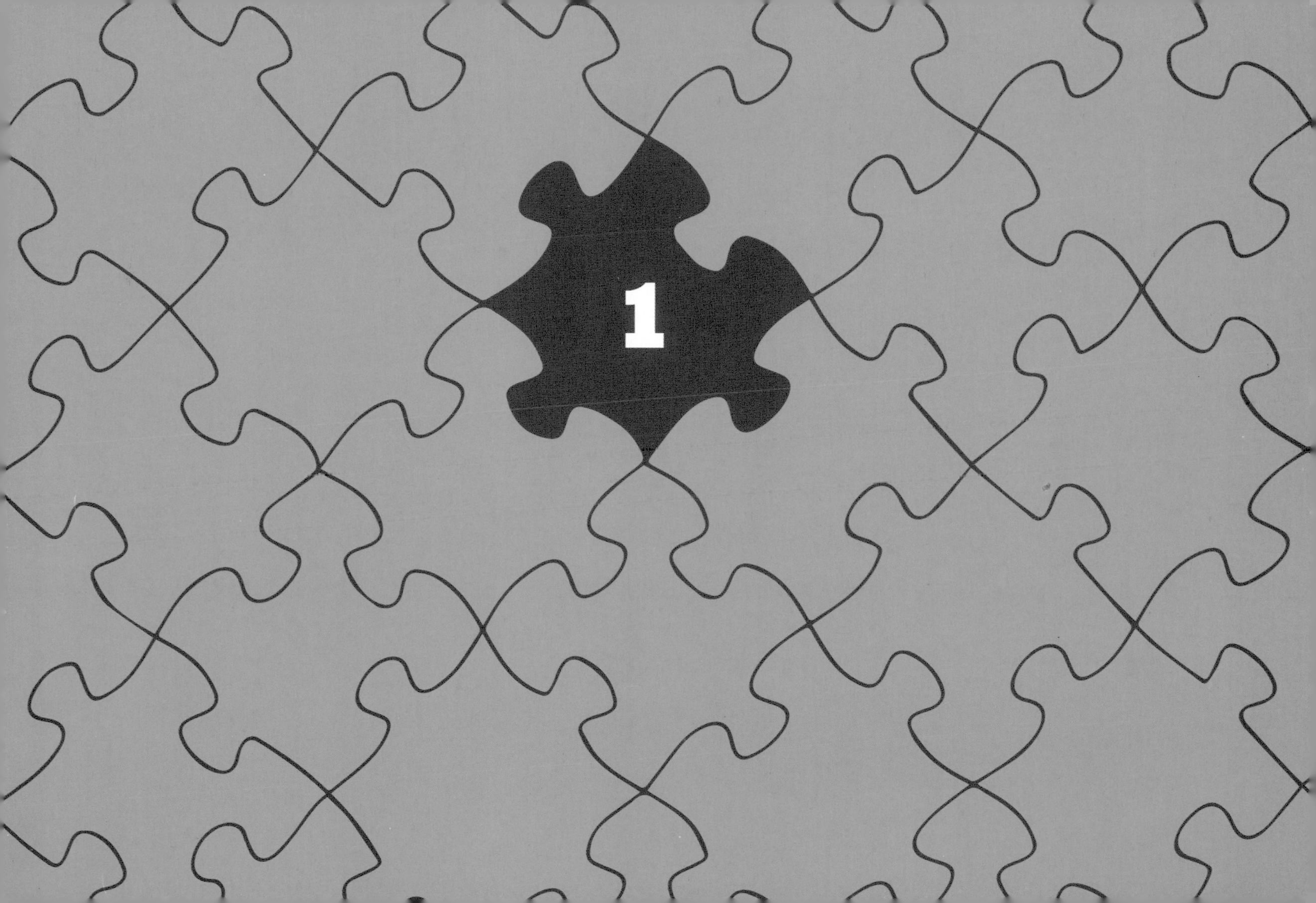
1

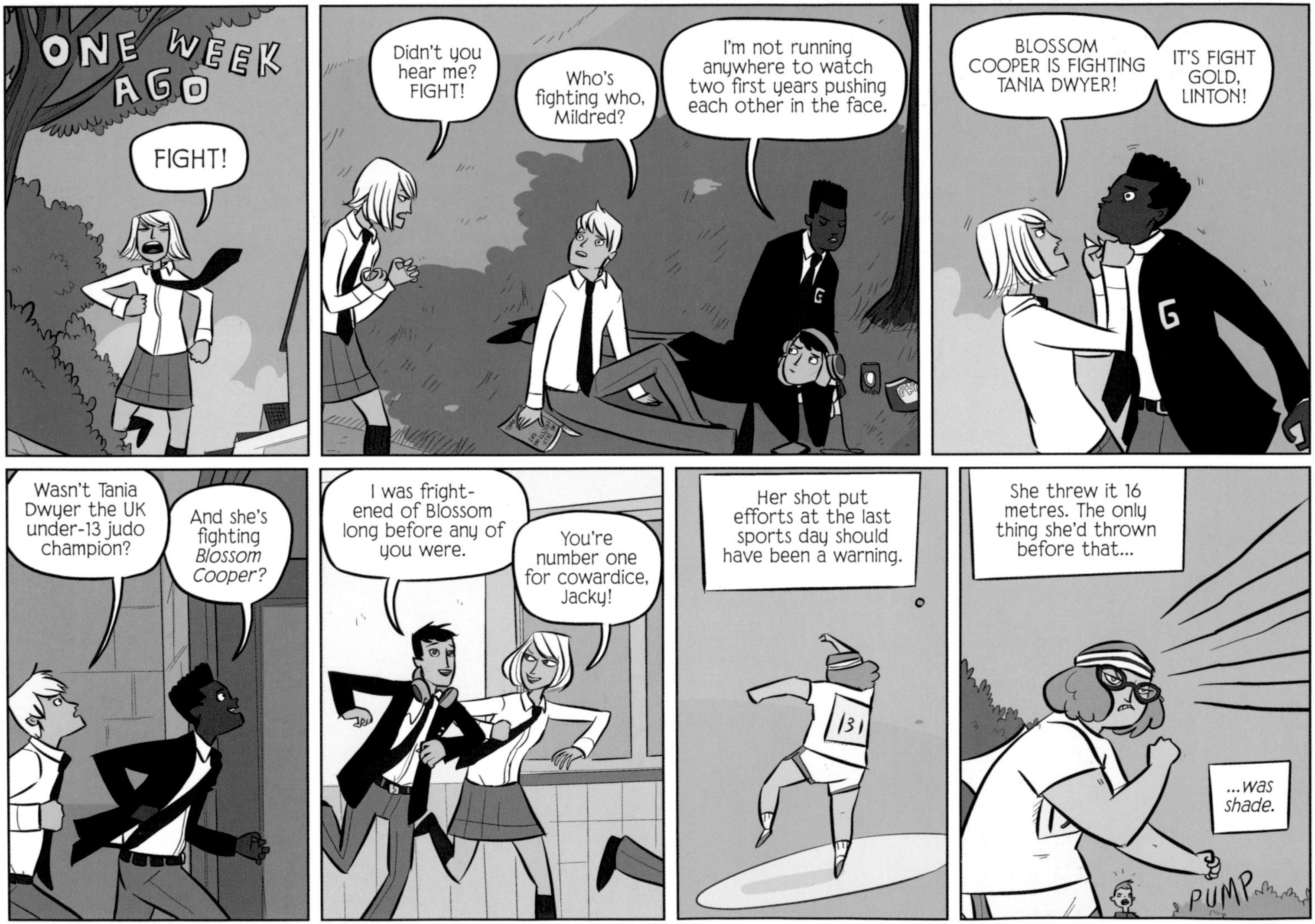
ONE WEEK AGO
FIGHT!
Didn't you hear me? FIGHT!
Who's fighting who, Mildred?
I'm not running anywhere to watch two first years pushing each other in the face.
BLOSSOM COOPER IS FIGHTING TANIA DWYER!
IT'S FIGHT GOLD, LINTON!
Wasn't Tania Dwyer the UK under-13 judo champion?
And she's fighting *Blossom Cooper?*
I was fright-ened of Blossom long before any of you were.
You're number one for cowardice, Jacky!
Her shot put efforts at the last sports day should have been a warning.
She threw it 16 metres. The only thing she'd thrown before that...
...*was shade.*
PUMP

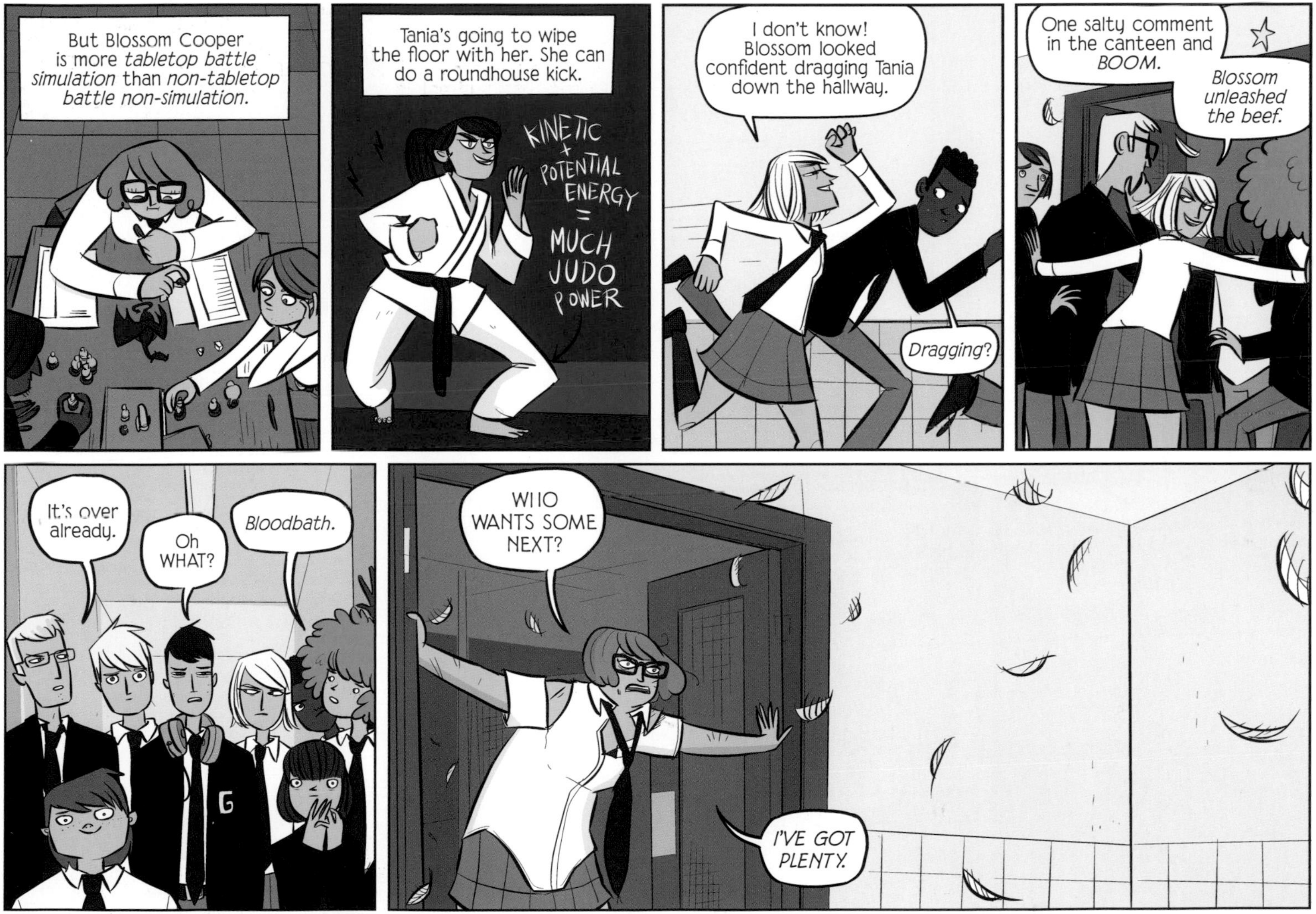
But Blossom Cooper is more *tabletop battle simulation* than *non-tabletop battle non-simulation.*
Tania's going to wipe the floor with her. She can do a roundhouse kick.
KINETIC + POTENTIAL ENERGY = MUCH JUDO POWER
I don't know! Blossom looked confident dragging Tania down the hallway.
Dragging?
One salty comment in the canteen and *BOOM.*
Blossom unleashed the beef.
It's over already.
Oh WHAT?
Bloodbath.
WHO WANTS SOME NEXT?
I'VE GOT PLENTY.

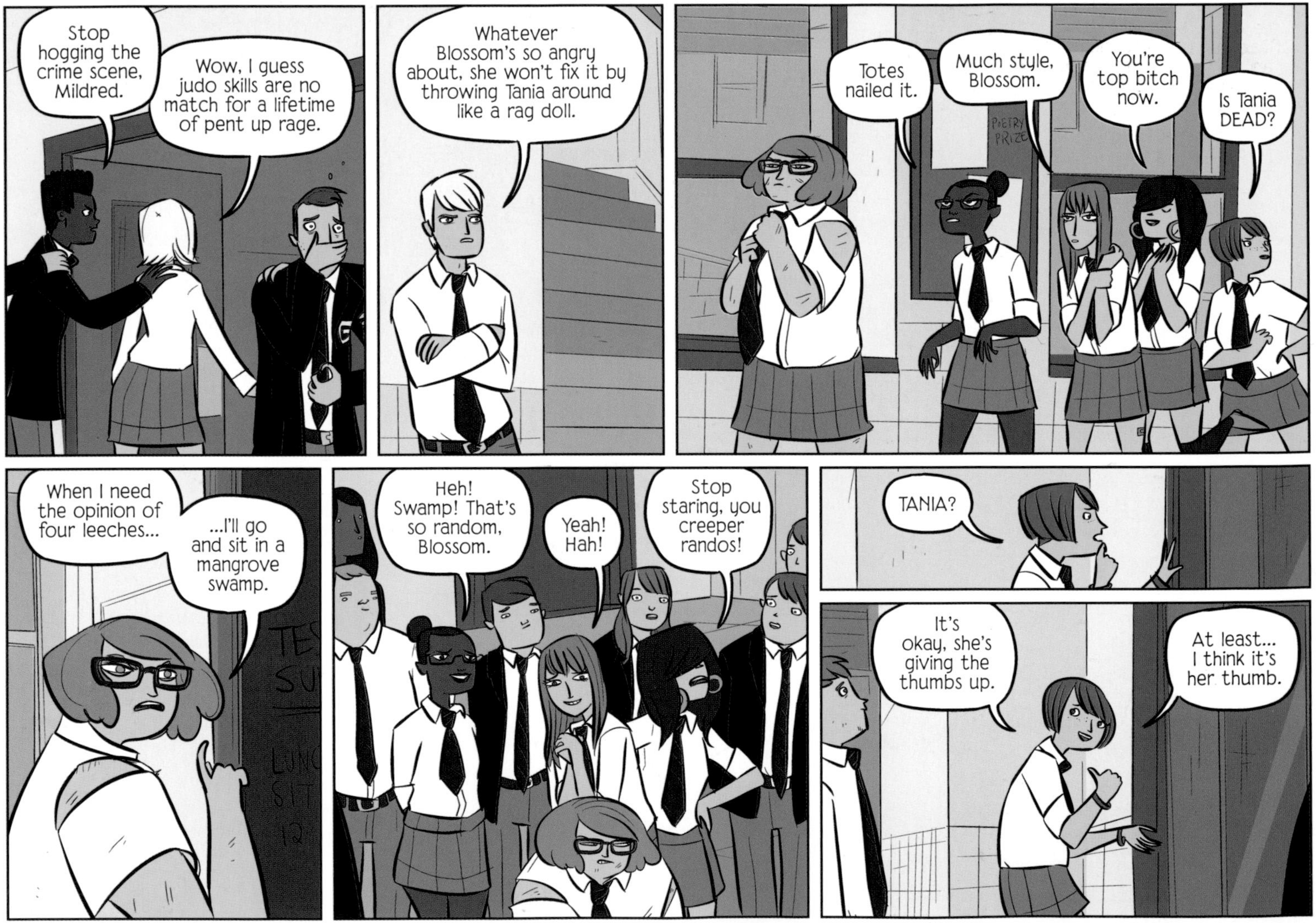
Stop hogging the crime scene, Mildred.
Wow, I guess judo skills are no match for a lifetime of pent up rage.
Whatever Blossom's so angry about, she won't fix it by throwing Tania around like a rag doll.
Totes nailed it.
Much style, Blossom.
You're top bitch now.
Is Tania DEAD?
POETRY PRIZE
When I need the opinion of four leeches...
...I'll go and sit in a mangrove swamp.
Heh! Swamp! That's so random, Blossom.
Yeah! Hah!
Stop staring, you creeper randos!
TANIA?
It's okay, she's giving the thumbs up.
At least... I think it's her thumb.

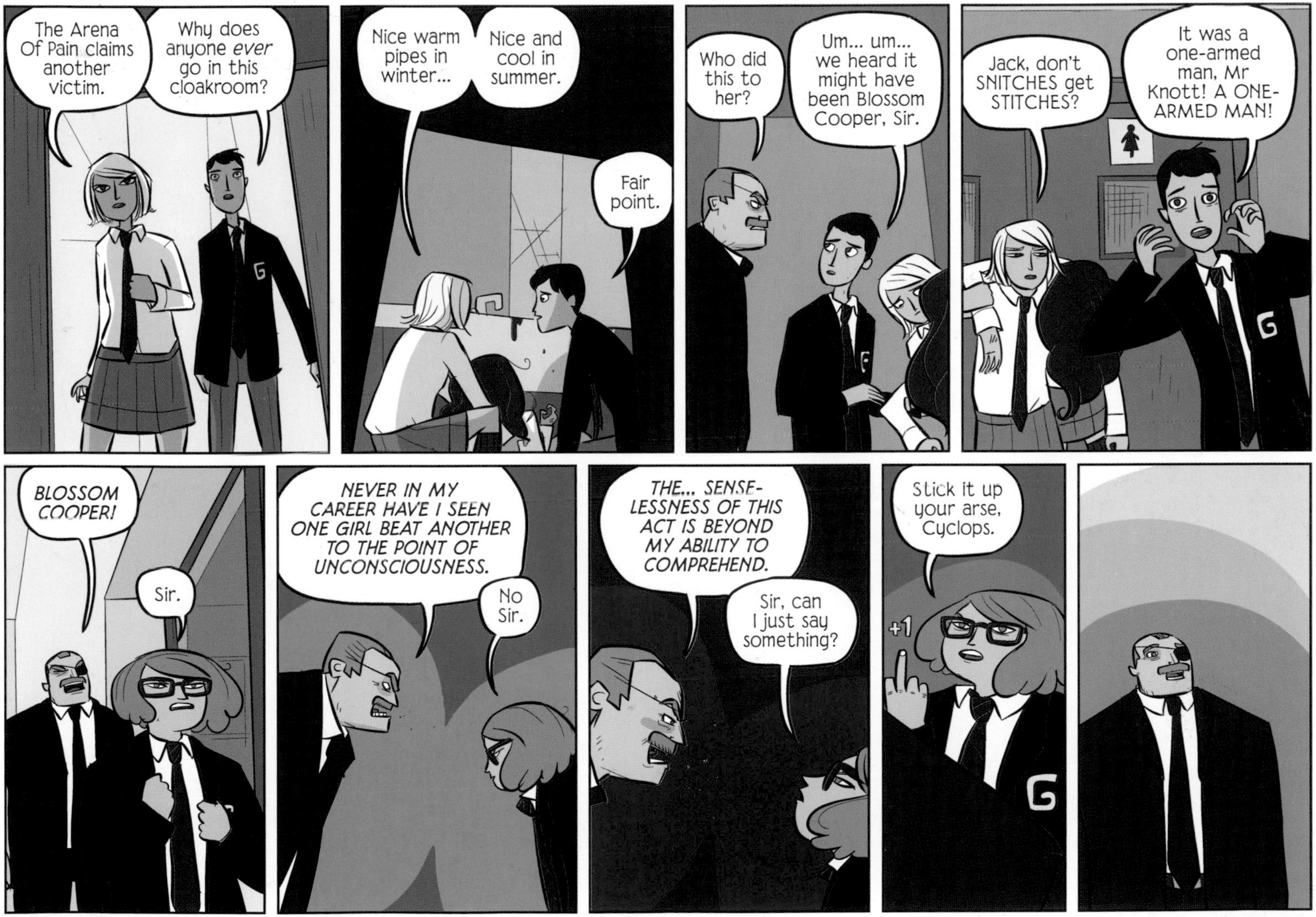
The Arena Of Pain claims another victim.
Why does anyone *ever* go in this cloakroom?
Nice warm pipes in winter...
Nice and cool in summer.
Fair point.
Who did this to her?
Um... um... we heard it might have been Blossom Cooper, Sir.
Jack, don't SNITCHES get STITCHES?
It was a one-armed man, Mr Knott! A ONE-ARMED MAN!
BLOSSOM COOPER!
Sir.
NEVER IN MY CAREER HAVE I SEEN ONE GIRL BEAT ANOTHER TO THE POINT OF UNCONSCIOUSNESS.
No Sir.
THE... SENSE-LESSNESS OF THIS ACT IS BEYOND MY ABILITY TO COMPREHEND.
Sir, can I just say something?
Stick it up your arse, Cyclops.
+1

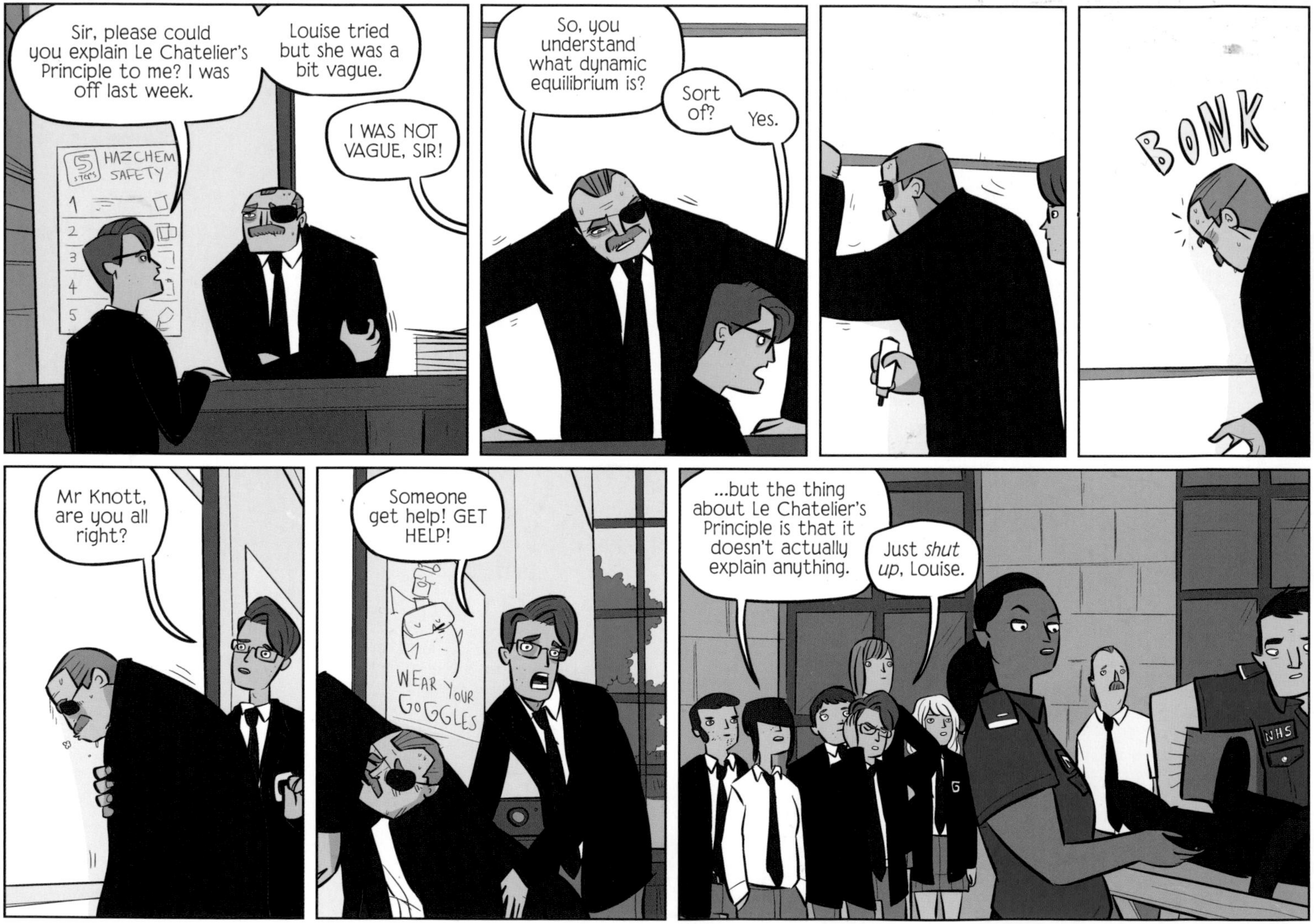
Sir, please could you explain Le Chatelier's Principle to me? I was off last week.
Louise tried but she was a bit vague.
I WAS NOT VAGUE, SIR!
HAZCHEM SAFETY
So, you understand what dynamic equilibrium is?
Sort of?
Yes.
BONK
Mr Knott, are you all right?
Someone get help! GET HELP!
WEAR YOUR GOGGLES
...but the thing about Le Chatelier's Principle is that it doesn't actually explain anything.
Just *shut up*, Louise.
NHS

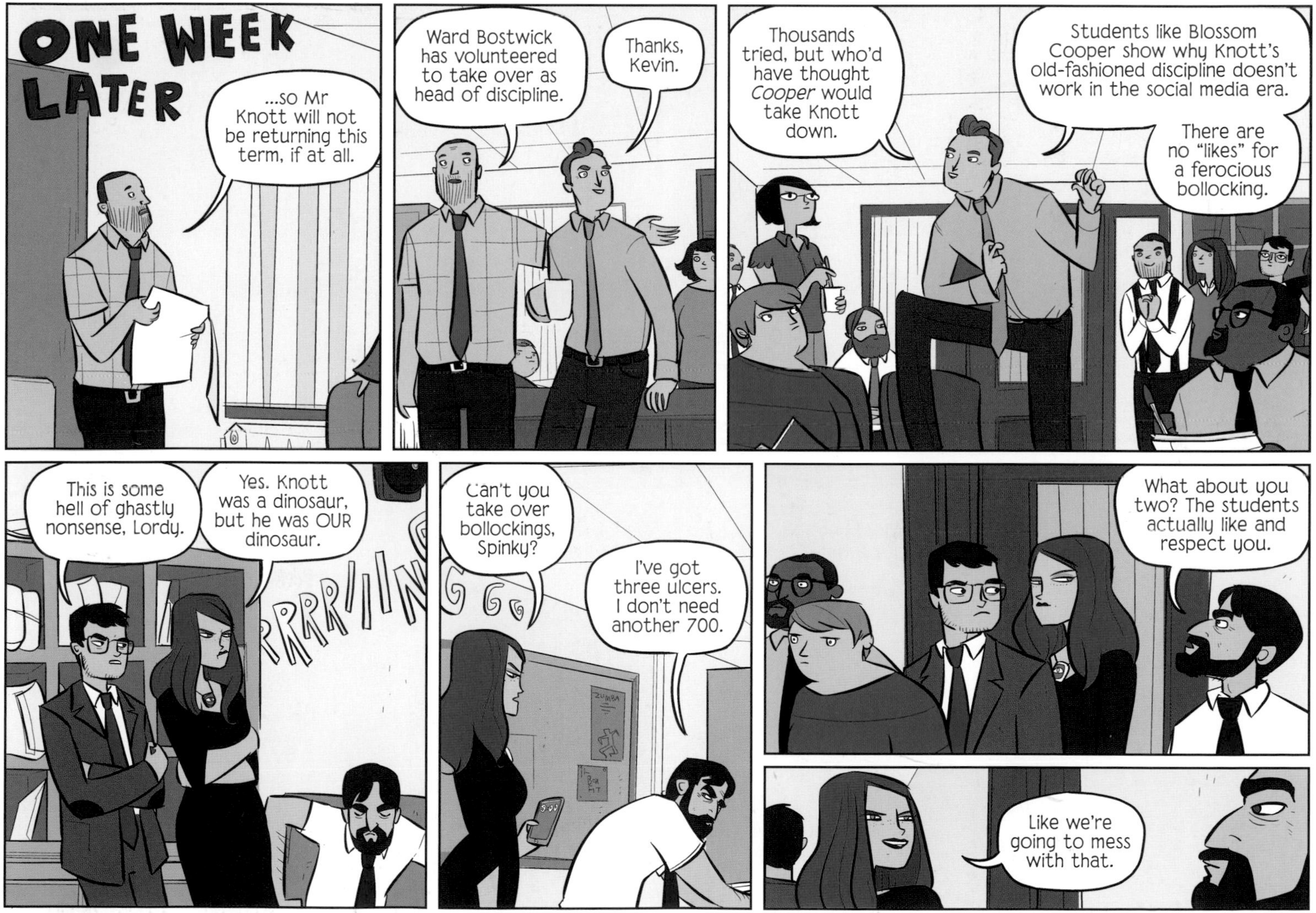
ONE WEEK LATER
...so Mr Knott will not be returning this term, if at all.
Ward Bostwick has volunteered to take over as head of discipline.
Thanks, Kevin.
Thousands tried, but who'd have thought *Cooper* would take Knott down.
Students like Blossom Cooper show why Knott's old-fashioned discipline doesn't work in the social media era.
There are no "likes" for a ferocious bollocking.
This is some hell of ghastly nonsense, Lordy.
Yes. Knott was a dinosaur, but he was OUR dinosaur.
RRRRIIINGGG
Can't you take over bollockings, Spinky?
I've got three ulcers. I don't need another 700.
What about you two? The students actually like and respect you.
Like we're going to mess with that.

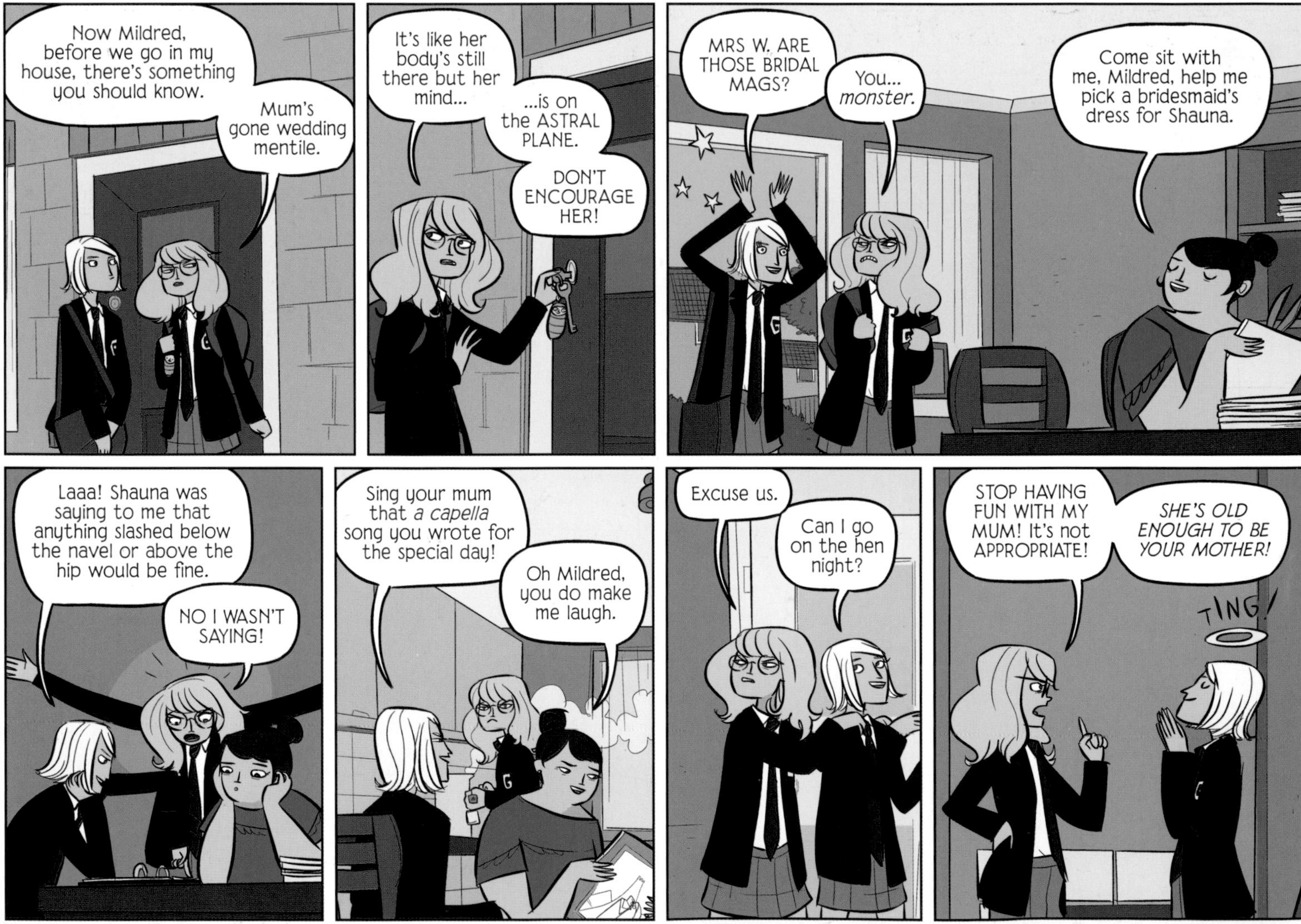
Now Mildred, before we go in my house, there's something you should know.
Mum's gone wedding mentile.
It's like her body's still there but her mind...
...is on the ASTRAL PLANE.
DON'T ENCOURAGE HER!
MRS W. ARE THOSE BRIDAL MAGS?
You... *monster.*
Come sit with me, Mildred, help me pick a bridesmaid's dress for Shauna.
Laaa! Shauna was saying to me that anything slashed below the navel or above the hip would be fine.
NO I WASN'T SAYING!
Sing your mum that *a capella* song you wrote for the special day!
Oh Mildred, you do make me laugh.
Excuse us.
Can I go on the hen night?
STOP HAVING FUN WITH MY MUM! It's not APPROPRIATE!
SHE'S OLD ENOUGH TO BE YOUR MOTHER!
TING!

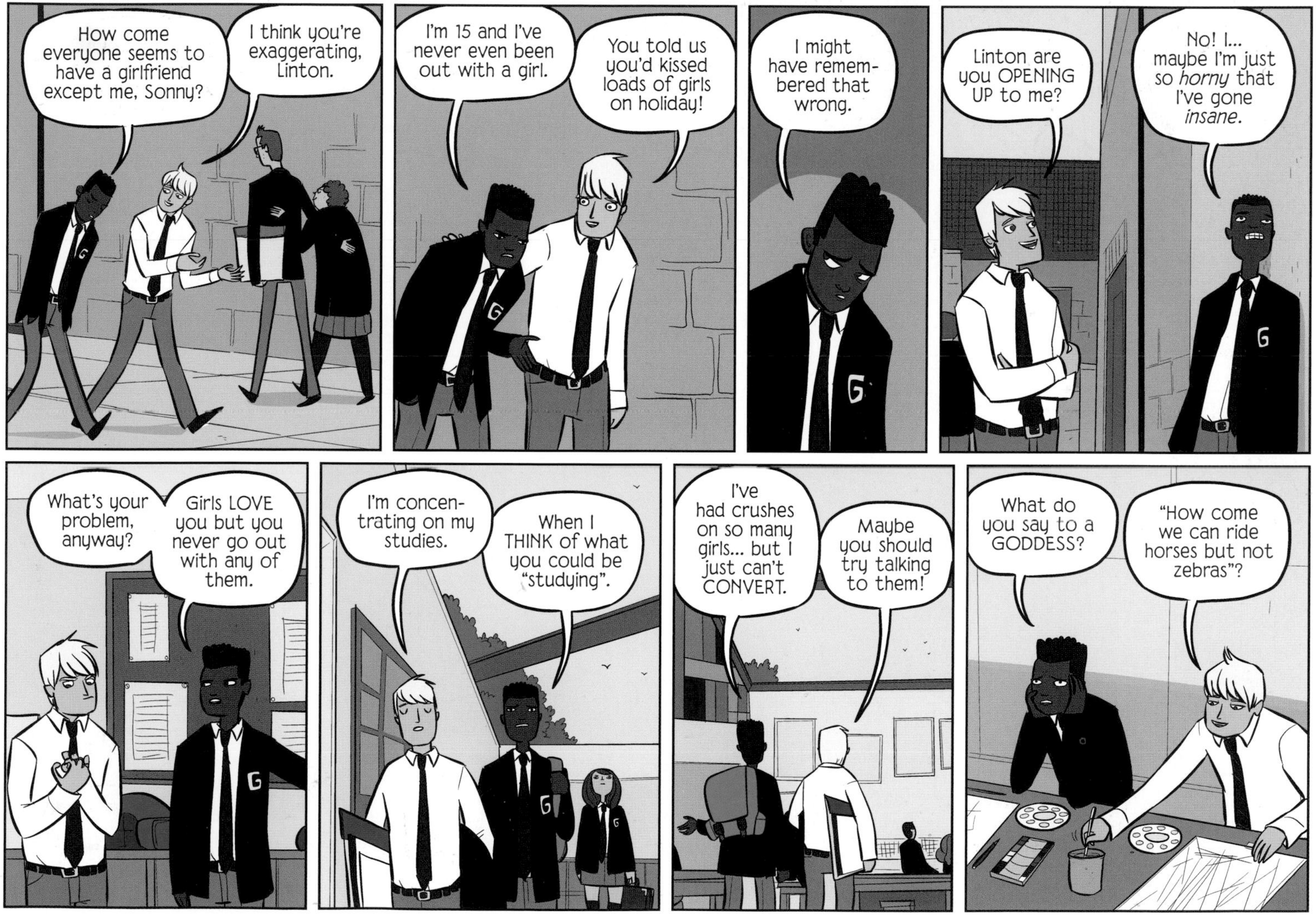
How come everyone seems to have a girlfriend except me, Sonny?
I think you're exaggerating, Linton.
I'm 15 and I've never even been out with a girl.
You told us you'd kissed loads of girls on holiday!
I might have remem-bered that wrong.
Linton are you OPENING UP to me?
No! I... maybe I'm just so *horny* that I've gone *insane*.
What's your problem, anyway?
Girls LOVE you but you never go out with any of them.
I'm concen-trating on my studies.
When I THINK of what you could be "studying".
I've had crushes on so many girls... but I just can't CONVERT.
Maybe you should try talking to them!
What do you say to a GODDESS?
"How come we can ride horses but not zebras"?

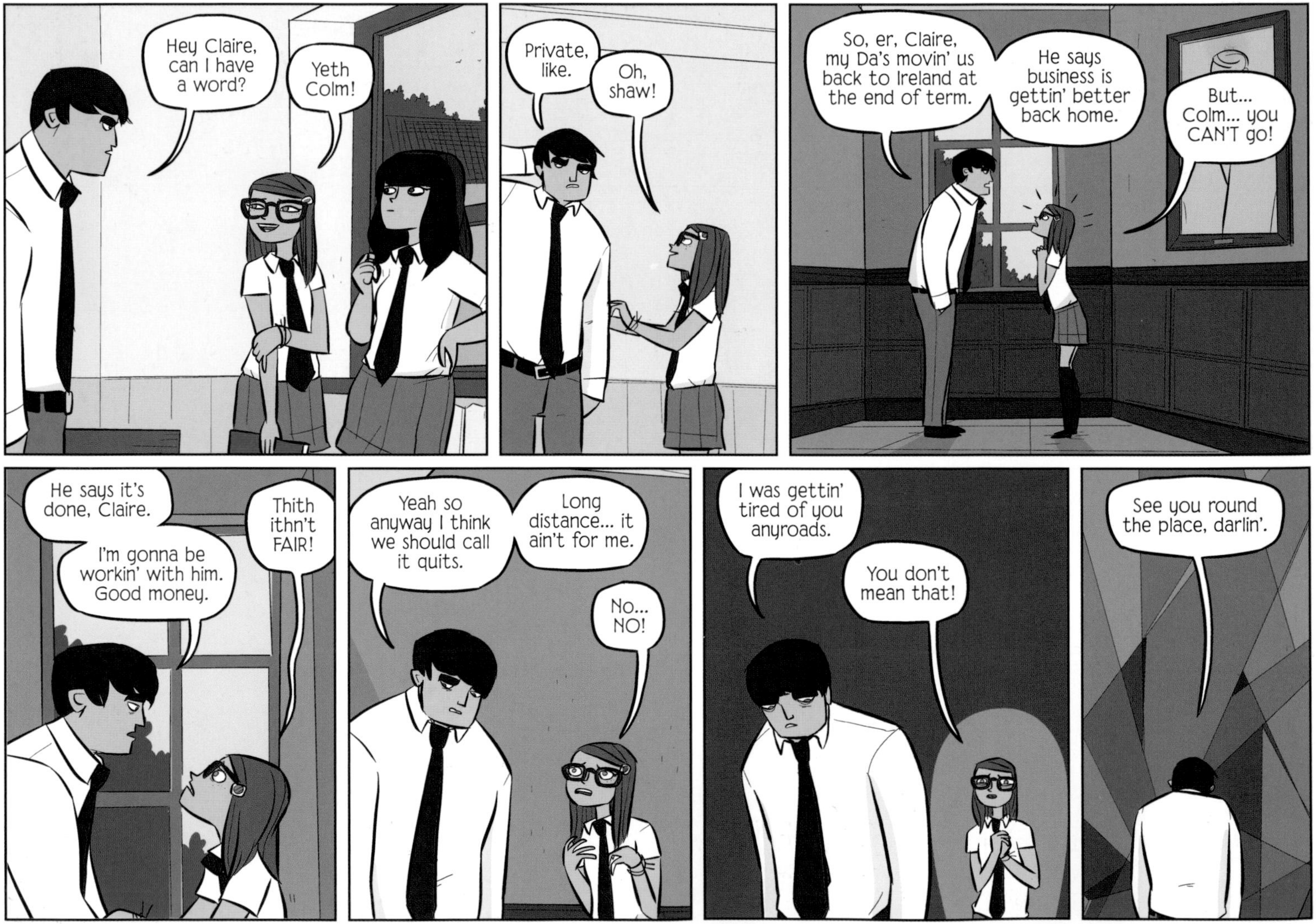
Hey Claire, can I have a word?
Yeth Colm!
Private, like.
Oh, shaw!
So, er, Claire, my Da's movin' us back to Ireland at the end of term.
He says business is gettin' better back home.
But... Colm... you CAN'T go!
He says it's done, Claire.
I'm gonna be workin' with him. Good money.
Thith ithn't FAIR!
Yeah so anyway I think we should call it quits.
Long distance... it ain't for me.
No... NO!
I was gettin' tired of you anyroads.
You don't mean that!
See you round the place, darlin'.

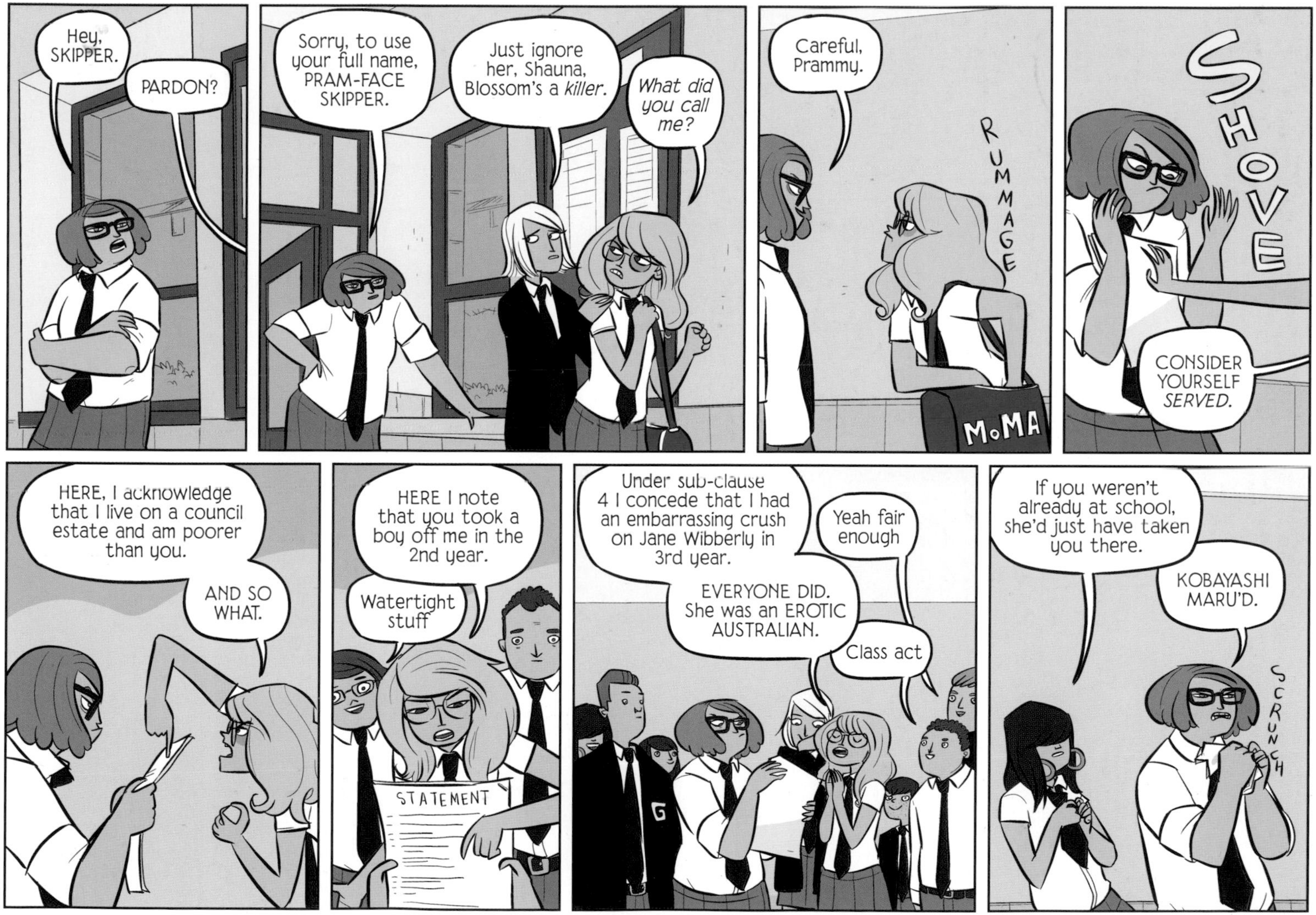
Hey, SKIPPER.
PARDON?
Sorry, to use your full name, PRAM-FACE SKIPPER.
Just ignore her, Shauna, Blossom's a *killer*.
What did you call me?
Careful, Prammy.
RUMMAGE
SHOVE
CONSIDER YOURSELF *SERVED*.
MoMA
HERE, I acknowledge that I live on a council estate and am poorer than you.
AND SO WHAT.
HERE I note that you took a boy off me in the 2nd year.
Watertight stuff
STATEMENT
Under sub-clause 4 I concede that I had an embarrassing crush on Jane Wibberly in 3rd year.
Yeah fair enough
EVERYONE DID. She was an EROTIC AUSTRALIAN.
Class act
G
If you weren't already at school, she'd just have taken you there.
KOBAYASHI MARU'D.
SCRUNCH

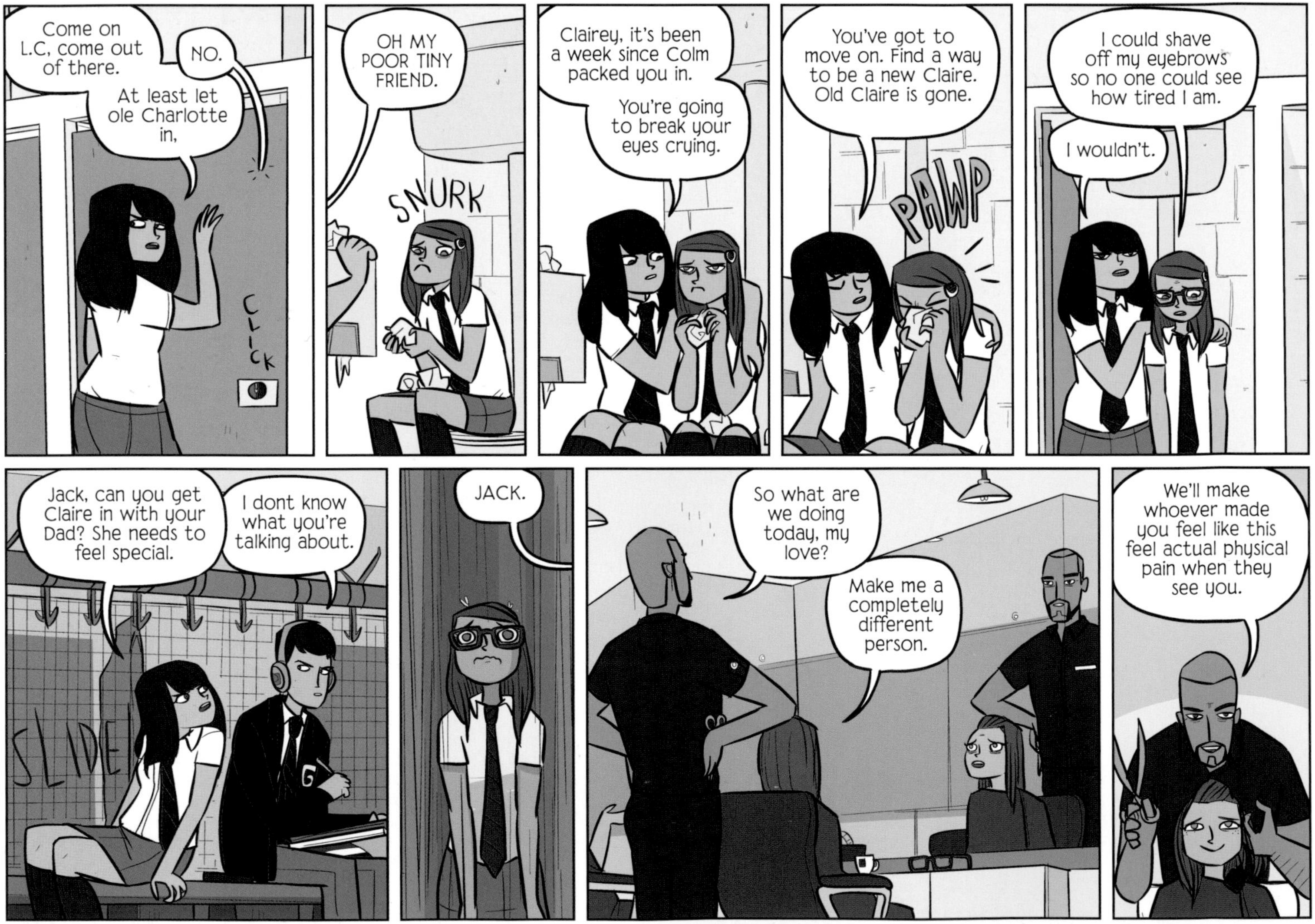
Come on L.C, come out of there.
NO.
At least let ole Charlotte in,
CLICK
OH MY POOR TINY FRIEND.
SNURK
Clairey, it's been a week since Colm packed you in.
You're going to break your eyes crying.
You've got to move on. Find a way to be a new Claire. Old Claire is gone.
PAWP
I could shave off my eyebrows so no one could see how tired I am.
I wouldn't.
Jack, can you get Claire in with your Dad? She needs to feel special.
I dont know what you're talking about.
SLIDE
JACK.
So what are we doing today, my love?
Make me a completely different person.
We'll make whoever made you feel like this feel actual physical pain when they see you.

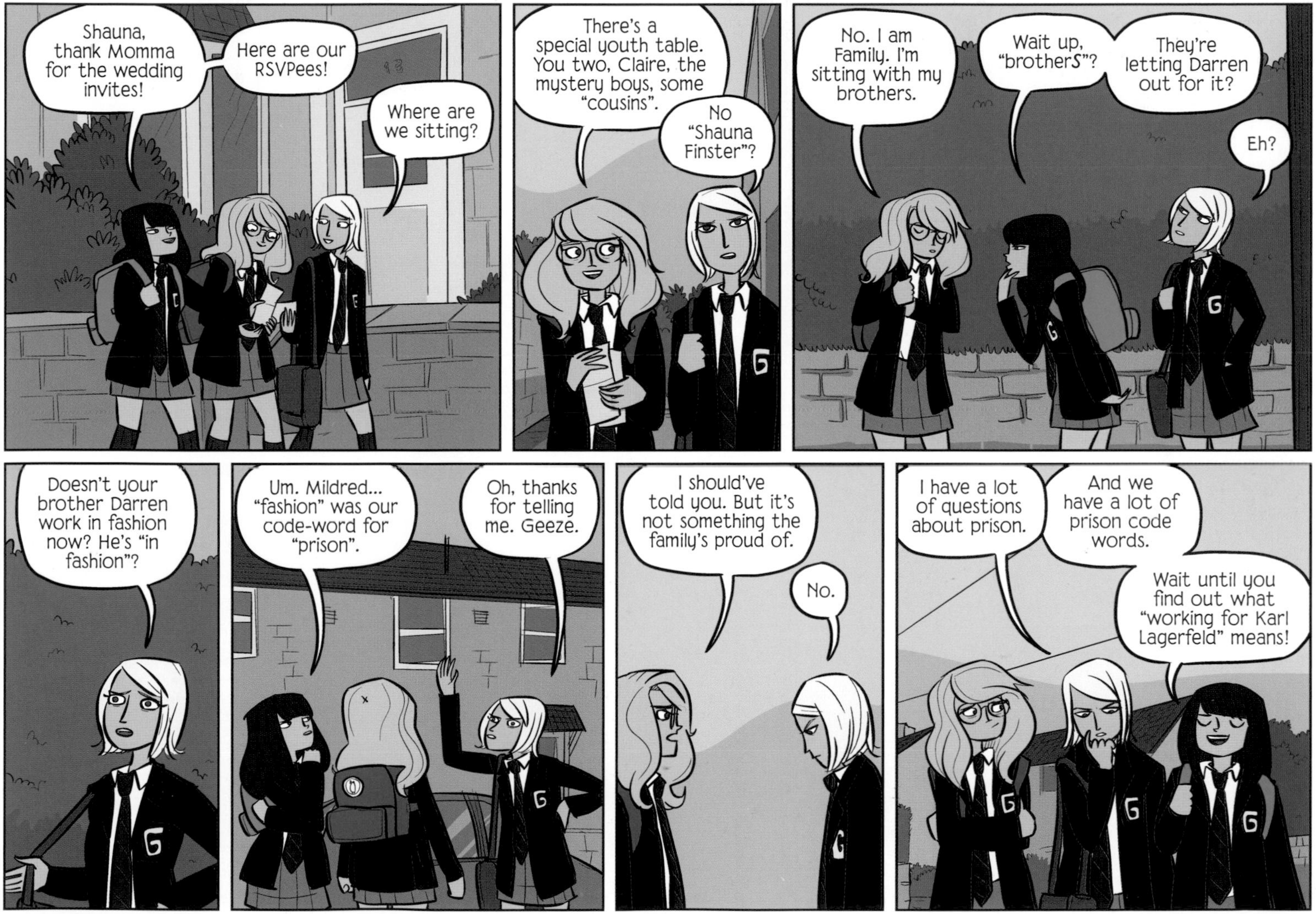
Shauna, thank Momma for the wedding invites!
Here are our RSVPees!
Where are we sitting?
There's a special youth table. You two, Claire, the mystery boys, some "cousins".
No "Shauna Finster"?
No. I am Family. I'm sitting with my brothers.
Wait up, "brotherS"?
They're letting Darren out for it?
Eh?
Doesn't your brother Darren work in fashion now? He's "in fashion"?
Um. Mildred... "fashion" was our code-word for "prison".
Oh, thanks for telling me. Geeze.
I should've told you. But it's not something the family's proud of.
No.
I have a lot of questions about prison.
And we have a lot of prison code words.
Wait until you find out what "working for Karl Lagerfeld" means!

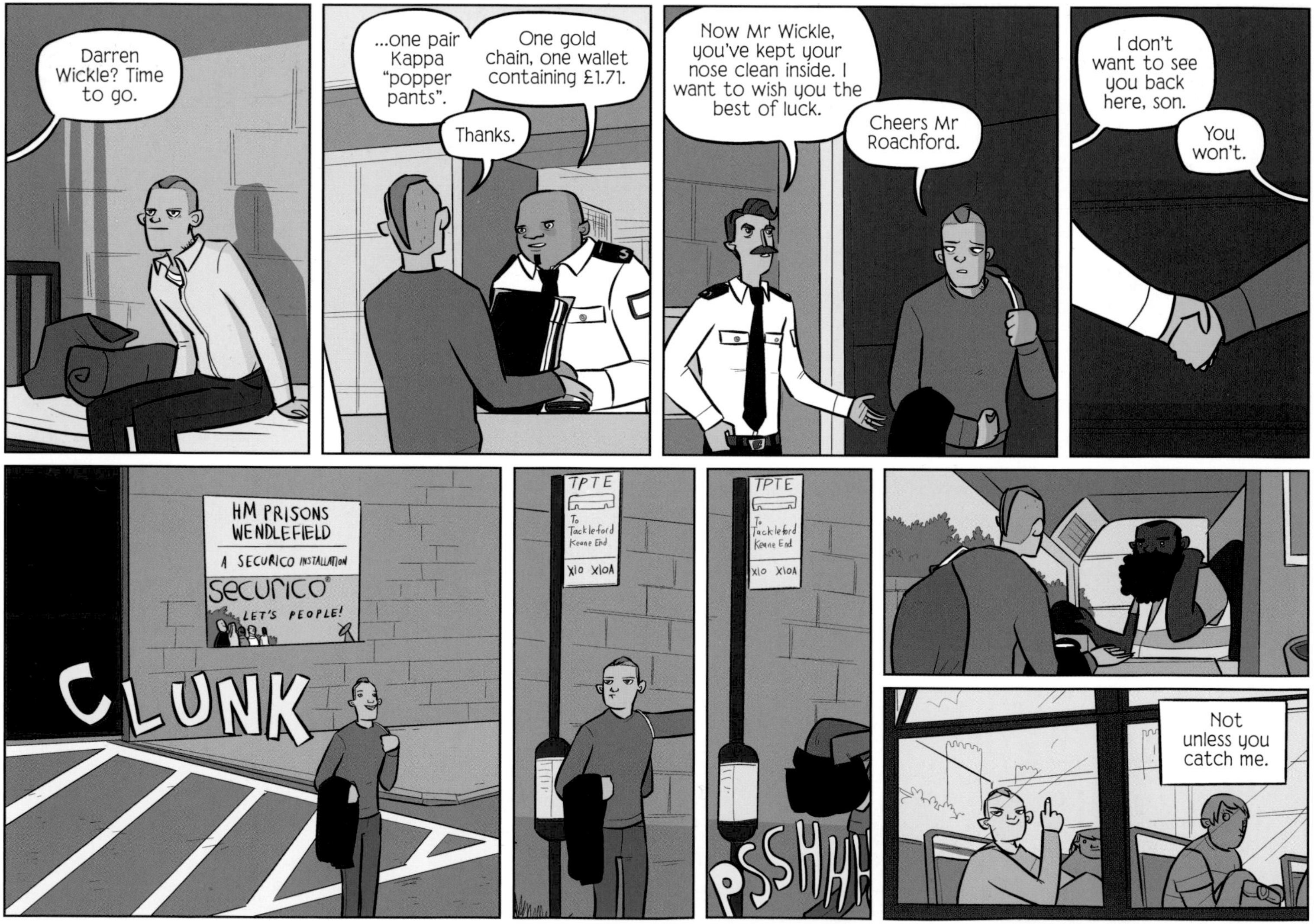
Darren Wickle? Time to go.
...one pair Kappa "popper pants".
One gold chain, one wallet containing £1.71.
Thanks.
Now Mr Wickle, you've kept your nose clean inside. I want to wish you the best of luck.
Cheers Mr Roachford.
I don't want to see you back here, son.
You won't.
HM PRISONS WENDLEFIELD
A SECURICO INSTALLATION
securico
LET'S PEOPLE!
CLUNK
TPTE
To Tackleford Keane End
X10 X10A
TPTE
To Tackleford Keane End
X10 X10A
PSSHHH
Not unless you catch me.

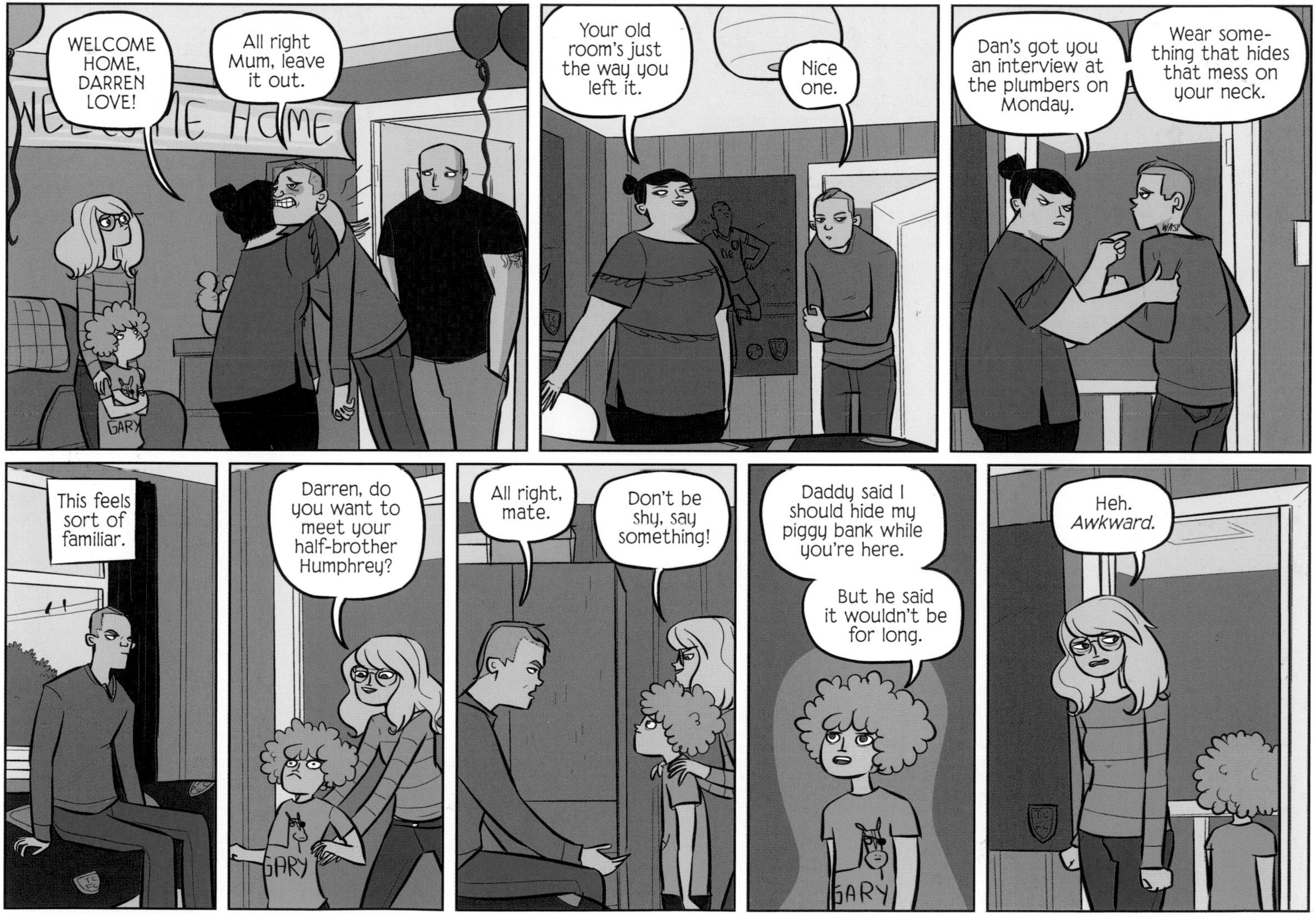
WELCOME HOME, DARREN LOVE!
All right Mum, leave it out.
WELCOME HOME
Your old room's just the way you left it.
Nice one.
Dan's got you an interview at the plumbers on Monday.
Wear something that hides that mess on your neck.
WASP
GARY
This feels sort of familiar.
Darren, do you want to meet your half-brother Humphrey?
GARY
All right, mate.
Don't be shy, say something!
Daddy said I should hide my piggy bank while you're here.
But he said it wouldn't be for long.
GARY
Heh. *Awkward.*

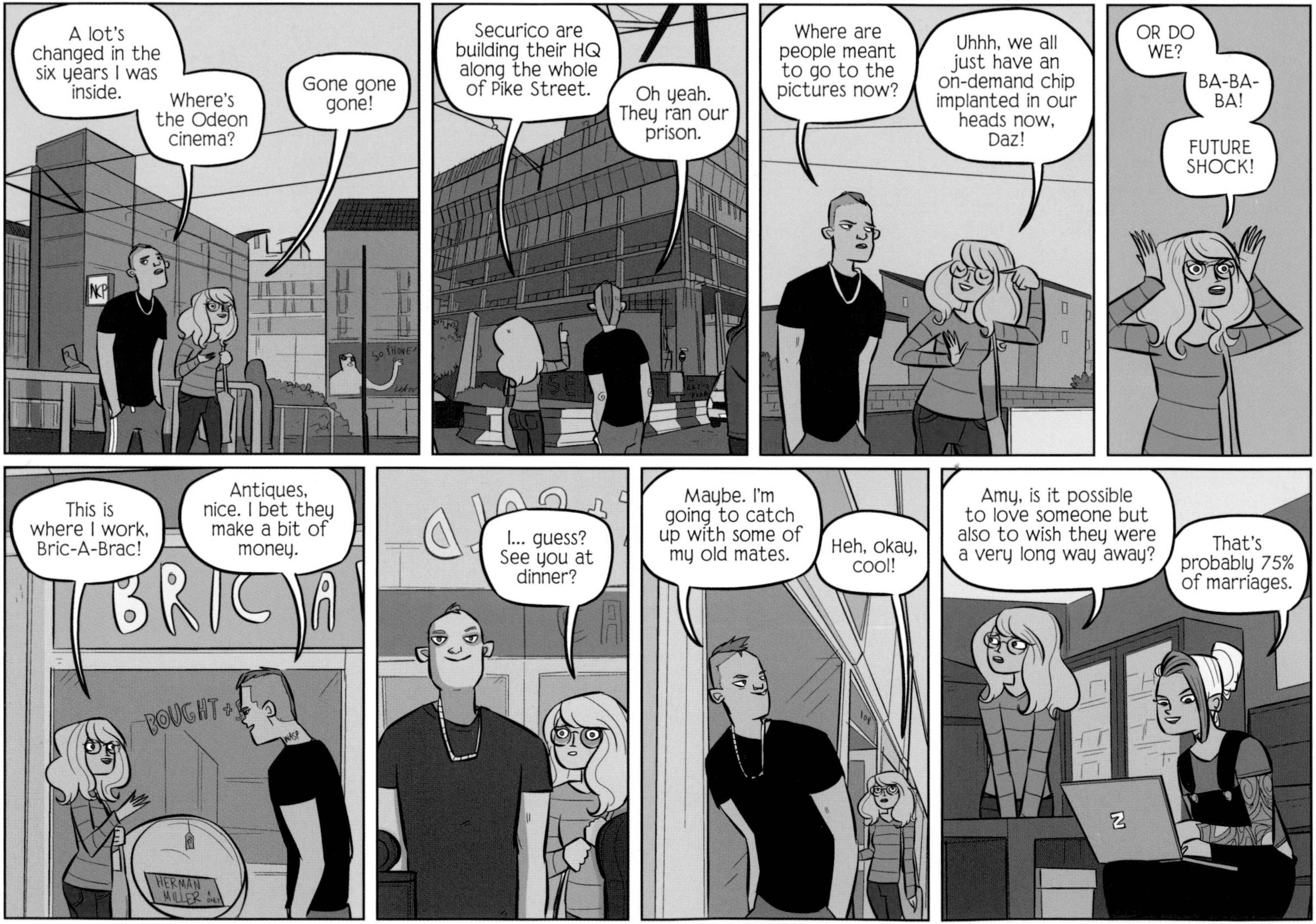
A lot's changed in the six years I was inside.
Where's the Odeon cinema?
Gone gone gone!
Securico are building their HQ along the whole of Pike Street.
Oh yeah. They ran our prison.
Where are people meant to go to the pictures now?
Uhhh, we all just have an on-demand chip implanted in our heads now, Daz!
OR DO WE?
BA-BA-BA!
FUTURE SHOCK!
This is where I work, Bric-A-Brac!
Antiques, nice. I bet they make a bit of money.
I... guess? See you at dinner?
Maybe. I'm going to catch up with some of my old mates.
Heh, okay, cool!
Amy, is it possible to love someone but also to wish they were a very long way away?
That's probably 75% of marriages.

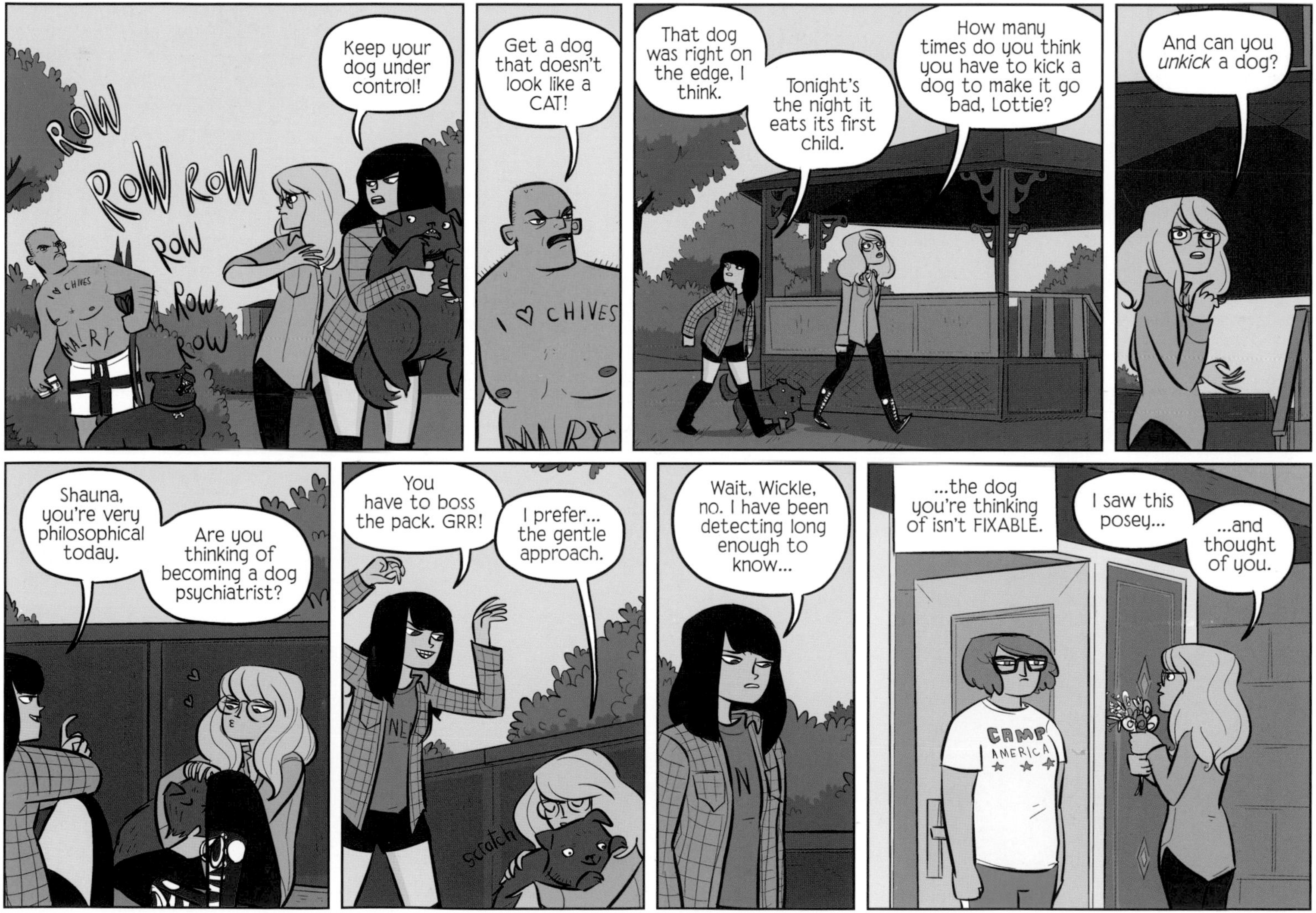
ROW
ROW ROW
ROW
ROW
ROW
I ♡ CHIVES
MARY
Keep your dog under control!
Get a dog that doesn't look like a CAT!
I ♡ CHIVES
MARY
That dog was right on the edge, I think.
Tonight's the night it eats its first child.
How many times do you think you have to kick a dog to make it go bad, Lottie?
And can you *unkick* a dog?
Shauna, you're very philosophical today.
Are you thinking of becoming a dog psychiatrist?
You have to boss the pack. GRR!
I prefer... the gentle approach.
scratch
Wait, Wickle, no. I have been detecting long enough to know...
...the dog you're thinking of isn't FIXABLE.
I saw this posey...
...and thought of you.
CAMP AMERICA

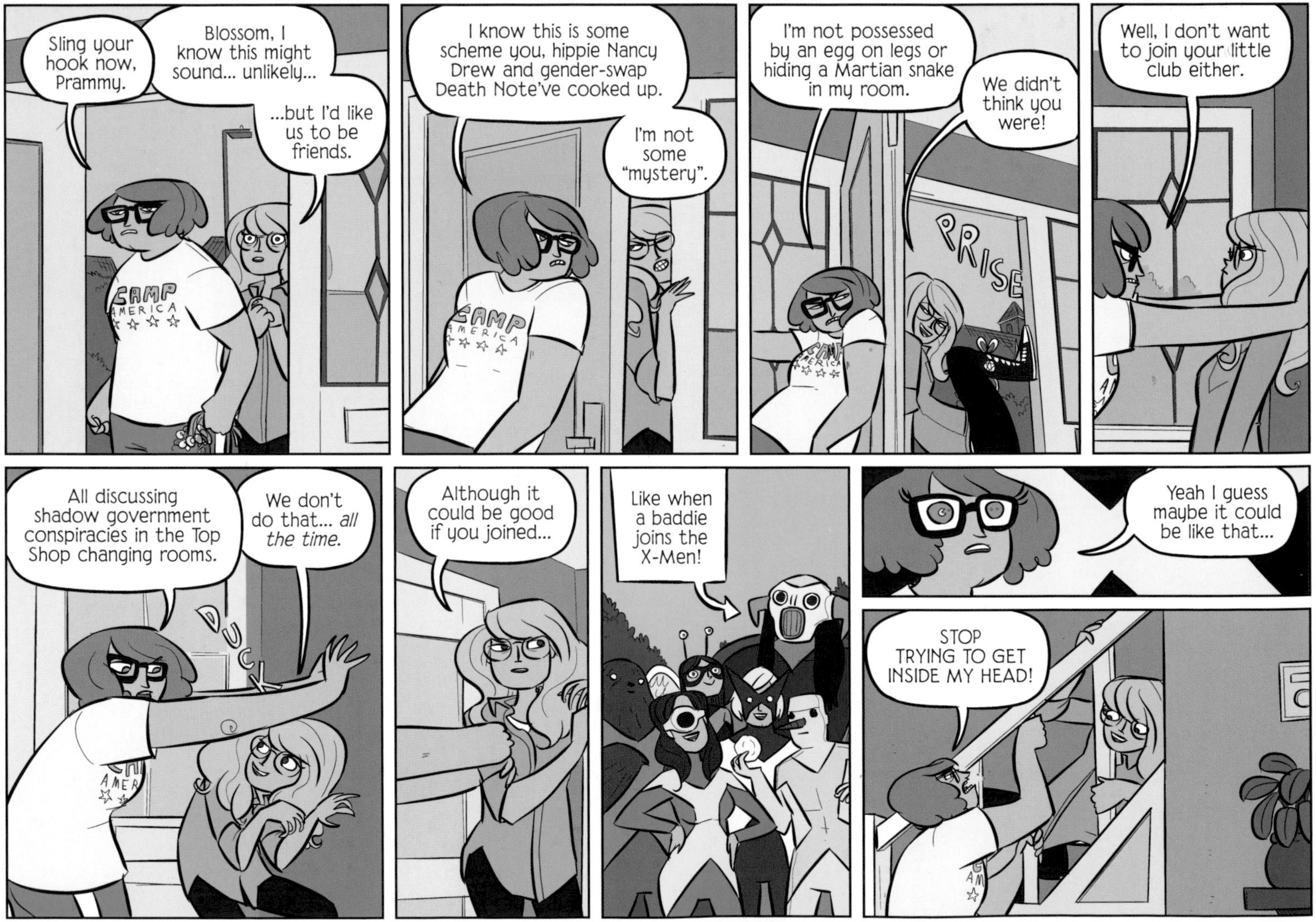

Sling your hook now, Prammy.
Blossom, I know this might sound... unlikely...
...but I'd like us to be friends.
CAMP AMERICA
I know this is some scheme you, hippie Nancy Drew and gender-swap Death Note've cooked up.
I'm not some "mystery".
I'm not possessed by an egg on legs or hiding a Martian snake in my room.
We didn't think you were!
PRISE
Well, I don't want to join your little club either.
All discussing shadow government conspiracies in the Top Shop changing rooms.
We don't do that... *all the time.*
DUCK
Although it could be good if you joined...
Like when a baddie joins the X-Men!
Yeah I guess maybe it could be like that...
STOP TRYING TO GET INSIDE MY HEAD!

The Case of the Missing Piece

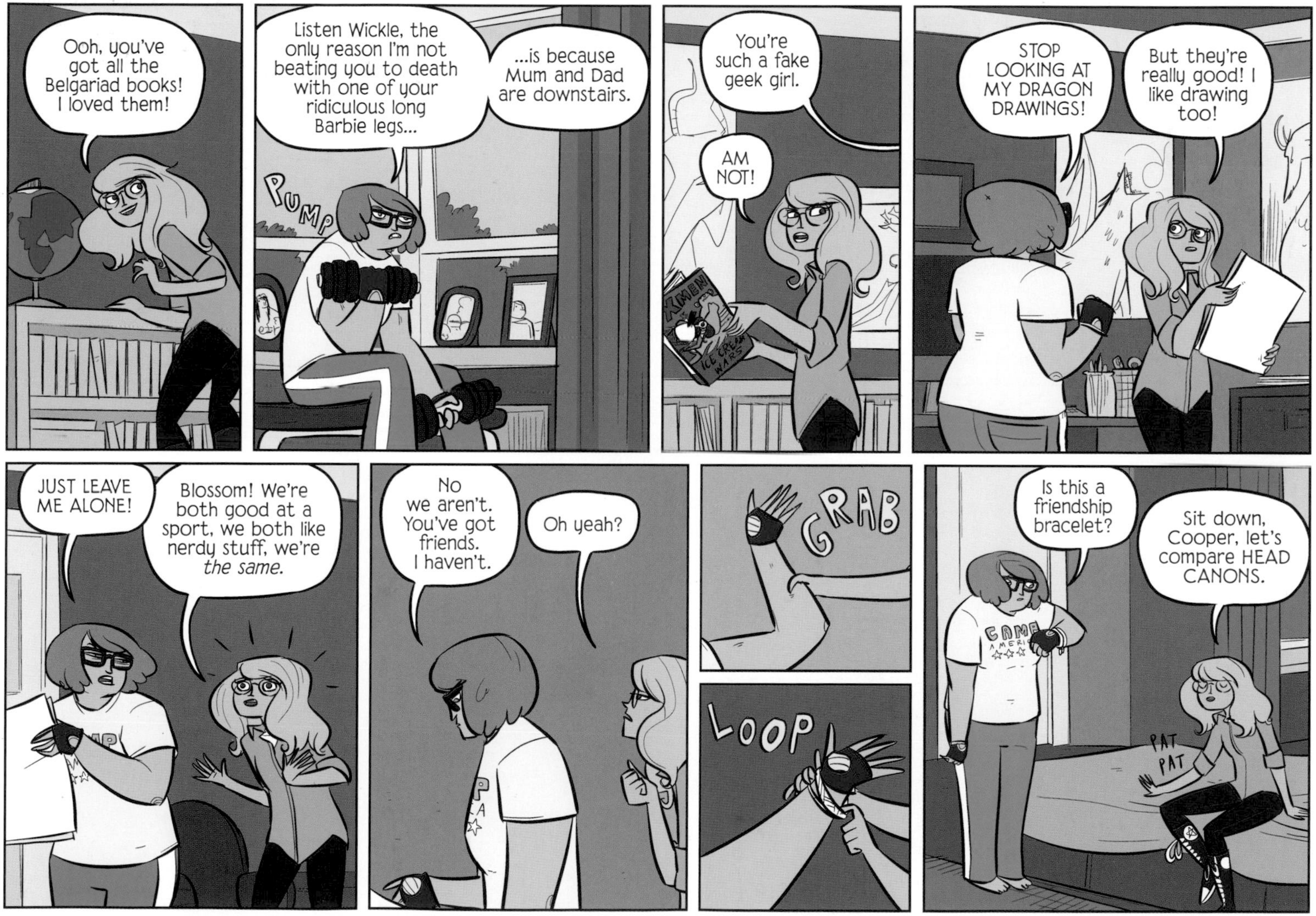

Ooh, you've got all the Belgariad books! I loved them!
Listen Wickle, the only reason I'm not beating you to death with one of your ridiculous long Barbie legs...
...is because Mum and Dad are downstairs.
PUMP
You're such a fake geek girl.
AM NOT!
X-MEN
ICE CREAM WARS
STOP LOOKING AT MY DRAGON DRAWINGS!
But they're really good! I like drawing too!
JUST LEAVE ME ALONE!
Blossom! We're both good at a sport, we both like nerdy stuff, we're *the same.*
No we aren't. You've got friends. I haven't.
Oh yeah?
GRAB
LOOP
Is this a friendship bracelet?
Sit down, Cooper, let's compare HEAD CANONS.
PAT PAT

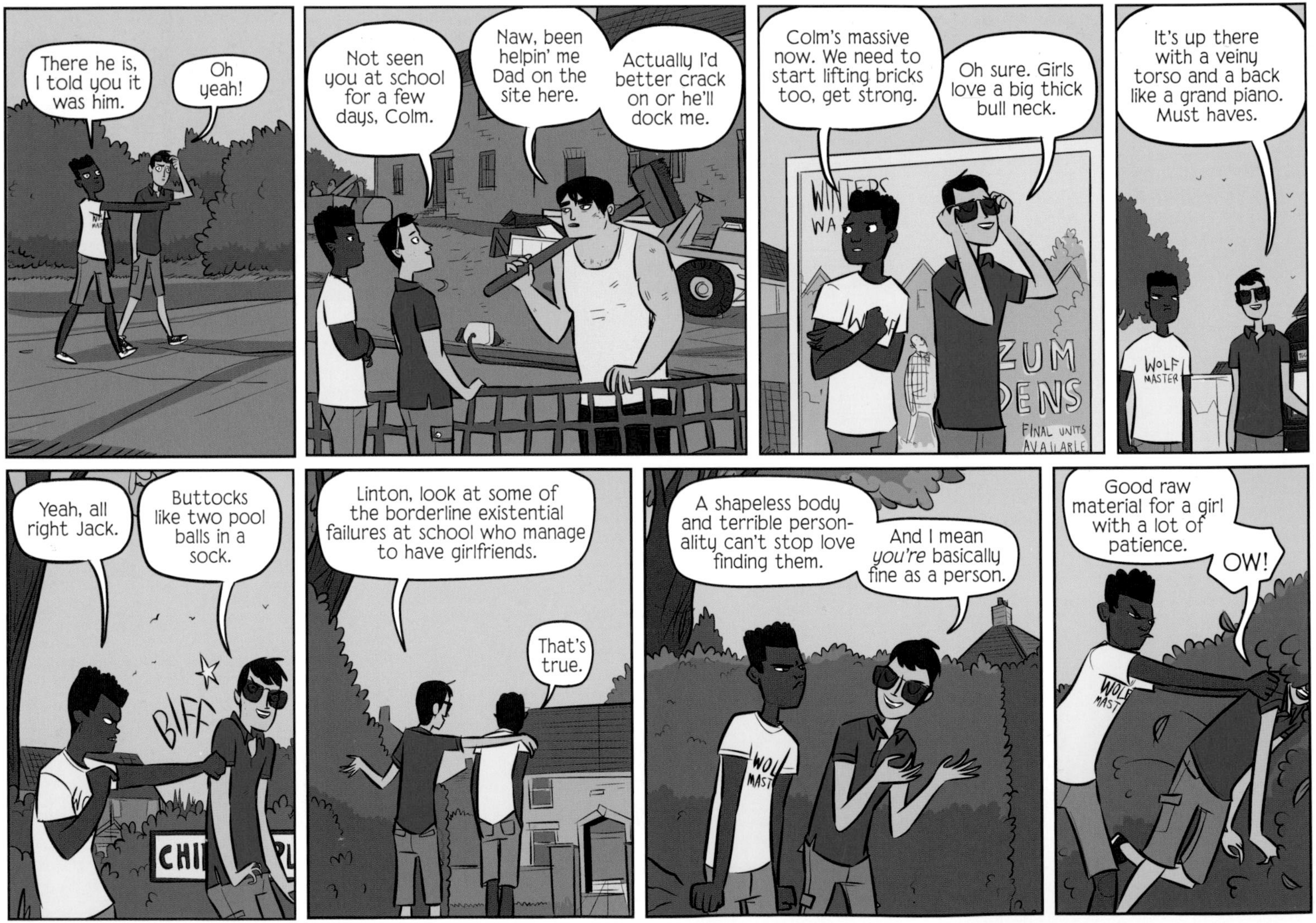
There he is, I told you it was him.
Oh yeah!
Not seen you at school for a few days, Colm.
Naw, been helpin' me Dad on the site here.
Actually I'd better crack on or he'll dock me.
Colm's massive now. We need to start lifting bricks too, get strong.
Oh sure. Girls love a big thick bull neck.
ZUM
DENS
FINAL UNITS AVAILABLE
It's up there with a veiny torso and a back like a grand piano. Must haves.
WOLF MASTER
Yeah, all right Jack.
Buttocks like two pool balls in a sock.
BIFF
Linton, look at some of the borderline existential failures at school who manage to have girlfriends.
That's true.
A shapeless body and terrible personality can't stop love finding them.
And I mean *you're* basically fine as a person.
Good raw material for a girl with a lot of patience.
OW!

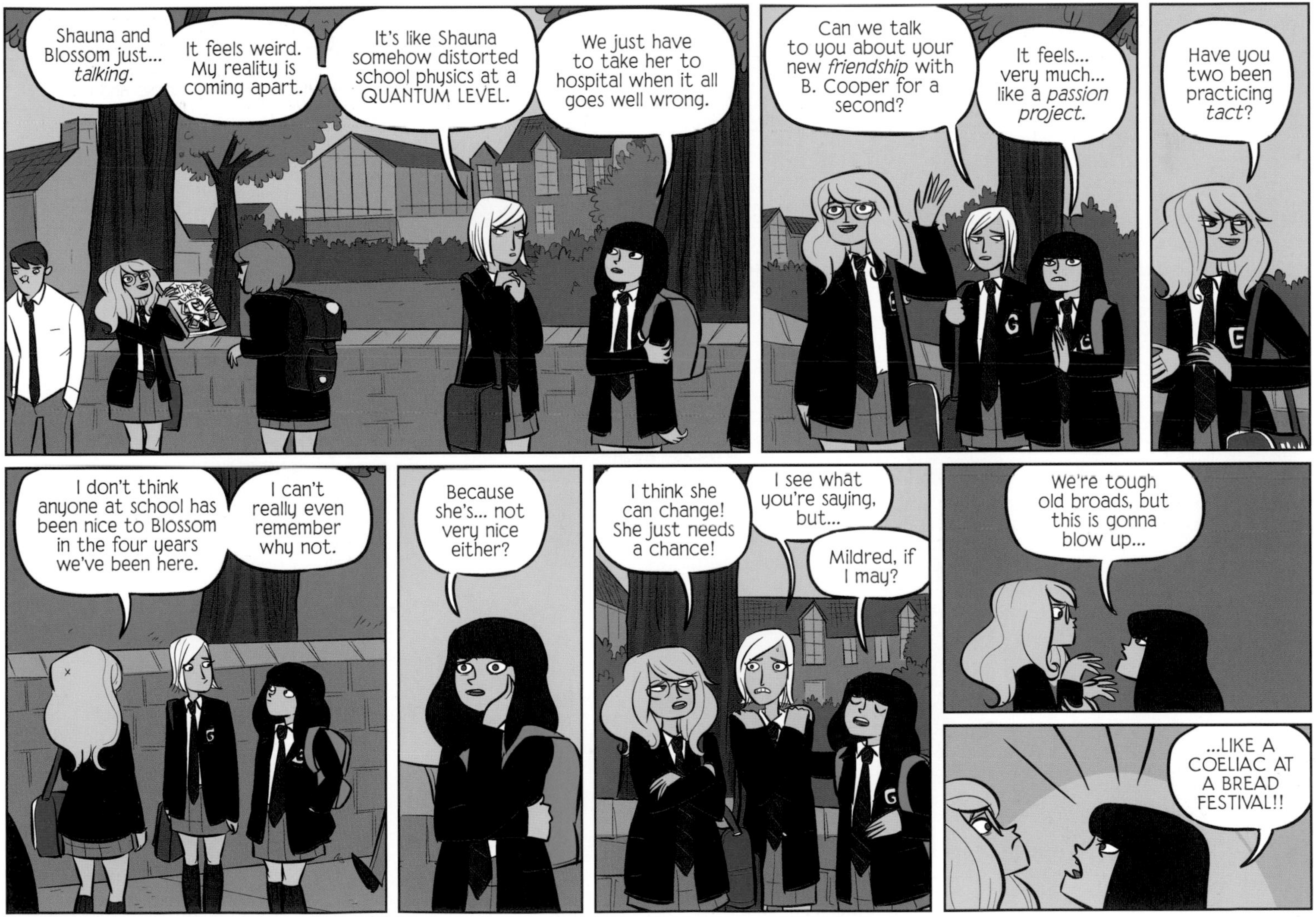

Shauna and Blossom just... *talking*.
It feels weird. My reality is coming apart.
It's like Shauna somehow distorted school physics at a QUANTUM LEVEL.
We just have to take her to hospital when it all goes well wrong.
Can we talk to you about your new *friendship* with B. Cooper for a second?
It feels... very much... like a *passion project*.
Have you two been practicing *tact*?
I don't think anyone at school has been nice to Blossom in the four years we've been here.
I can't really even remember why not.
Because she's... not very nice either?
I think she can change! She just needs a chance!
I see what you're saying, but...
Mildred, if I may?
We're tough old broads, but this is gonna blow up...
...LIKE A COELIAC AT A BREAD FESTIVAL!!

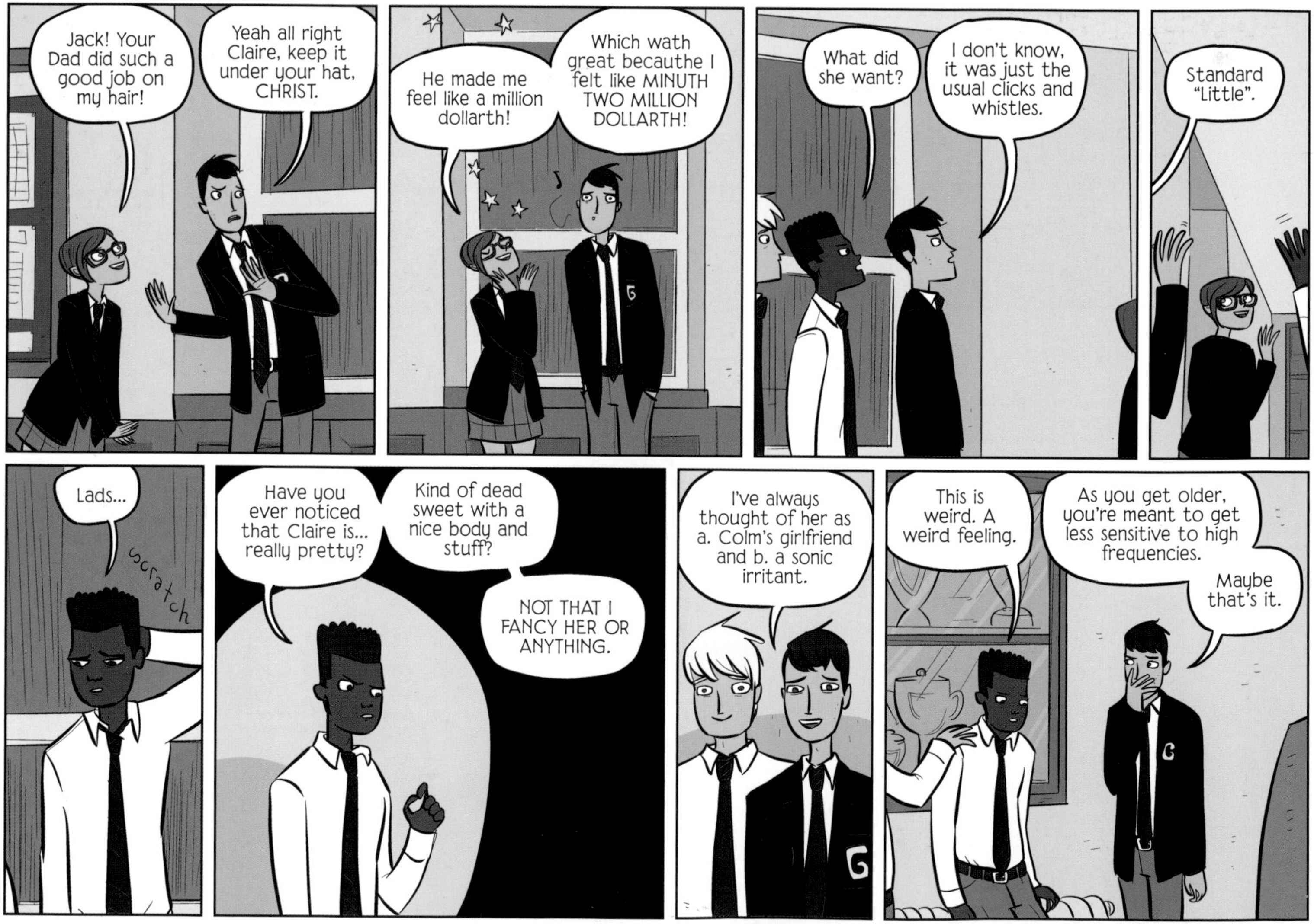
Jack! Your Dad did such a good job on my hair!
Yeah all right Claire, keep it under your hat, CHRIST.
He made me feel like a million dollarth!
Which wath great becauthe I felt like MINUTH TWO MILLION DOLLARTH!
What did she want?
I don't know, it was just the usual clicks and whistles.
Standard "Little".
Lads...
scratch
Have you ever noticed that Claire is... really pretty?
Kind of dead sweet with a nice body and stuff?
NOT THAT I FANCY HER OR ANYTHING.
I've always thought of her as a. Colm's girlfriend and b. a sonic irritant.
This is weird. A weird feeling.
As you get older, you're meant to get less sensitive to high frequencies.
Maybe that's it.

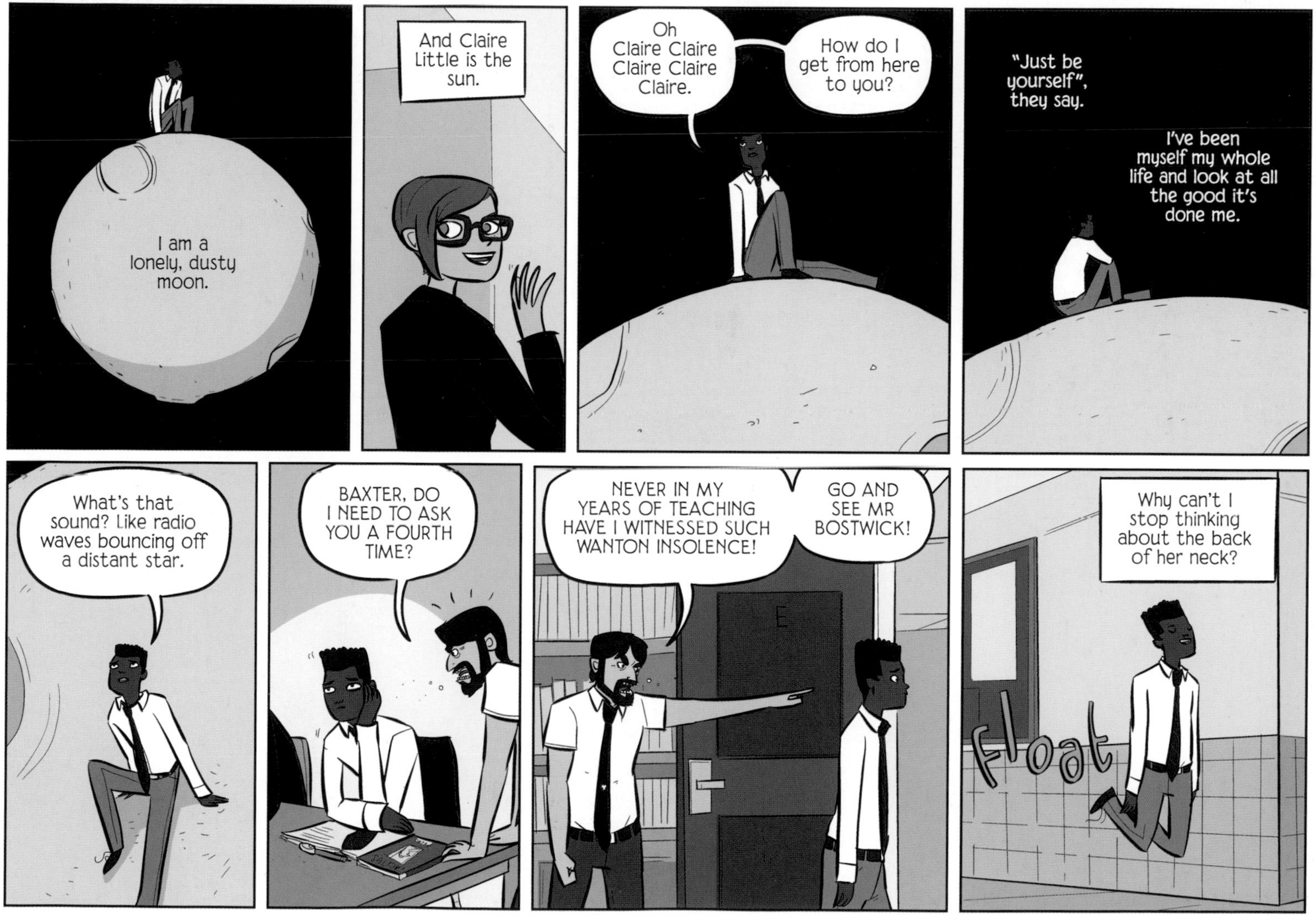
I am a lonely, dusty moon.
And Claire Little is the sun.
Oh Claire Claire Claire Claire Claire.
How do I get from here to you?
"Just be yourself", they say.
I've been myself my whole life and look at all the good it's done me.
What's that sound? Like radio waves bouncing off a distant star.
BAXTER, DO I NEED TO ASK YOU A FOURTH TIME?
NEVER IN MY YEARS OF TEACHING HAVE I WITNESSED SUCH WANTON INSOLENCE!
GO AND SEE MR BOSTWICK!
Why can't I stop thinking about the back of her neck?
Float

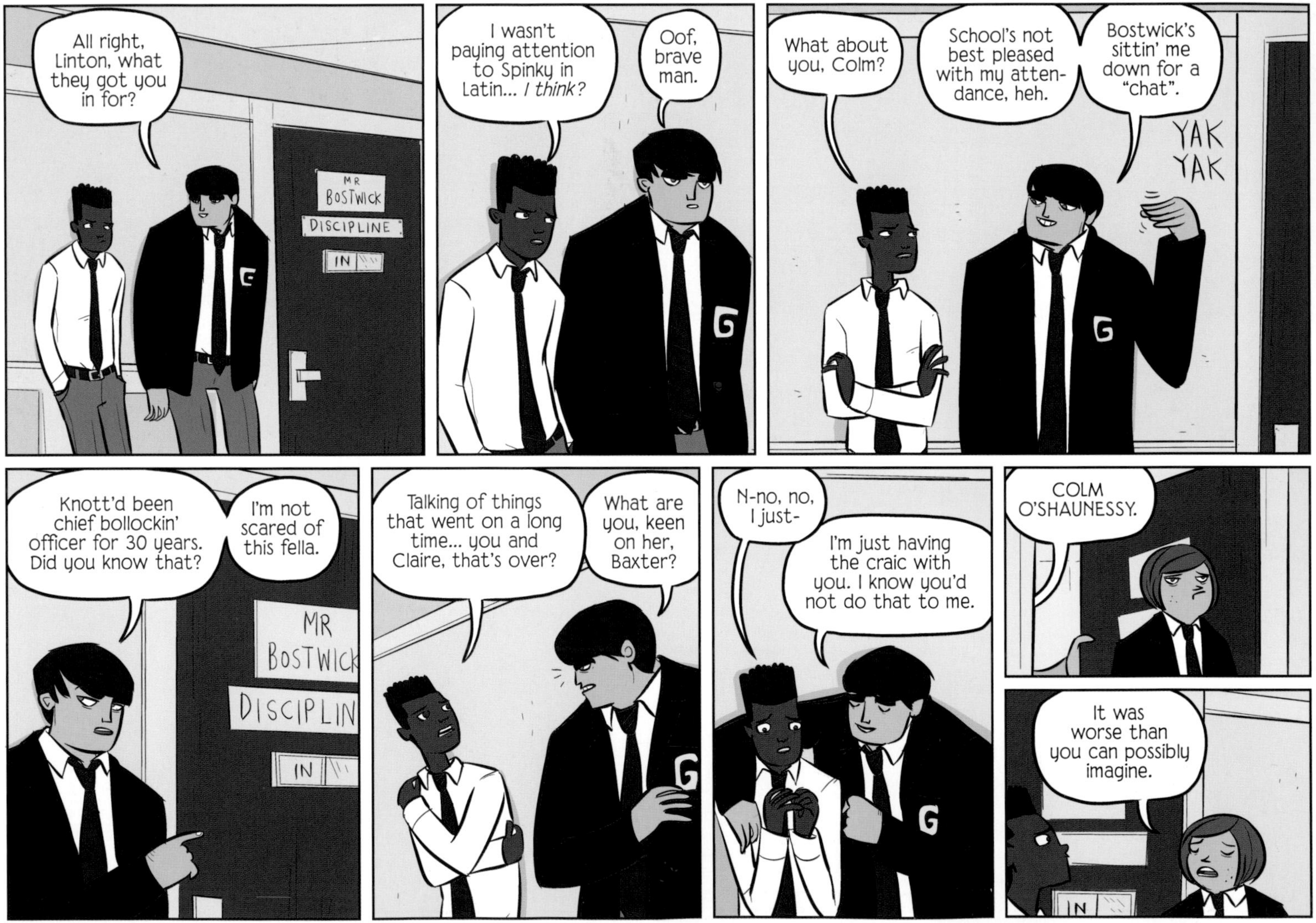
All right, Linton, what they got you in for?
MR BOSTWICK
DISCIPLINE
IN
I wasn't paying attention to Spinky in Latin... *I think?*
Oof, brave man.
What about you, Colm?
School's not best pleased with my attendance, heh.
Bostwick's sittin' me down for a "chat".
YAK YAK
Knott'd been chief bollockin' officer for 30 years. Did you know that?
I'm not scared of this fella.
MR BOSTWICK
DISCIPLIN
IN
Talking of things that went on a long time... you and Claire, that's over?
What are you, keen on her, Baxter?
N-no, no, I just-
I'm just having the craic with you. I know you'd not do that to me.
COLM O'SHAUNESSY.
It was worse than you can possibly imagine.
IN

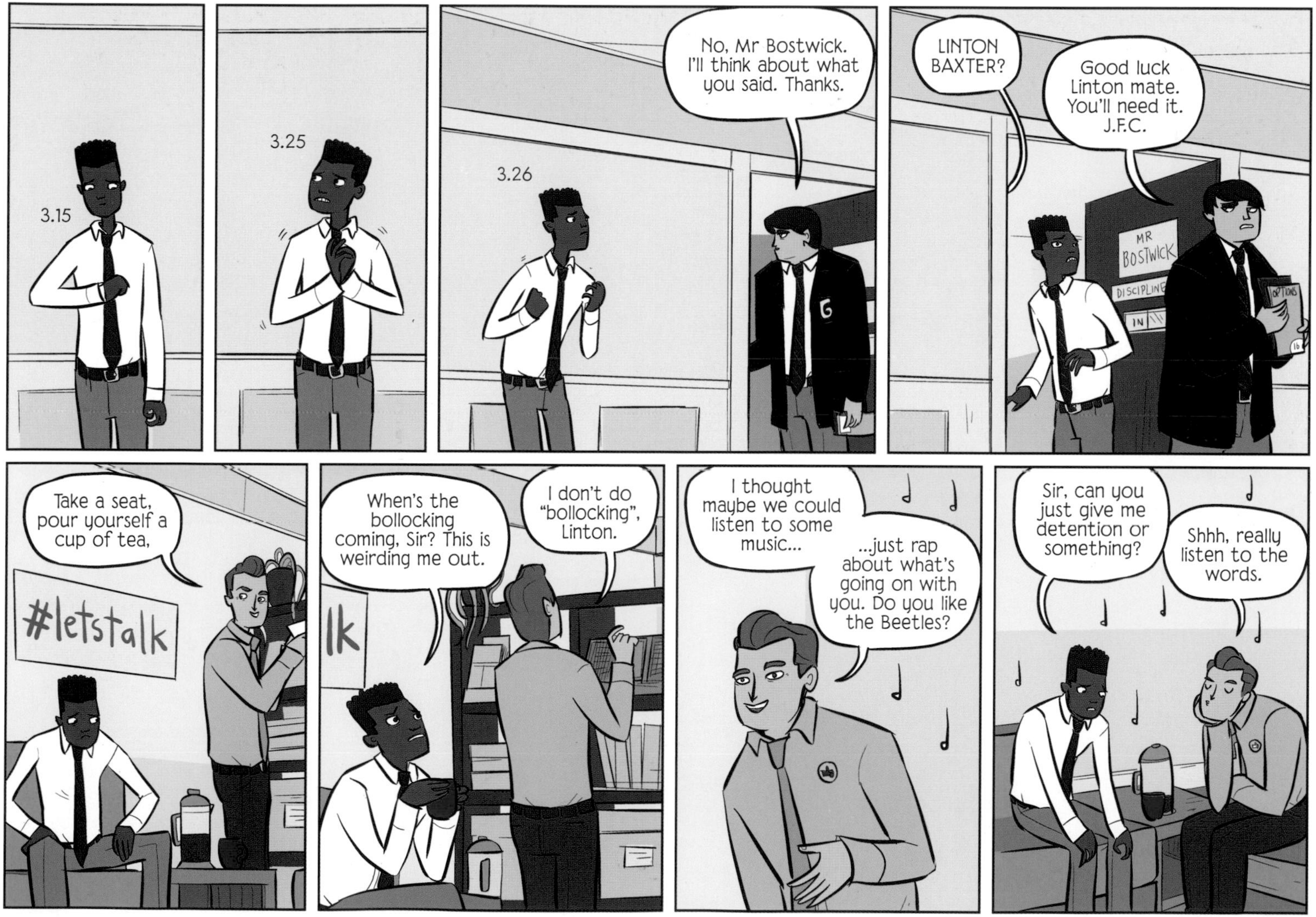
3.15
3.25
3.26
No, Mr Bostwick. I'll think about what you said. Thanks.
LINTON BAXTER?
Good luck Linton mate. You'll need it. J.F.C.
MR BOSTWICK
DISCIPLINE
IN
OPTIONS
Take a seat, pour yourself a cup of tea,
#letstalk
When's the bollocking coming, Sir? This is weirding me out.
I don't do "bollocking", Linton.
I thought maybe we could listen to some music...
...just rap about what's going on with you. Do you like the Beetles?
Sir, can you just give me detention or something?
Shhh, really listen to the words.

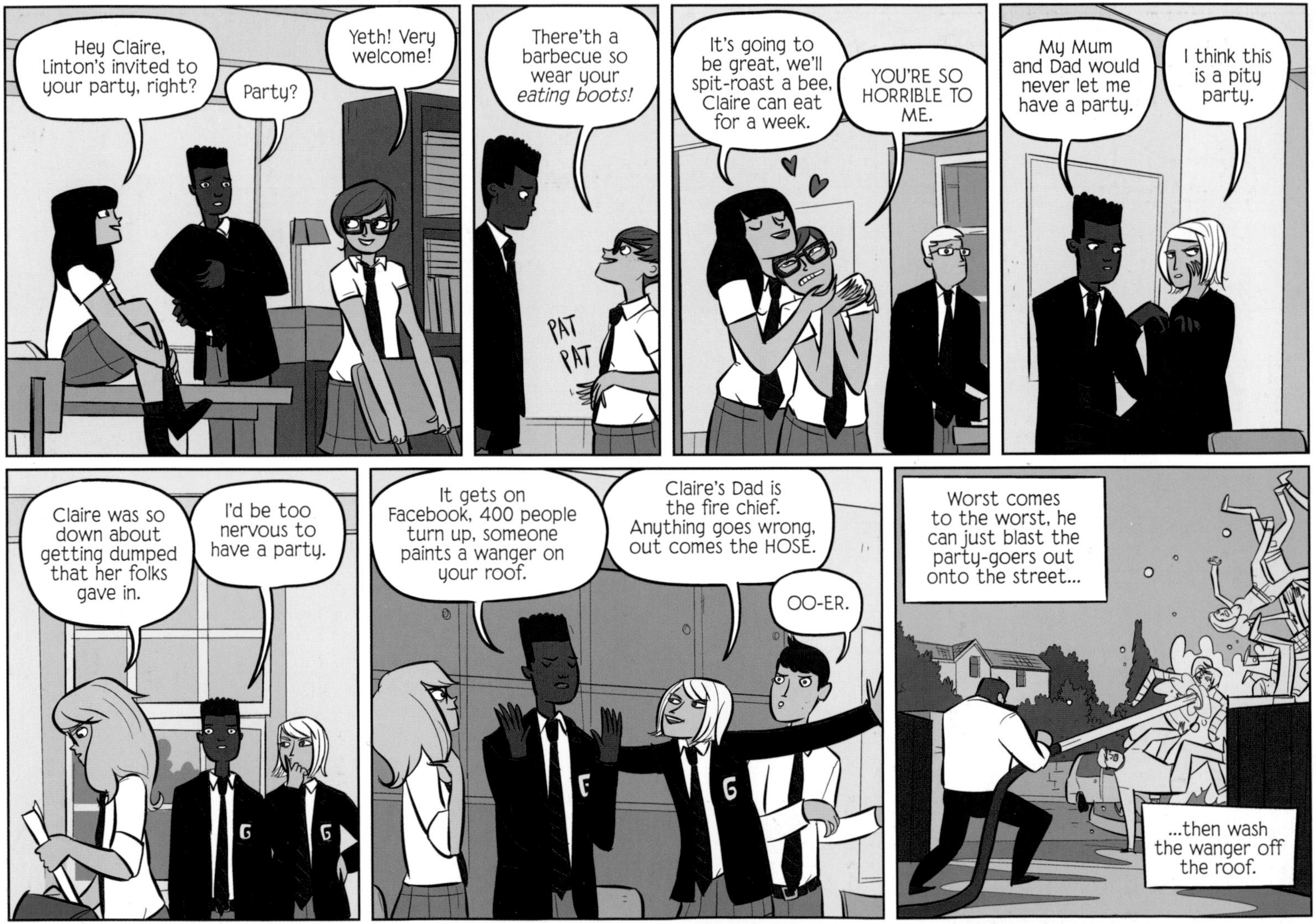
Hey Claire, Linton's invited to your party, right?
Party?
Yeth! Very welcome!
There'th a barbecue so wear your *eating boots!*
PAT PAT
It's going to be great, we'll spit-roast a bee, Claire can eat for a week.
YOU'RE SO HORRIBLE TO ME.
My Mum and Dad would never let me have a party.
I think this is a pity party.
Claire was so down about getting dumped that her folks gave in.
I'd be too nervous to have a party.
It gets on Facebook, 400 people turn up, someone paints a wanger on your roof.
Claire's Dad is the fire chief. Anything goes wrong, out comes the HOSE.
OO-ER.
Worst comes to the worst, he can just blast the party-goers out onto the street...
...then wash the wanger off the roof.

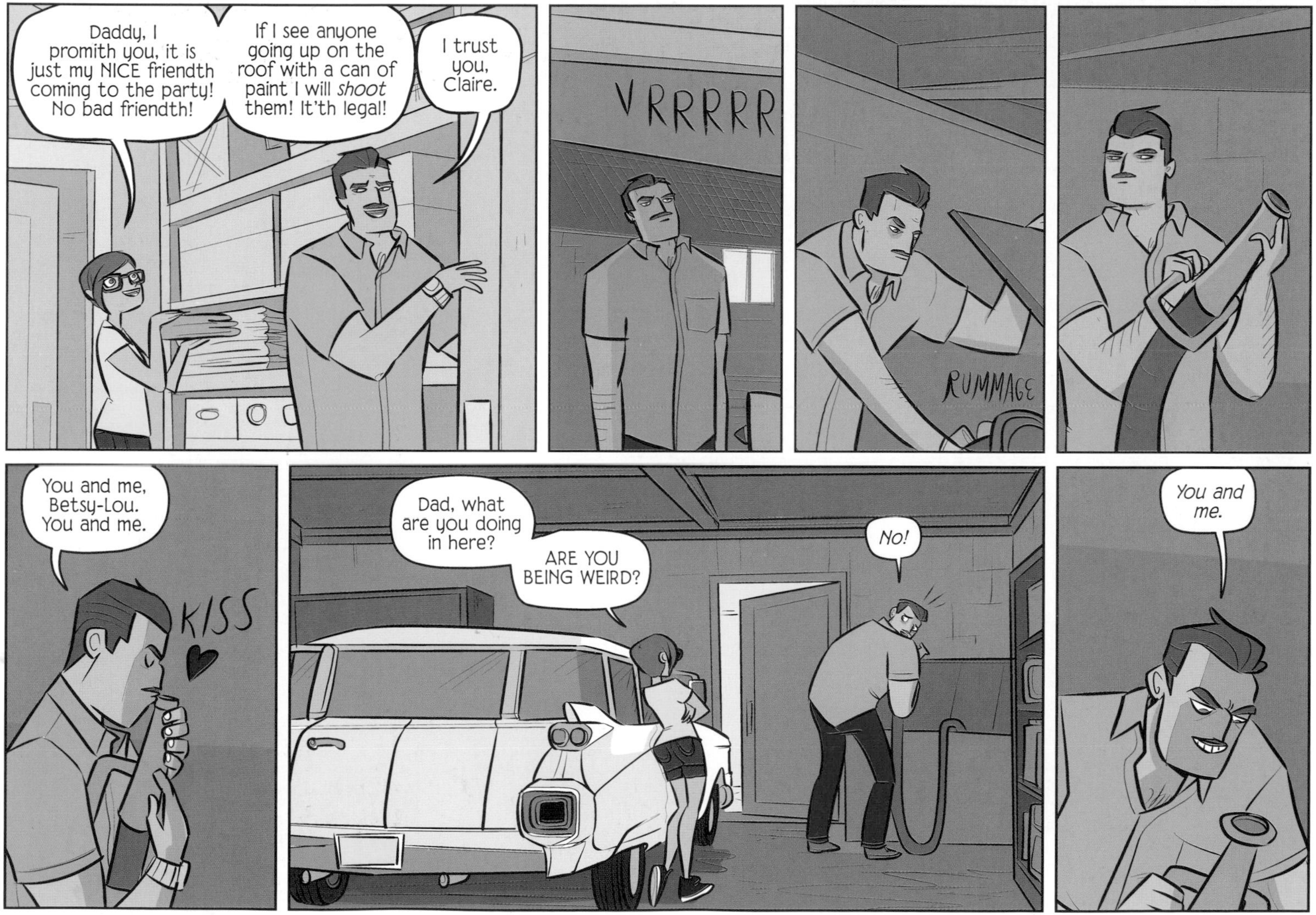

Daddy, I promith you, it is just my NICE friendth coming to the party! No bad friendth!
If I see anyone going up on the roof with a can of paint I will *shoot* them! It'th legal!
I trust you, Claire.
VRRRRR
RUMMAGE
You and me, Betsy-Lou. You and me.
KISS
Dad, what are you doing in here?
ARE YOU BEING WEIRD?
No!
You and me.

Bad Machinery, Volume Nine

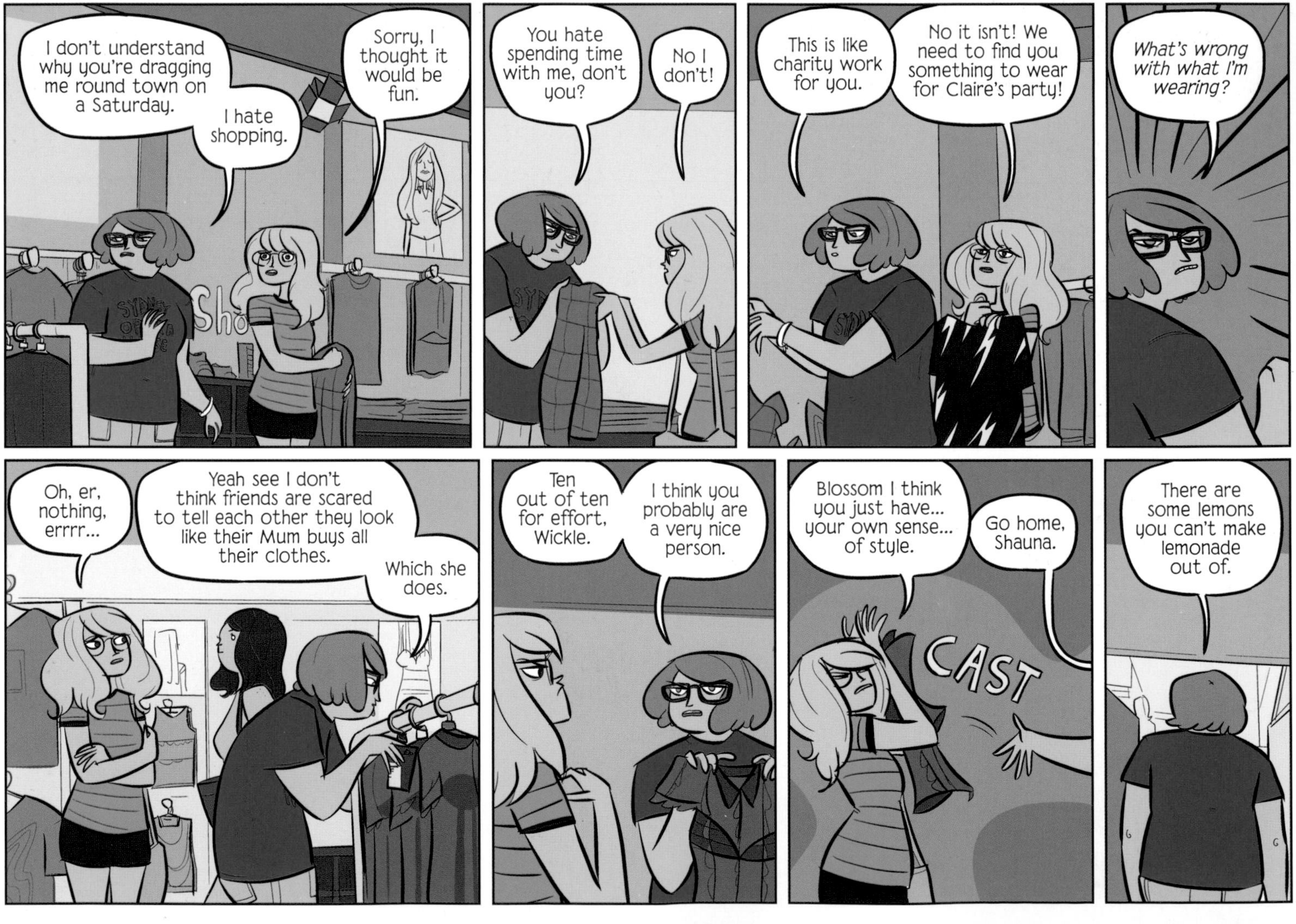

I don't understand why you're dragging me round town on a Saturday.
I hate shopping.
Sorry, I thought it would be fun.
You hate spending time with me, don't you?
No I don't!
This is like charity work for you.
No it isn't! We need to find you something to wear for Claire's party!
What's wrong with what I'm wearing?
Oh, er, nothing, errrr...
Yeah see I don't think friends are scared to tell each other they look like their Mum buys all their clothes.
Which she does.
Ten out of ten for effort, Wickle.
I think you probably are a very nice person.
Blossom I think you just have... your own sense... of style.
Go home, Shauna.
CAST
There are some lemons you can't make lemonade out of.

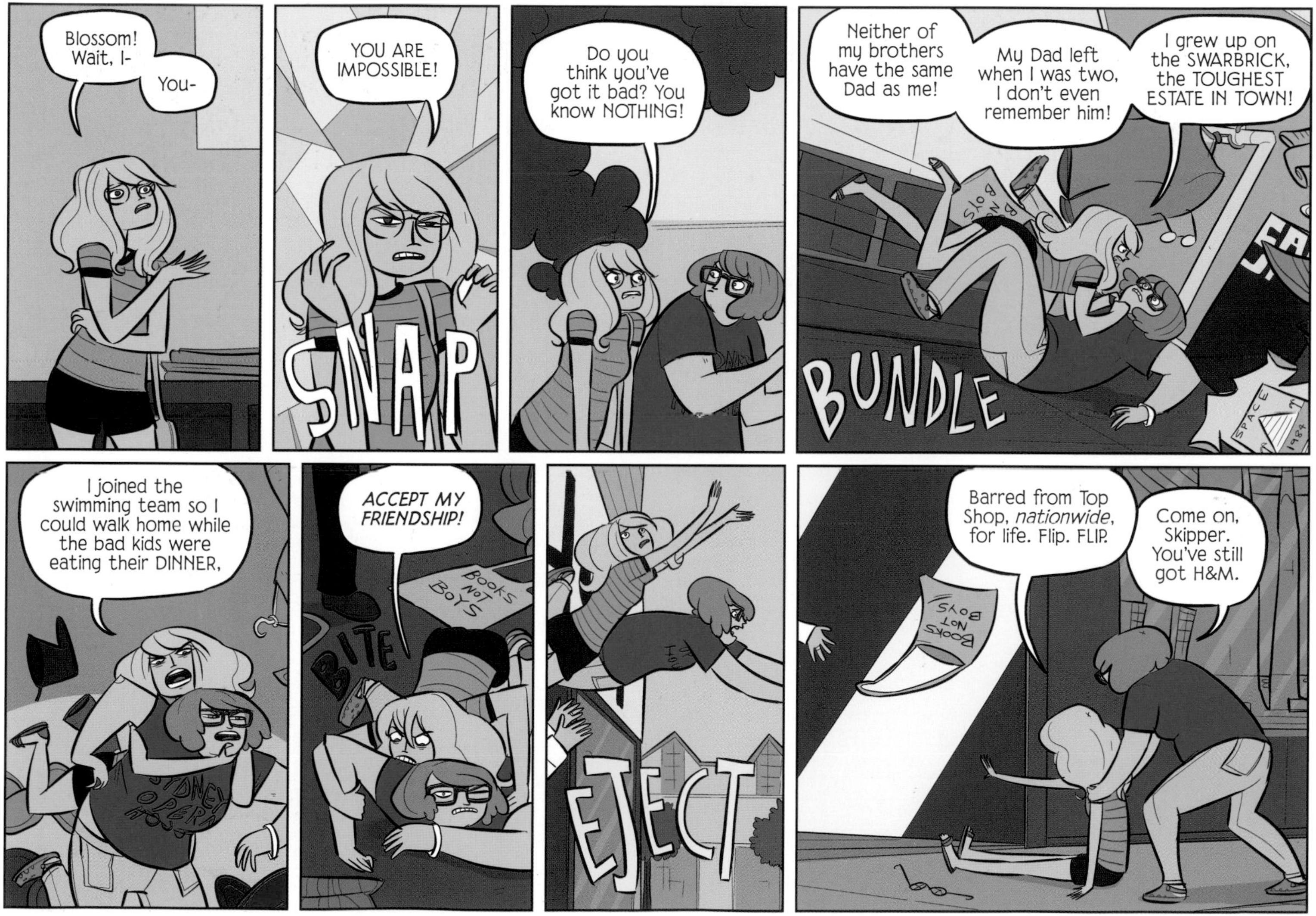
Blossom! Wait, I-
You-
YOU ARE IMPOSSIBLE!
SNAP
Do you think you've got it bad? You know NOTHING!
Neither of my brothers have the same Dad as me!
My Dad left when I was two, I don't even remember him!
I grew up on the SWARBRICK, the TOUGHEST ESTATE IN TOWN!
BOOKS NOT BOYS
BUNDLE
SPACE 1984
I joined the swimming team so I could walk home while the bad kids were eating their DINNER,
SYDNEY OPERA HOUSE
ACCEPT MY FRIENDSHIP!
BOOKS NOT BOYS
BITE
EJECT
Barred from Top Shop, *nationwide*, for life. Flip. FLIP.
Come on, Skipper. You've still got H&M.
BOOKS NOT BOYS

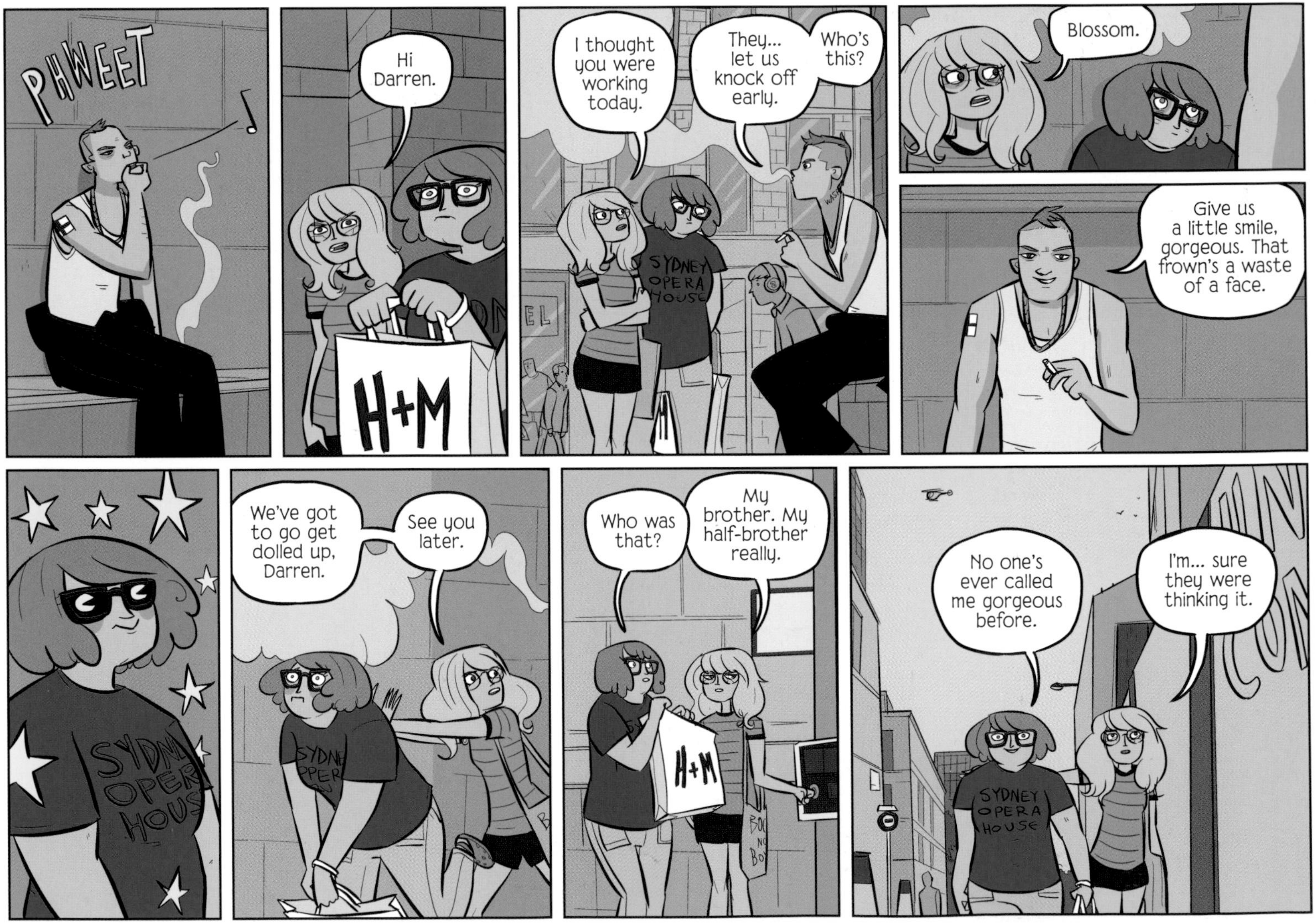
PHWEET
Hi Darren.
I thought you were working today.
They... let us knock off early.
Who's this?
Blossom.
Give us a little smile, gorgeous. That frown's a waste of a face.
We've got to go get dolled up, Darren.
See you later.
Who was that?
My brother. My half-brother really.
No one's ever called me gorgeous before.
I'm... sure they were thinking it.

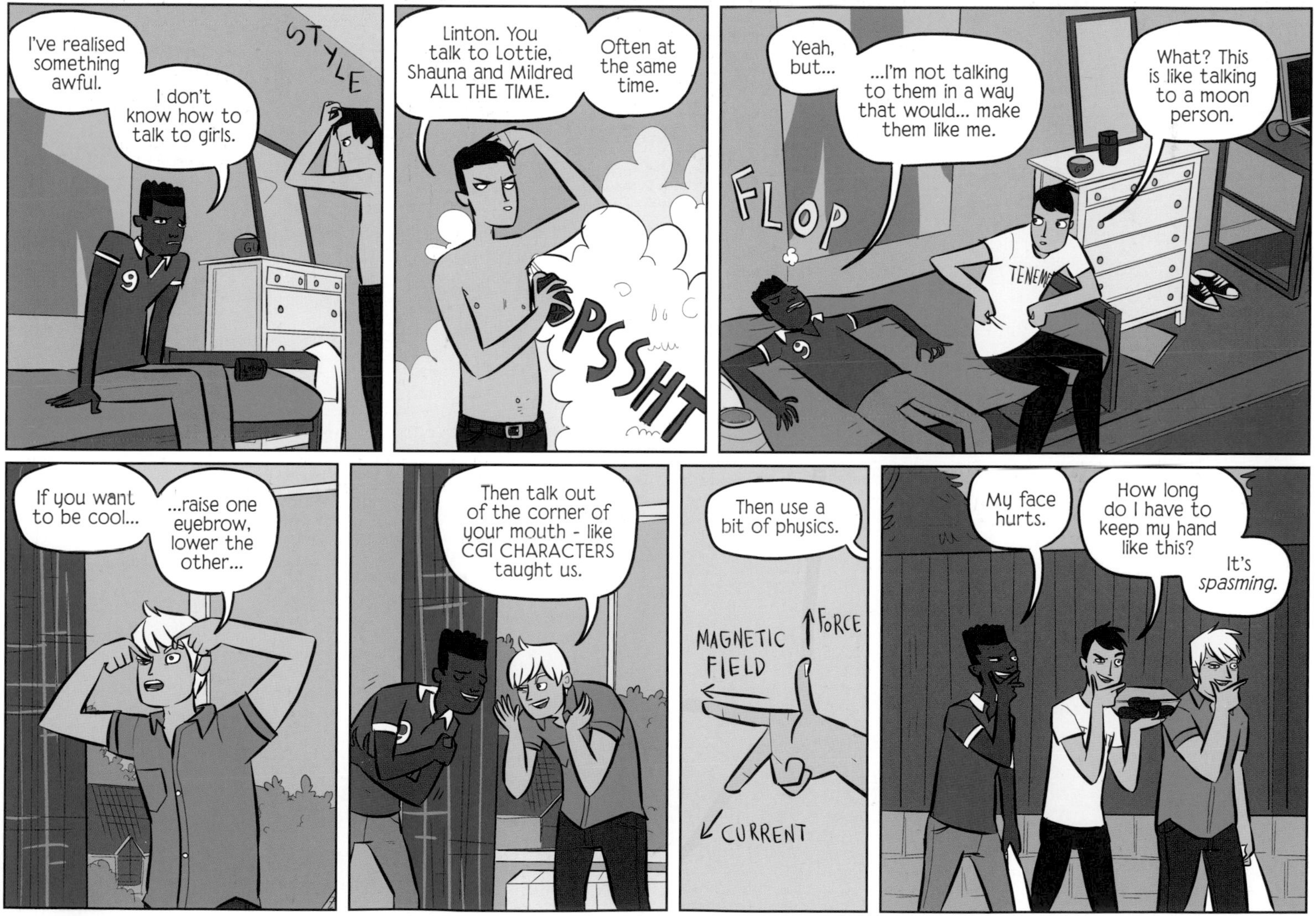
I've realised something awful.
I don't know how to talk to girls.
STYLE
Linton. You talk to Lottie, Shauna and Mildred ALL THE TIME.
Often at the same time.
PSSHT
Yeah, but...
...I'm not talking to them in a way that would... make them like me.
FLOP
What? This is like talking to a moon person.
TENEM
If you want to be cool...
...raise one eyebrow, lower the other...
Then talk out of the corner of your mouth - like CGI CHARACTERS taught us.
Then use a bit of physics.
FORCE
MAGNETIC FIELD
CURRENT
My face hurts.
How long do I have to keep my hand like this?
It's *spasming.*

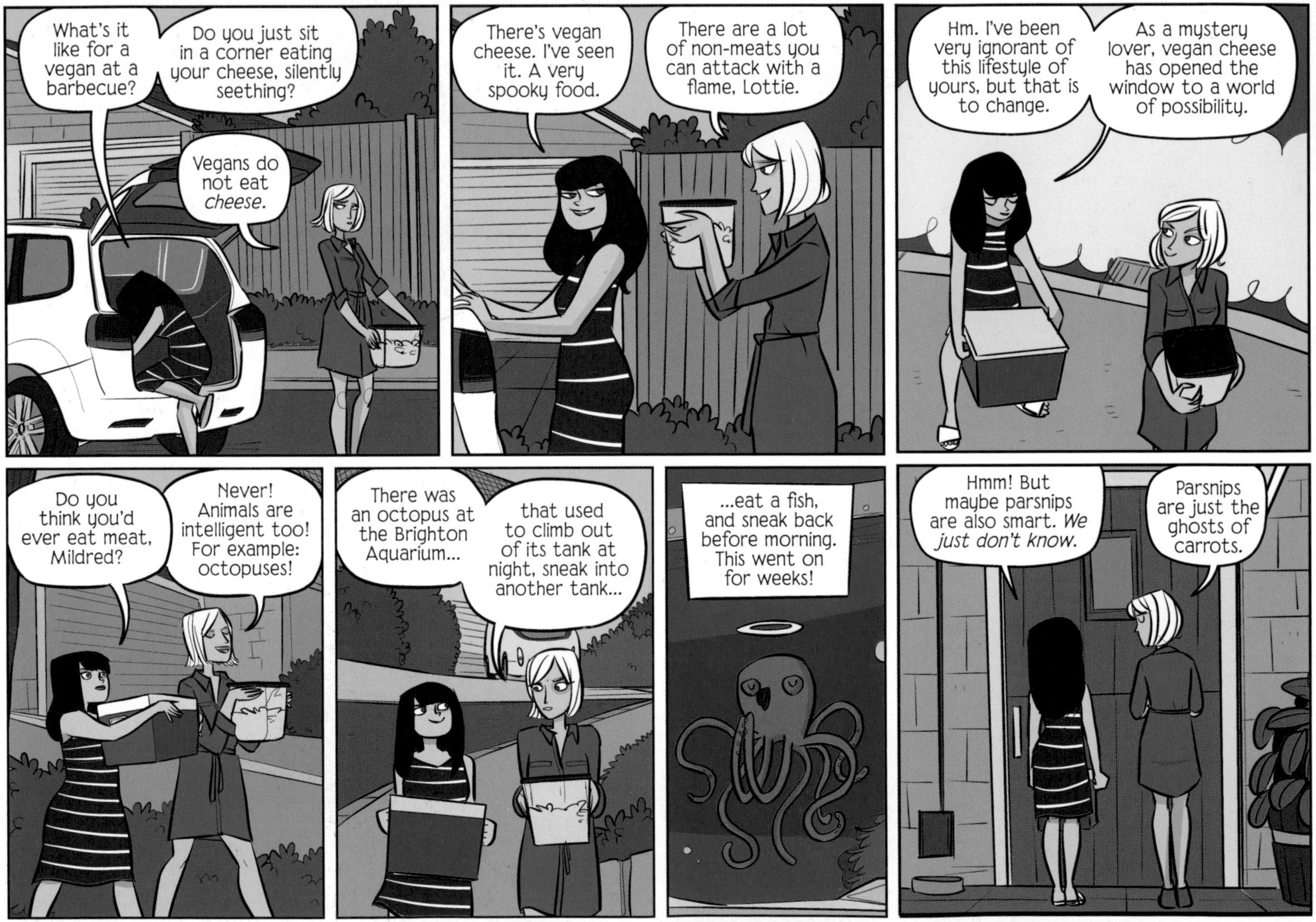
What's it like for a vegan at a barbecue?
Do you just sit in a corner eating your cheese, silently seething?
Vegans do not eat *cheese.*
There's vegan cheese. I've seen it. A very spooky food.
There are a lot of non-meats you can attack with a flame, Lottie.
Hm. I've been very ignorant of this lifestyle of yours, but that is to change.
As a mystery lover, vegan cheese has opened the window to a world of possibility.
Do you think you'd ever eat meat, Mildred?
Never! Animals are intelligent too! For example: octopuses!
There was an octopus at the Brighton Aquarium...
that used to climb out of its tank at night, sneak into another tank...
...eat a fish, and sneak back before morning. This went on for weeks!
Hmm! But maybe parsnips are also smart. *We just don't know.*
Parsnips are just the ghosts of carrots.

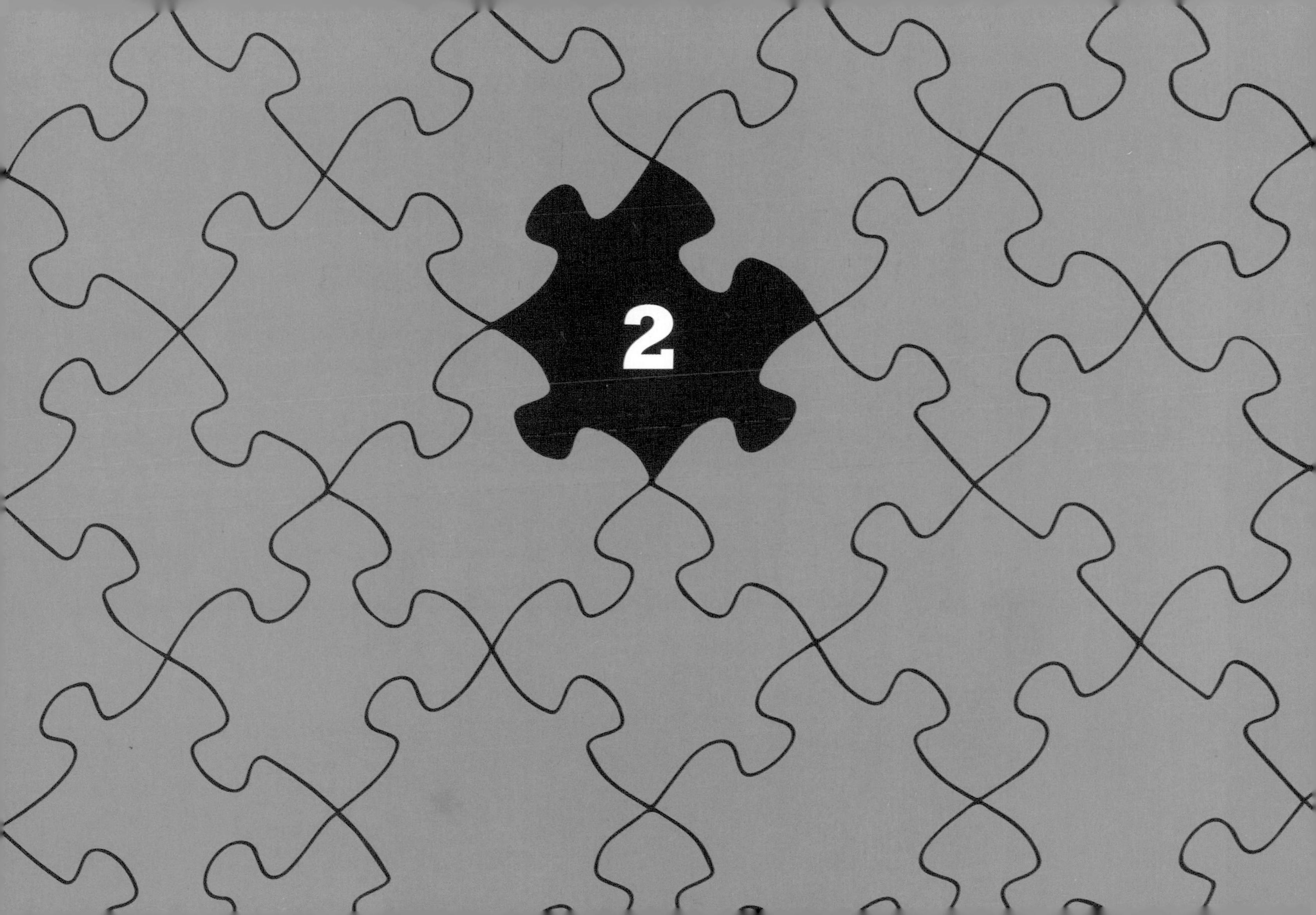
2

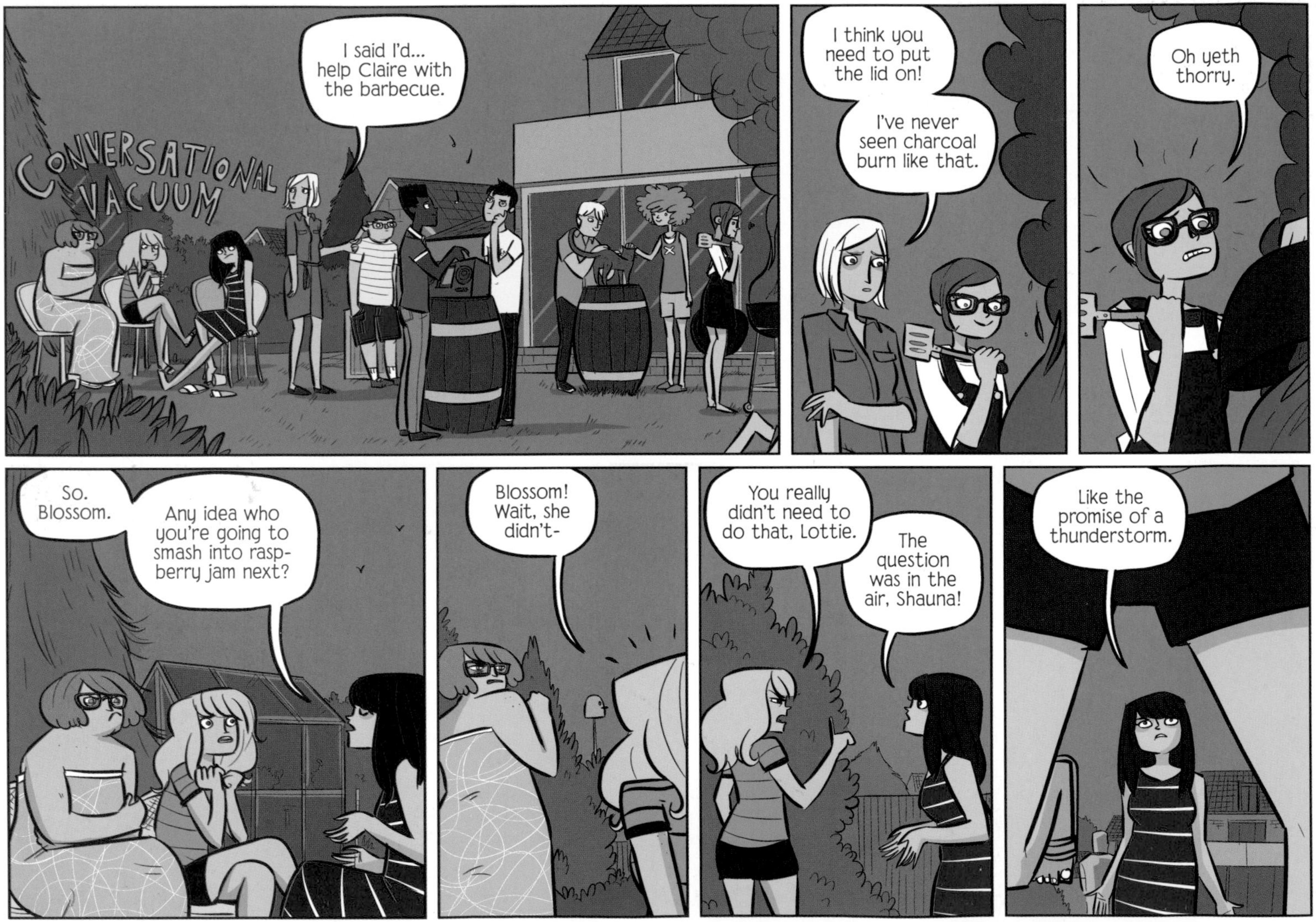
I said I'd... help Claire with the barbecue.
CONVERSATIONAL VACUUM
I think you need to put the lid on!
I've never seen charcoal burn like that.
Oh yeth thorry.
So. Blossom.
Any idea who you're going to smash into raspberry jam next?
Blossom! Wait, she didn't-
You really didn't need to do that, Lottie.
The question was in the air, Shauna!
Like the promise of a thunderstorm.

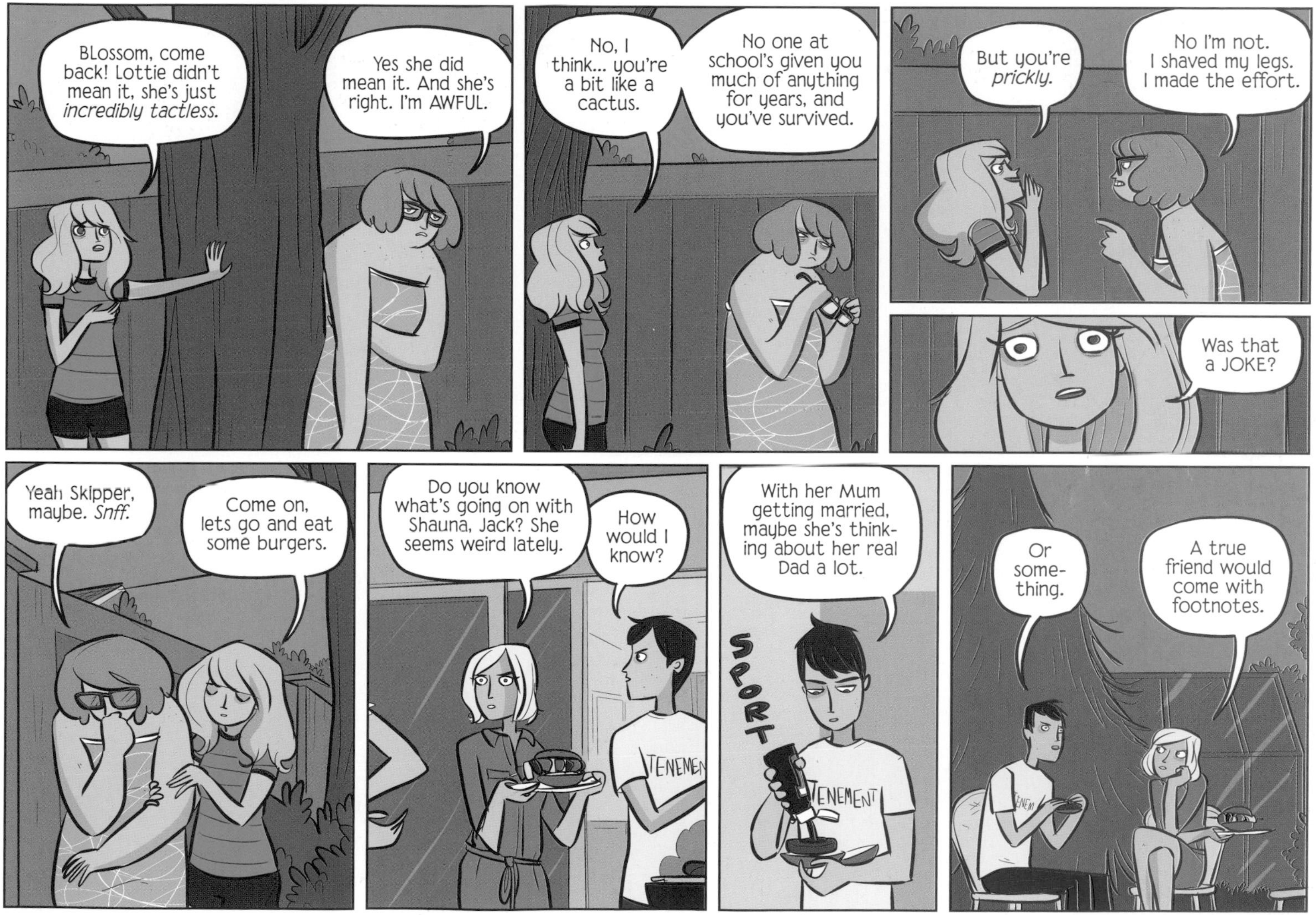

BLossom, come back! Lottie didn't mean it, she's just *incredibly tactless.*
Yes she did mean it. And she's right. I'm AWFUL.
No, I think... you're a bit like a cactus.
No one at school's given you much of anything for years, and you've survived.
But you're *prickly.*
No I'm not. I shaved my legs. I made the effort.
Was that a JOKE?
Yeah Skipper, maybe. *Snff.*
Come on, lets go and eat some burgers.
Do you know what's going on with Shauna, Jack? She seems weird lately.
How would I know?
TENEMEN
With her Mum getting married, maybe she's thinking about her real Dad a lot.
SPORT
TENEMENT
Or something.
A true friend would come with footnotes.

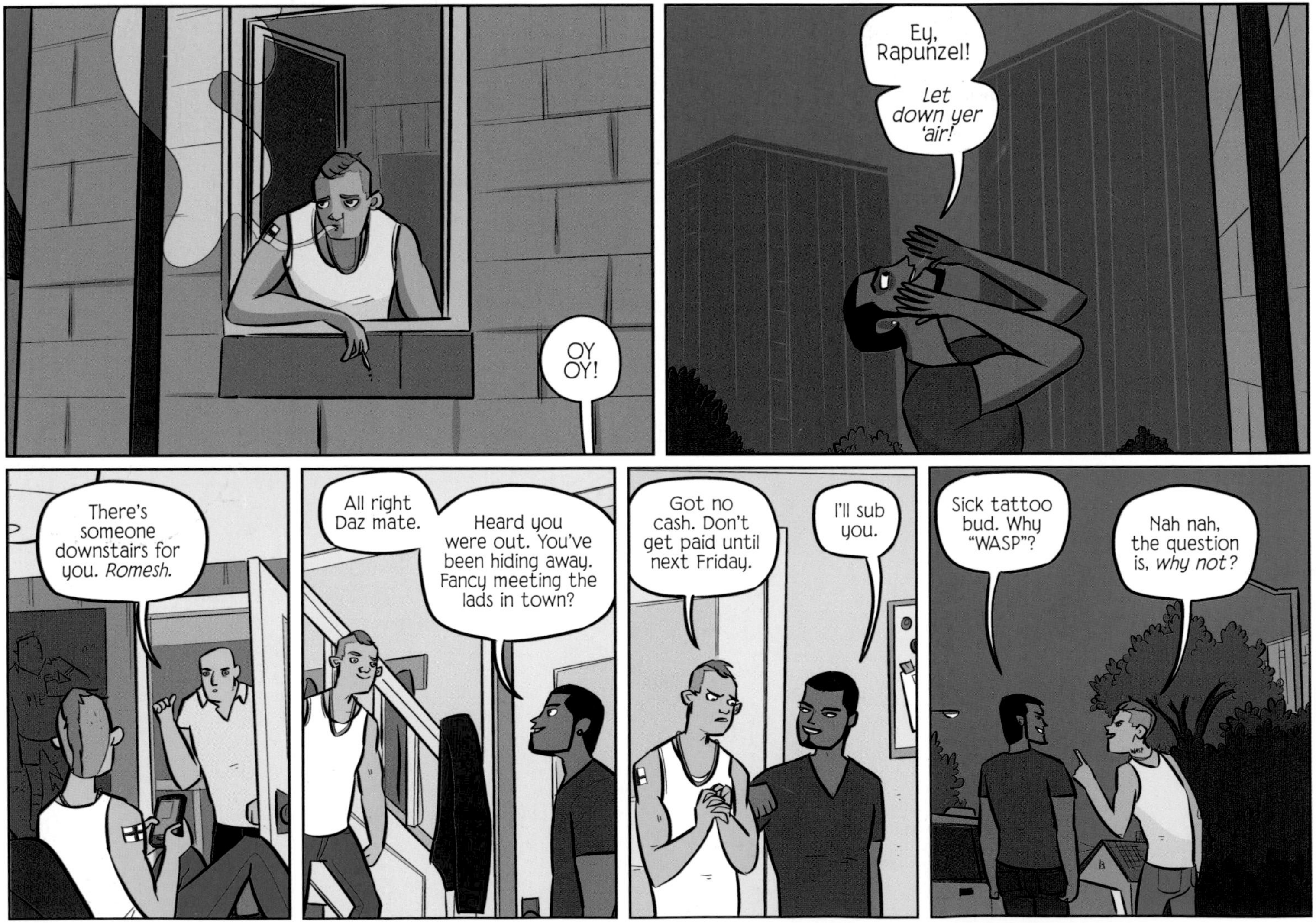
OY OY!
Ey, Rapunzel!
Let down yer 'air!
There's someone downstairs for you. *Romesh.*
All right Daz mate.
Heard you were out. You've been hiding away. Fancy meeting the lads in town?
Got no cash. Don't get paid until next Friday.
I'll sub you.
Sick tattoo bud. Why "WASP"?
Nah nah, the question is, *why not?*

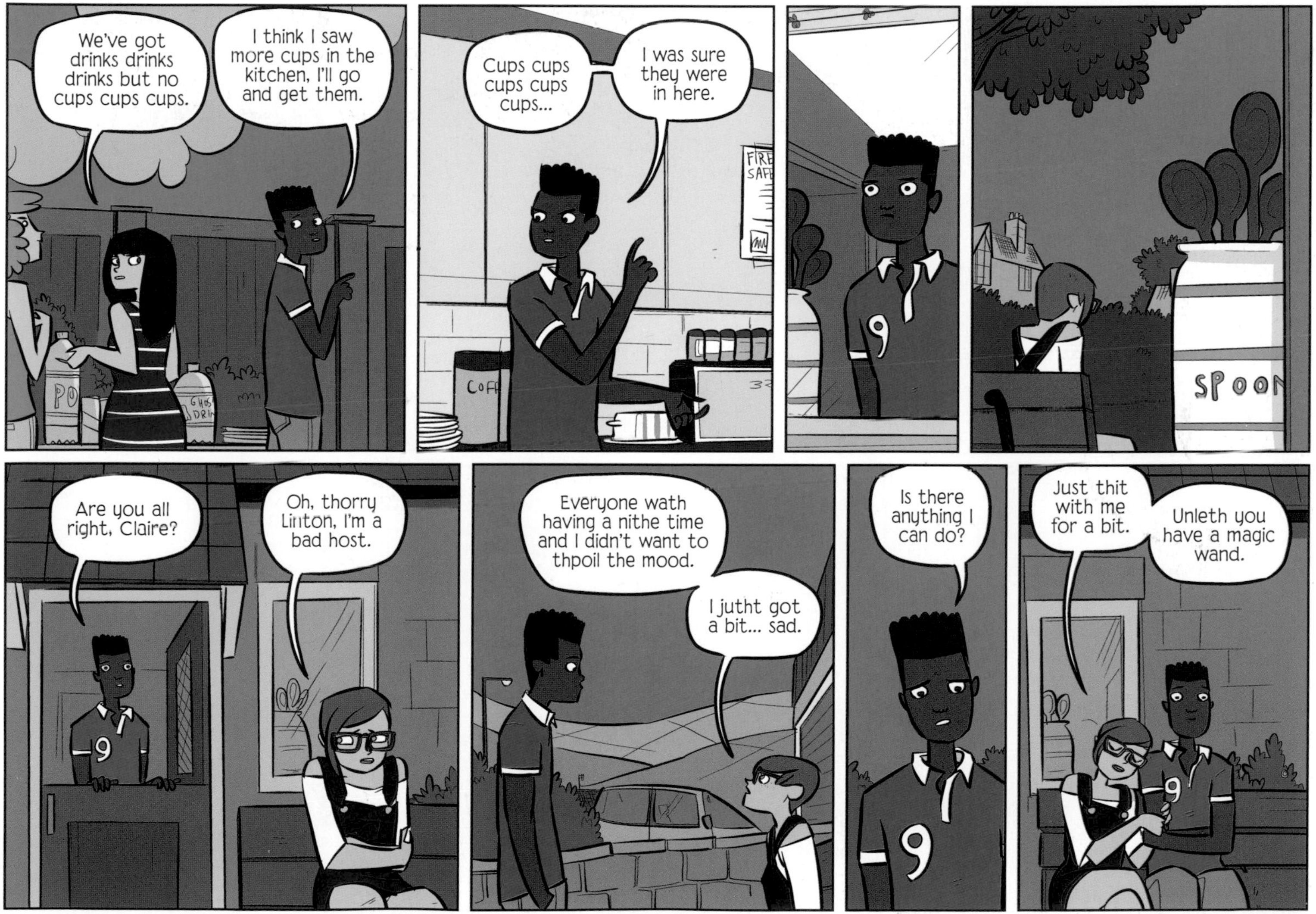
We've got drinks drinks drinks but no cups cups cups.
I think I saw more cups in the kitchen, I'll go and get them.
Cups cups cups cups cups...
I was sure they were in here.
SPOON
Are you all right, Claire?
Oh, thorry Linton, I'm a bad host.
Everyone wath having a nithe time and I didn't want to thpoil the mood.
I jutht got a bit... sad.
Is there anything I can do?
Just thit with me for a bit.
Unleth you have a magic wand.

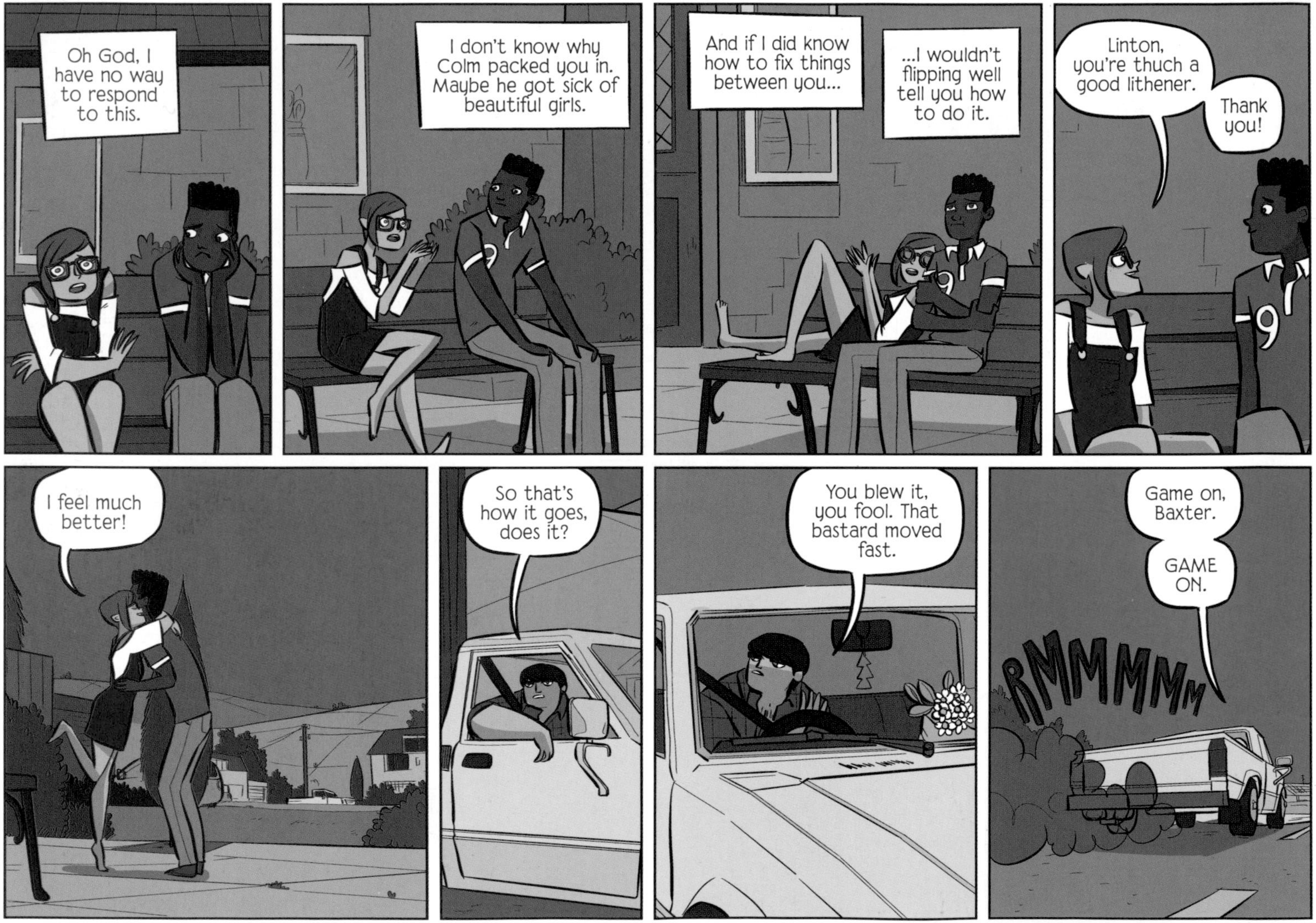
Oh God, I have no way to respond to this.
I don't know why Colm packed you in. Maybe he got sick of beautiful girls.
And if I did know how to fix things between you...
...I wouldn't flipping well tell you how to do it.
Linton, you're thuch a good lithener.
Thank you!
I feel much better!
So that's how it goes, does it?
You blew it, you fool. That bastard moved fast.
Game on, Baxter.
GAME ON.
RMMMMM

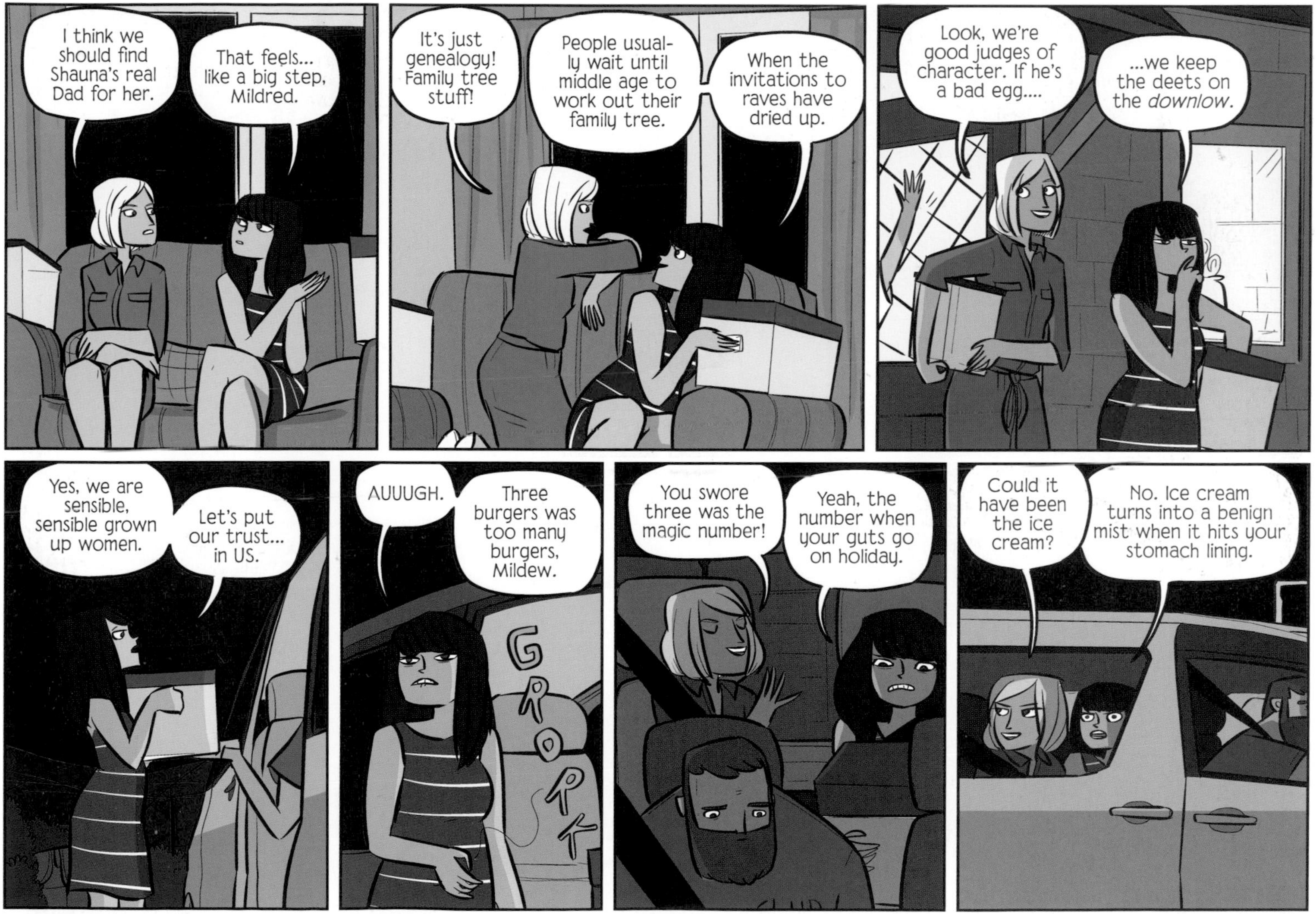
I think we should find Shauna's real Dad for her.
That feels... like a big step, Mildred.
It's just genealogy! Family tree stuff!
People usually wait until middle age to work out their family tree.
When the invitations to raves have dried up.
Look, we're good judges of character. If he's a bad egg....
...we keep the deets on the *downlow*.
Yes, we are sensible, sensible grown up women.
Let's put our trust... in US.
AUUUGH.
Three burgers was too many burgers, Mildew.
GRORK
You swore three was the magic number!
Yeah, the number when your guts go on holiday.
Could it have been the ice cream?
No. Ice cream turns into a benign mist when it hits your stomach lining.

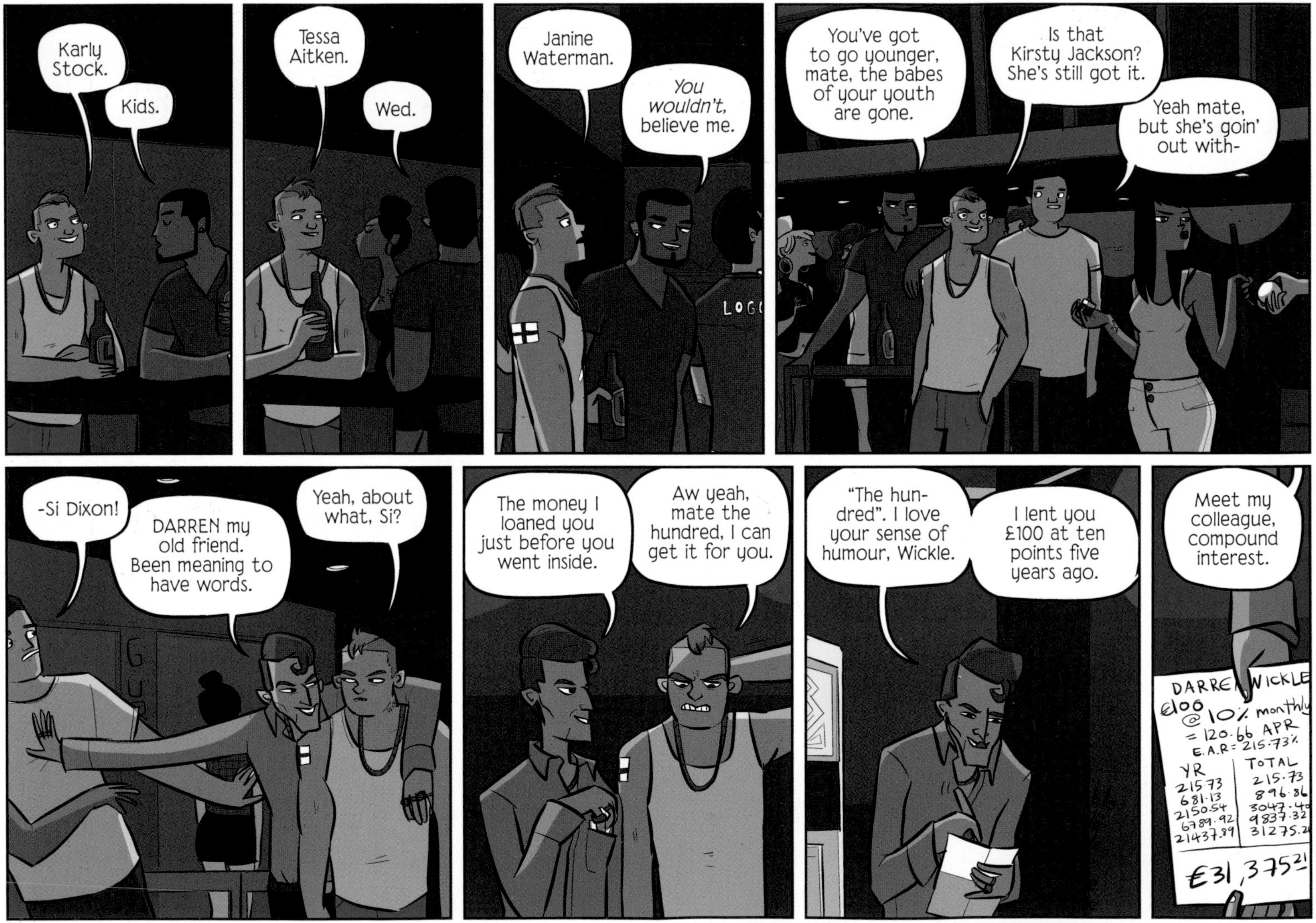
Karly Stock.
Kids.
Tessa Aitken.
Wed.
Janine Waterman.
You wouldn't, believe me.
LOGO
You've got to go younger, mate, the babes of your youth are gone.
Is that Kirsty Jackson? She's still got it.
Yeah mate, but she's goin' out with-
-Si Dixon!
DARREN my old friend. Been meaning to have words.
Yeah, about what, Si?
The money I loaned you just before you went inside.
Aw yeah, mate the hundred, I can get it for you.
"The hundred". I love your sense of humour, Wickle.
I lent you £100 at ten points five years ago.
Meet my colleague, compound interest.
DARRE WICKLE
£100 @ 10% monthly
= 120.66 APR
E.A.R = 215.73%
YR | TOTAL
215.73 | 215.73
681.13 | 896.86
2150.54 | 3047.40
6789.92 | 9837.32
21437.89 | 31275.21
£31,375.21

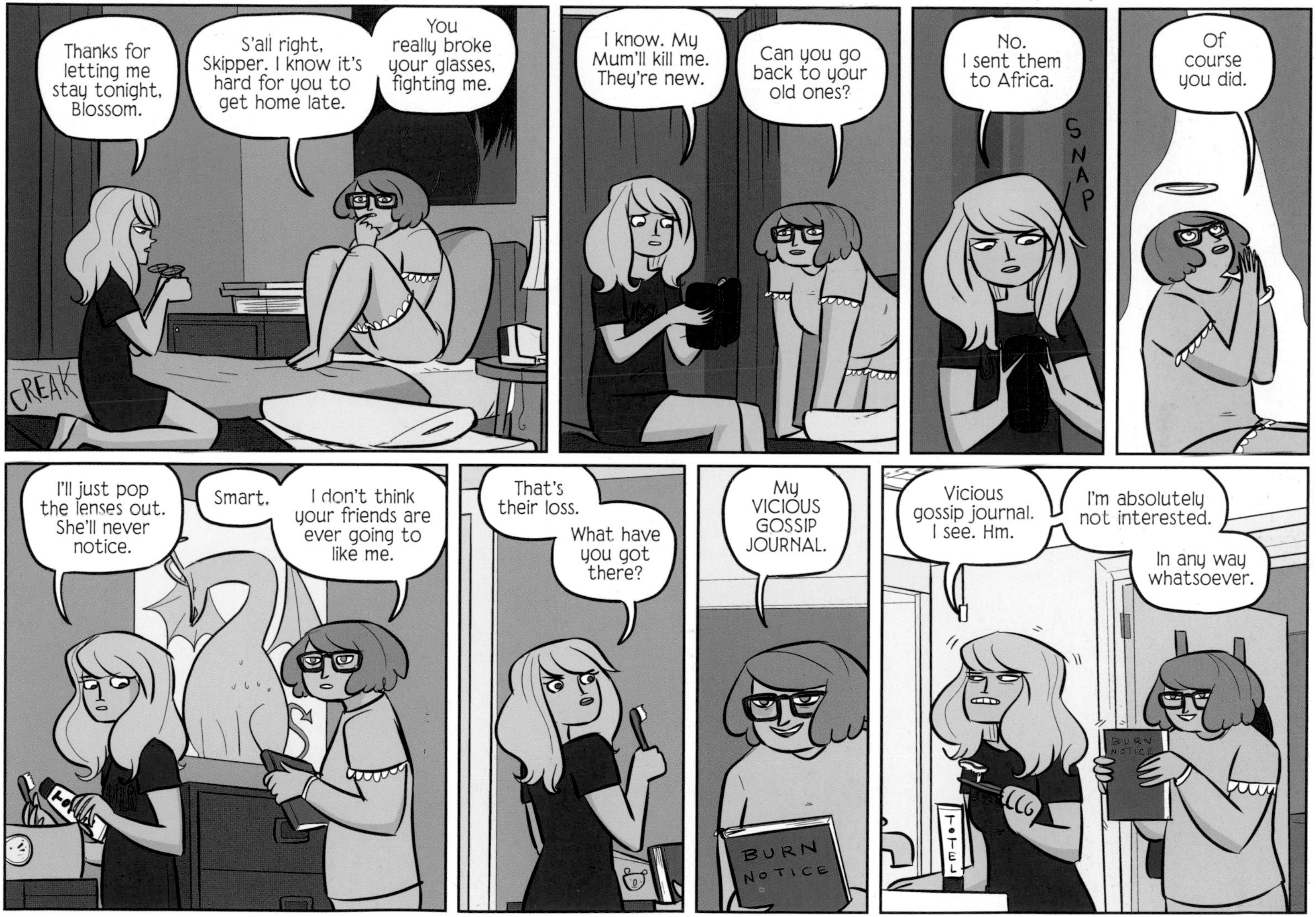
Thanks for letting me stay tonight, Blossom.
S'all right, Skipper. I know it's hard for you to get home late.
You really broke your glasses, fighting me.
CREAK
I know. My Mum'll kill me. They're new.
Can you go back to your old ones?
No. I sent them to Africa.
SNAP
Of course you did.
I'll just pop the lenses out. She'll never notice.
Smart.
I don't think your friends are ever going to like me.
That's their loss.
What have you got there?
My VICIOUS GOSSIP JOURNAL.
BURN NOTICE
Vicious gossip journal. I see. Hm.
I'm absolutely not interested.
In any way whatsoever.
BURN NOTICE

Bad Machinery, Volume Nine

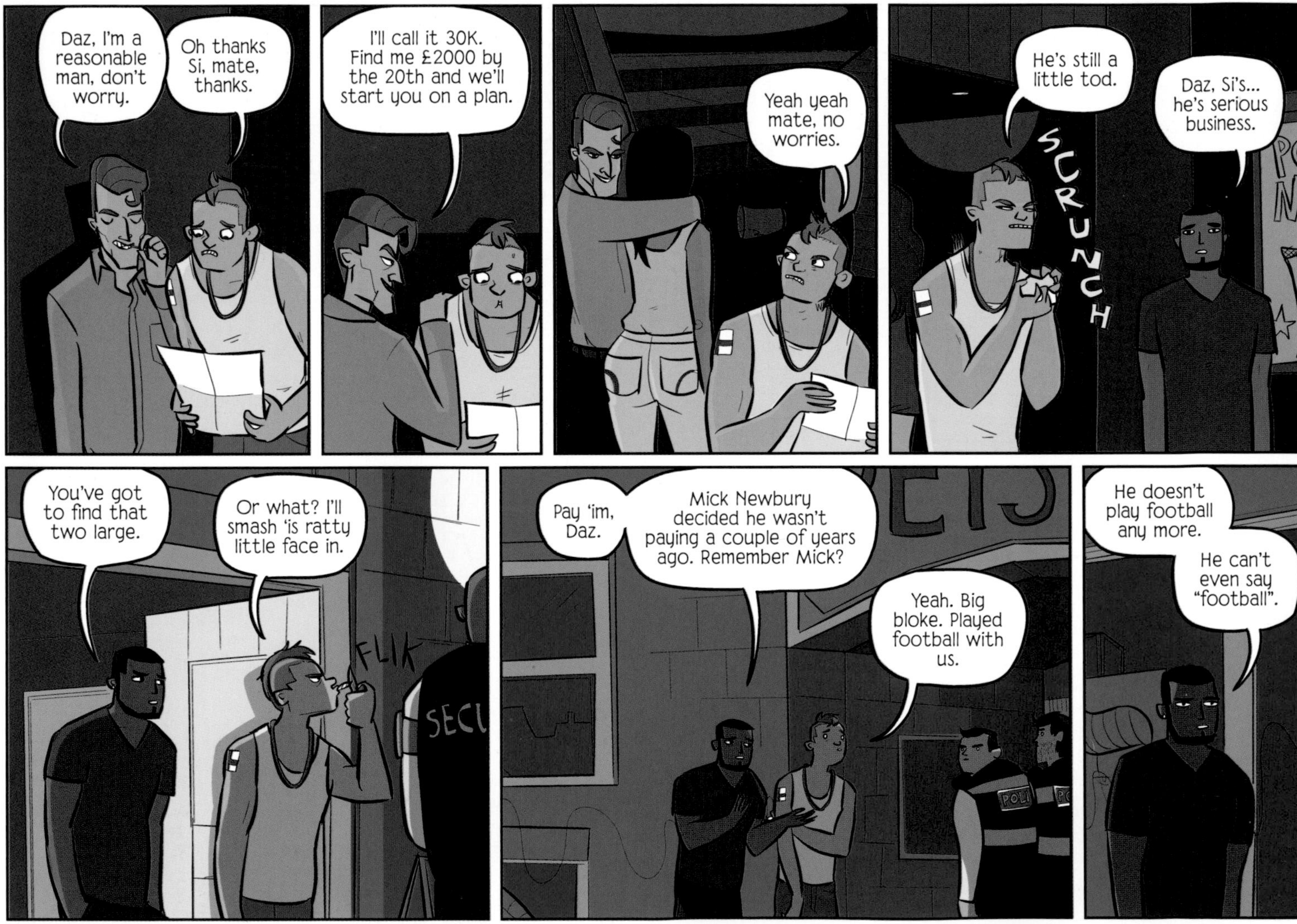
Daz, I'm a reasonable man, don't worry.
Oh thanks Si, mate, thanks.
I'll call it 30K. Find me £2000 by the 20th and we'll start you on a plan.
Yeah yeah mate, no worries.
He's still a little tod.
SCRUNCH
Daz, Si's... he's serious business.
You've got to find that two large.
Or what? I'll smash 'is ratty little face in.
FLIK
Pay 'im, Daz.
Mick Newbury decided he wasn't paying a couple of years ago. Remember Mick?
Yeah. Big bloke. Played football with us.
He doesn't play football any more.
He can't even say "football".

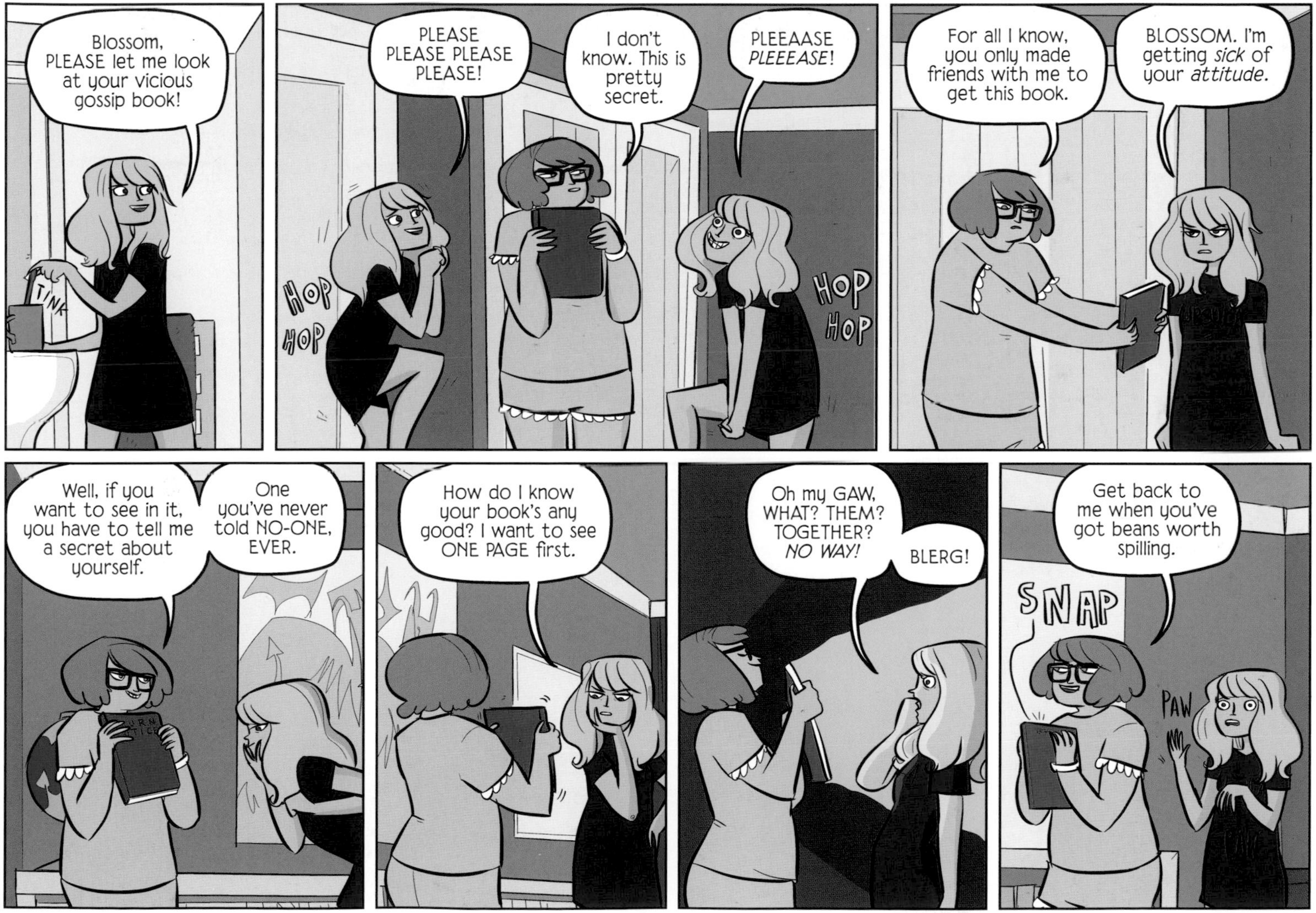
Blossom, PLEASE let me look at your vicious gossip book!
TINK
PLEASE PLEASE PLEASE PLEASE!
HOP HOP
I don't know. This is pretty secret.
PLEEAASE *PLEEEASE*!
HOP HOP
For all I know, you only made friends with me to get this book.
BLOSSOM. I'm getting *sick* of your *attitude*.
Well, if you want to see in it, you have to tell me a secret about yourself.
One you've never told NO-ONE, EVER.
How do I know your book's any good? I want to see ONE PAGE first.
Oh my GAW, WHAT? THEM? TOGETHER? *NO WAY!*
BLERG!
Get back to me when you've got beans worth spilling.
SNAP
PAW

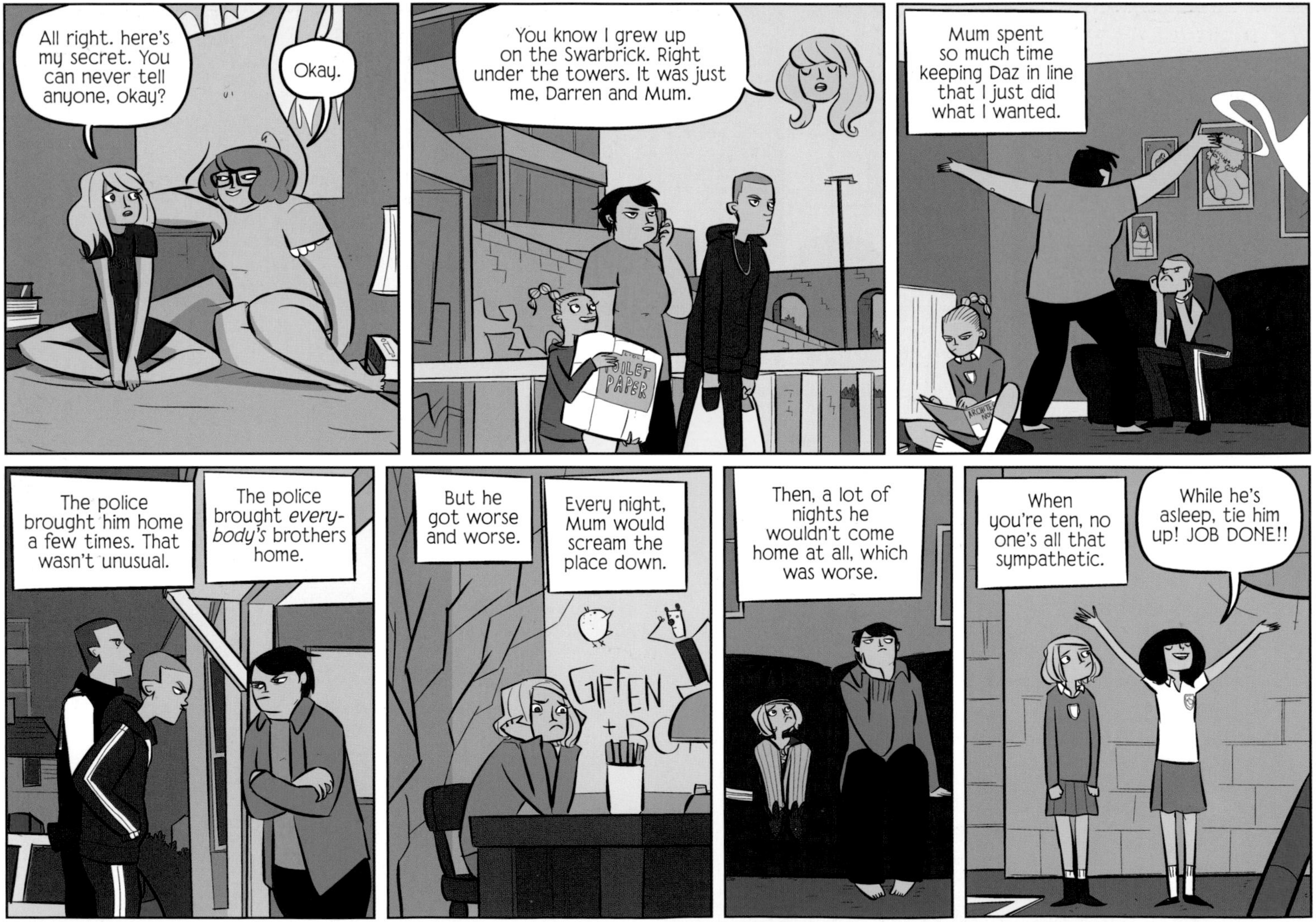
All right. here's my secret. You can never tell anyone, okay?
Okay.
You know I grew up on the Swarbrick. Right under the towers. It was just me, Darren and Mum.
TOILET PAPER
Mum spent so much time keeping Daz in line that I just did what I wanted.
The police brought him home a few times. That wasn't unusual.
The police brought *every-body's* brothers home.
But he got worse and worse.
Every night, Mum would scream the place down.
GIFFEN
Then, a lot of nights he wouldn't come home at all, which was worse.
When you're ten, no one's all that sympathetic.
While he's asleep, tie him up! JOB DONE!!

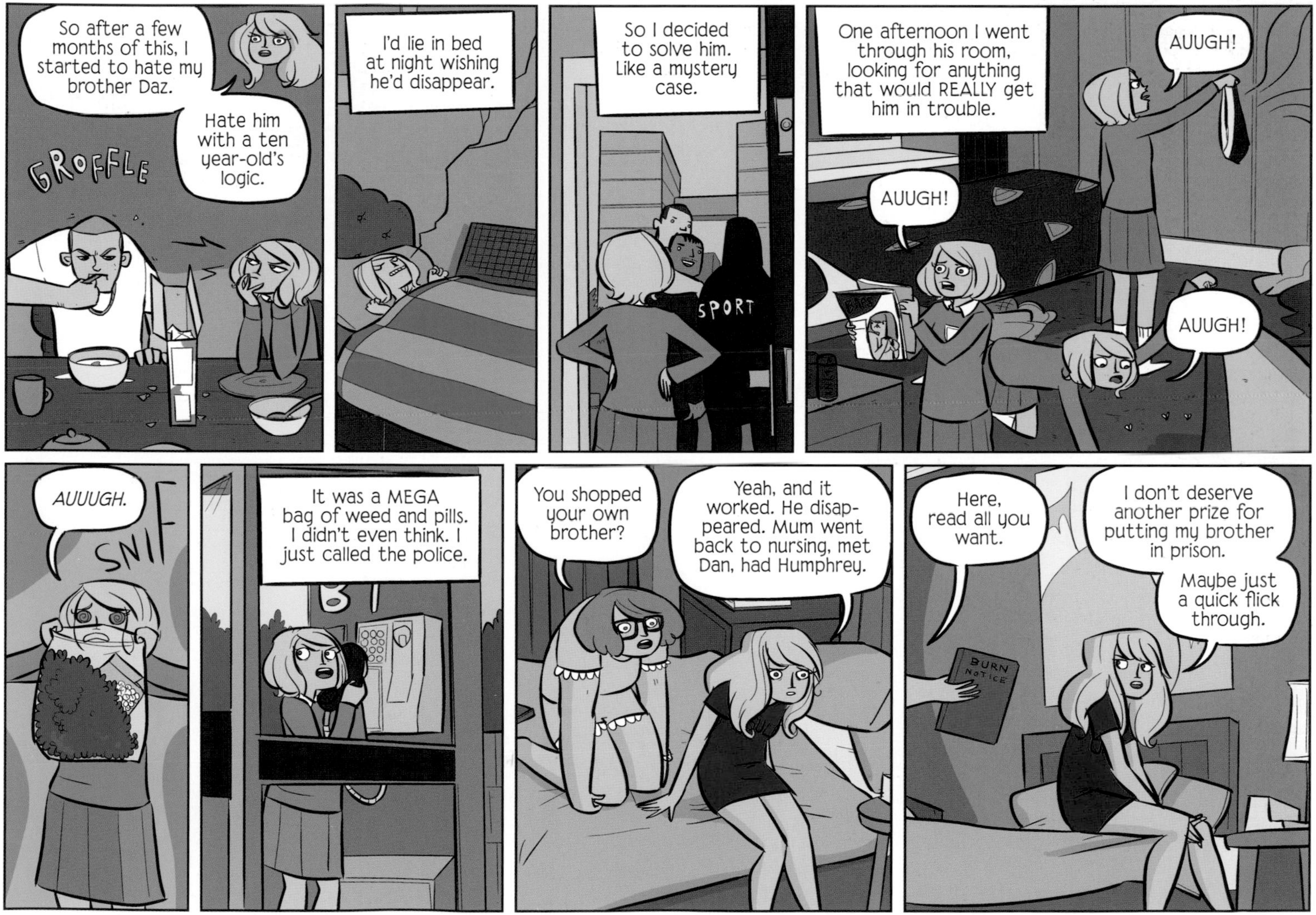
So after a few months of this, I started to hate my brother Daz.
Hate him with a ten year-old's logic.
GROFFLE
I'd lie in bed at night wishing he'd disappear.
So I decided to solve him. Like a mystery case.
SPORT
One afternoon I went through his room, looking for anything that would REALLY get him in trouble.
AUUGH!
AUUGH!
AUUGH!
AUUUGH.
SNIF
It was a MEGA bag of weed and pills. I didn't even think. I just called the police.
You shopped your own brother?
Yeah, and it worked. He disappeared. Mum went back to nursing, met Dan, had Humphrey.
Here, read all you want.
BURN NOTICE
I don't deserve another prize for putting my brother in prison.
Maybe just a quick flick through.

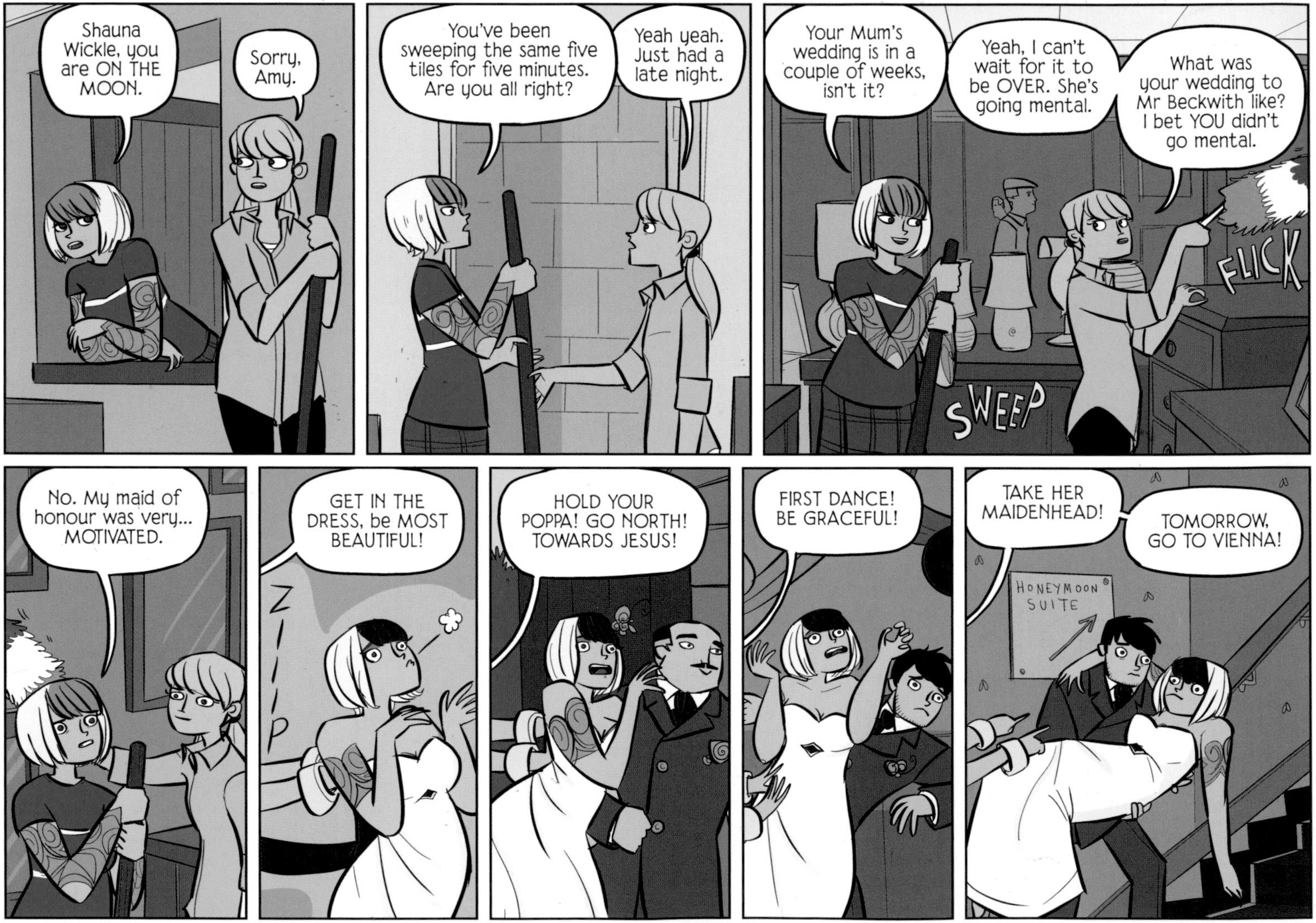
Shauna Wickle, you are ON THE MOON.
Sorry, Amy.
You've been sweeping the same five tiles for five minutes. Are you all right?
Yeah yeah. Just had a late night.
Your Mum's wedding is in a couple of weeks, isn't it?
Yeah, I can't wait for it to be OVER. She's going mental.
What was your wedding to Mr Beckwith like? I bet YOU didn't go mental.
FLICK
SWEEP
No. My maid of honour was very... MOTIVATED.
GET IN THE DRESS, be MOST BEAUTIFUL!
ZIP
HOLD YOUR POPPA! GO NORTH! TOWARDS JESUS!
FIRST DANCE! BE GRACEFUL!
TAKE HER MAIDENHEAD!
TOMORROW, GO TO VIENNA!
HONEYMOON SUITE

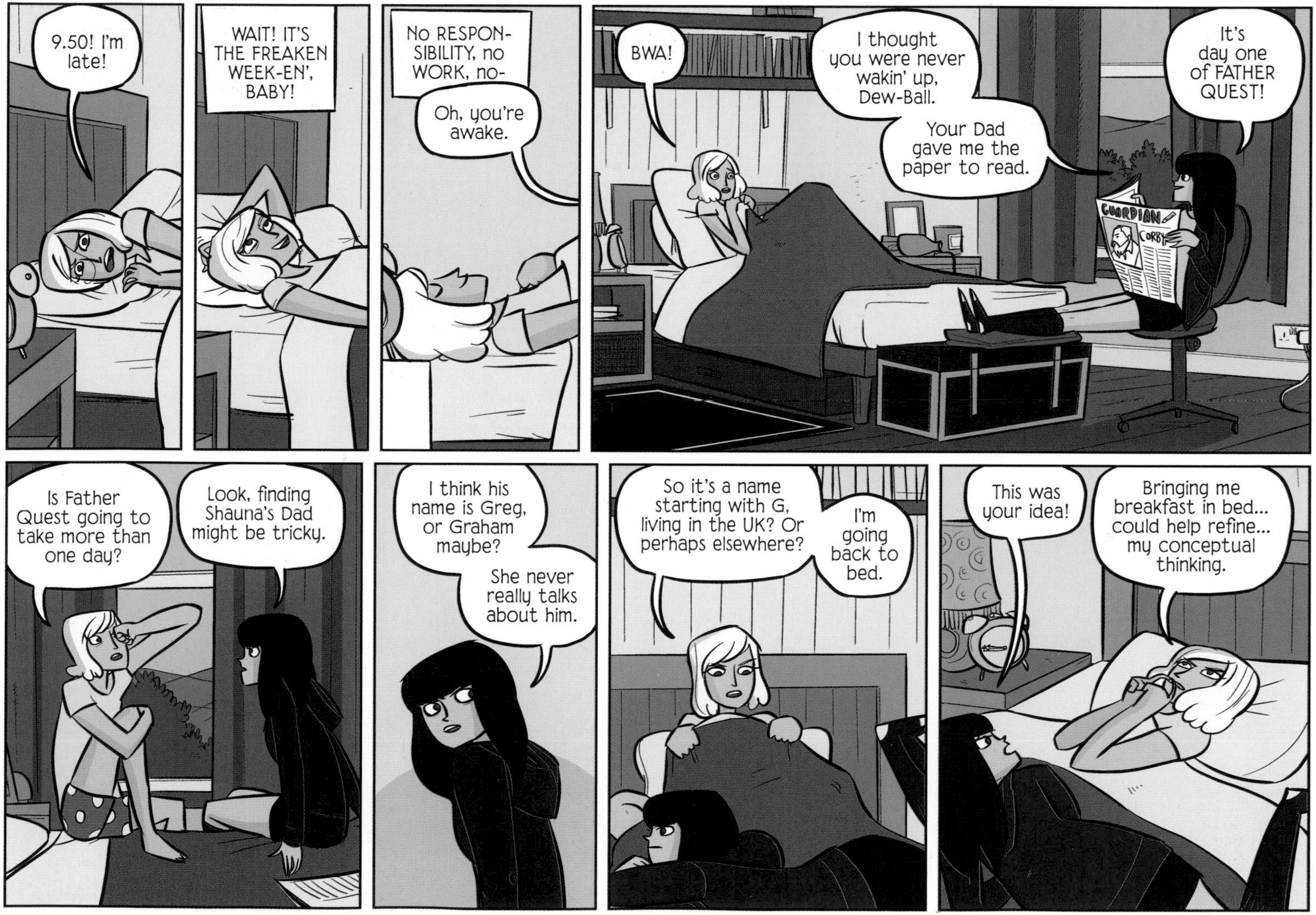
9.50! I'm late!
WAIT! IT'S THE FREAKEN WEEK-EN', BABY!
No RESPON-SIBILITY, no WORK, no-
Oh, you're awake.
BWA!
I thought you were never wakin' up, Dew-Ball.
Your Dad gave me the paper to read.
It's day one of FATHER QUEST!
GUARDIAN
CORBY
Is Father Quest going to take more than one day?
Look, finding Shauna's Dad might be tricky.
I think his name is Greg, or Graham maybe?
She never really talks about him.
So it's a name starting with G, living in the UK? Or perhaps elsewhere?
I'm going back to bed.
This was your idea!
Bringing me breakfast in bed... could help refine... my conceptual thinking.

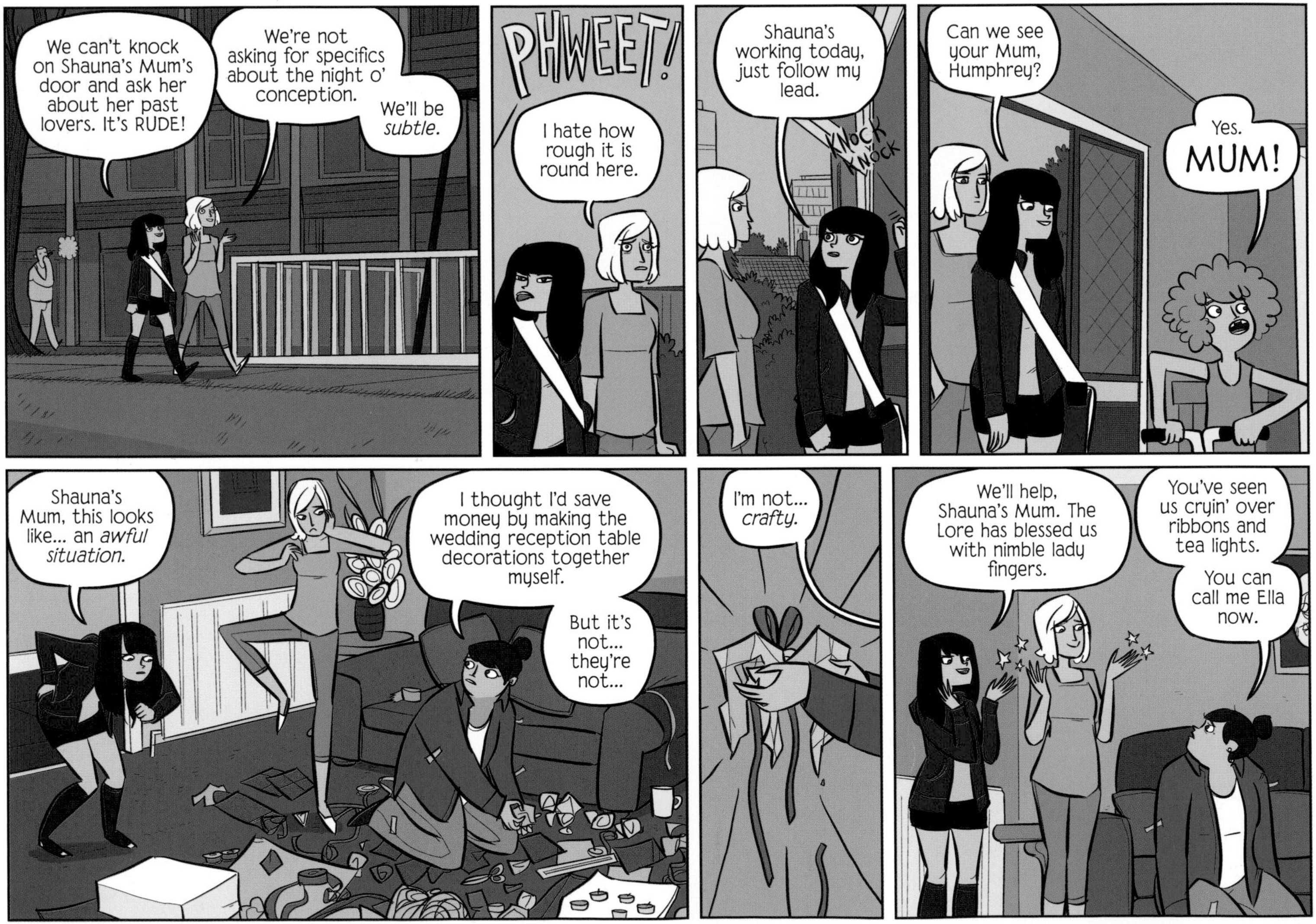

We can't knock on Shauna's Mum's door and ask her about her past lovers. It's RUDE!
We're not asking for specifics about the night o' conception.
We'll be *subtle*.
PHWEET!
I hate how rough it is round here.
Shauna's working today, just follow my lead.
KNOCK KNOCK
Can we see your Mum, Humphrey?
Yes.
MUM!
Shauna's Mum, this looks like... an *awful situation.*
I thought I'd save money by making the wedding reception table decorations together myself.
But it's not... they're not...
I'm not... *crafty.*
We'll help, Shauna's Mum. The Lore has blessed us with nimble lady fingers.
You've seen us cryin' over ribbons and tea lights.
You can call me Ella now.

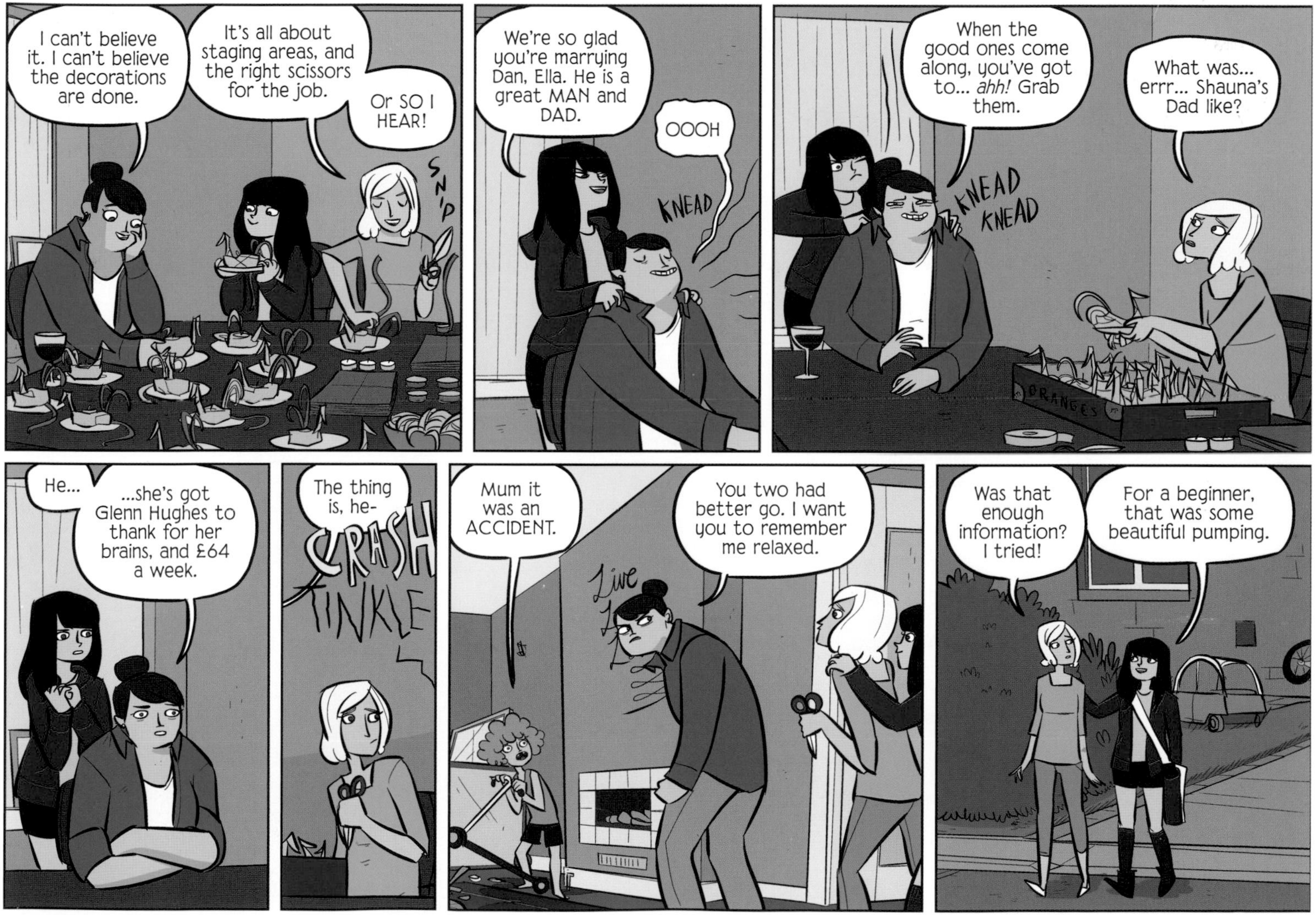

I can't believe it. I can't believe the decorations are done.
It's all about staging areas, and the right scissors for the job.
Or SO I HEAR!
SNIP
We're so glad you're marrying Dan, Ella. He is a great MAN and DAD.
OOOH
KNEAD
When the good ones come along, you've got to... *ahh!* Grab them.
KNEAD KNEAD
What was... errr... Shauna's Dad like?
ORANGES
He...
...she's got Glenn Hughes to thank for her brains, and £64 a week.
The thing is, he-
CRASH
TINKLE
Mum it was an ACCIDENT.
You two had better go. I want you to remember me relaxed.
Was that enough information? I tried!
For a beginner, that was some beautiful pumping.

Bad Machinery, Volume Nine

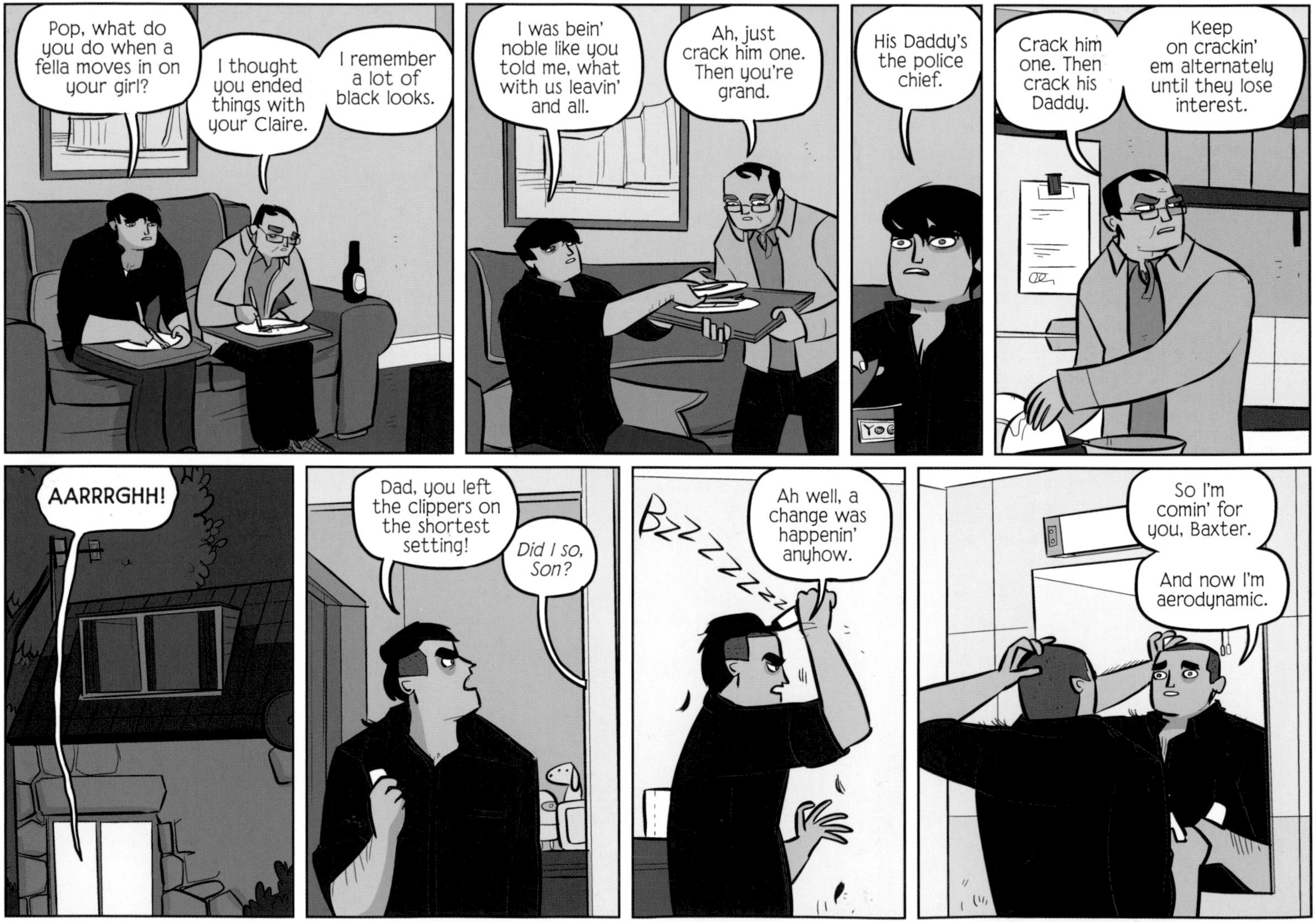
Pop, what do you do when a fella moves in on your girl?
I thought you ended things with your Claire.
I remember a lot of black looks.
I was bein' noble like you told me, what with us leavin' and all.
Ah, just crack him one. Then you're grand.
His Daddy's the police chief.
Crack him one. Then crack his Daddy.
Keep on crackin' em alternately until they lose interest.
AARRRGHH!
Dad, you left the clippers on the shortest setting!
Did I so, Son?
BZZZZZZZZZ
Ah well, a change was happenin' anyhow.
So I'm comin' for you, Baxter.
And now I'm aerodynamic.

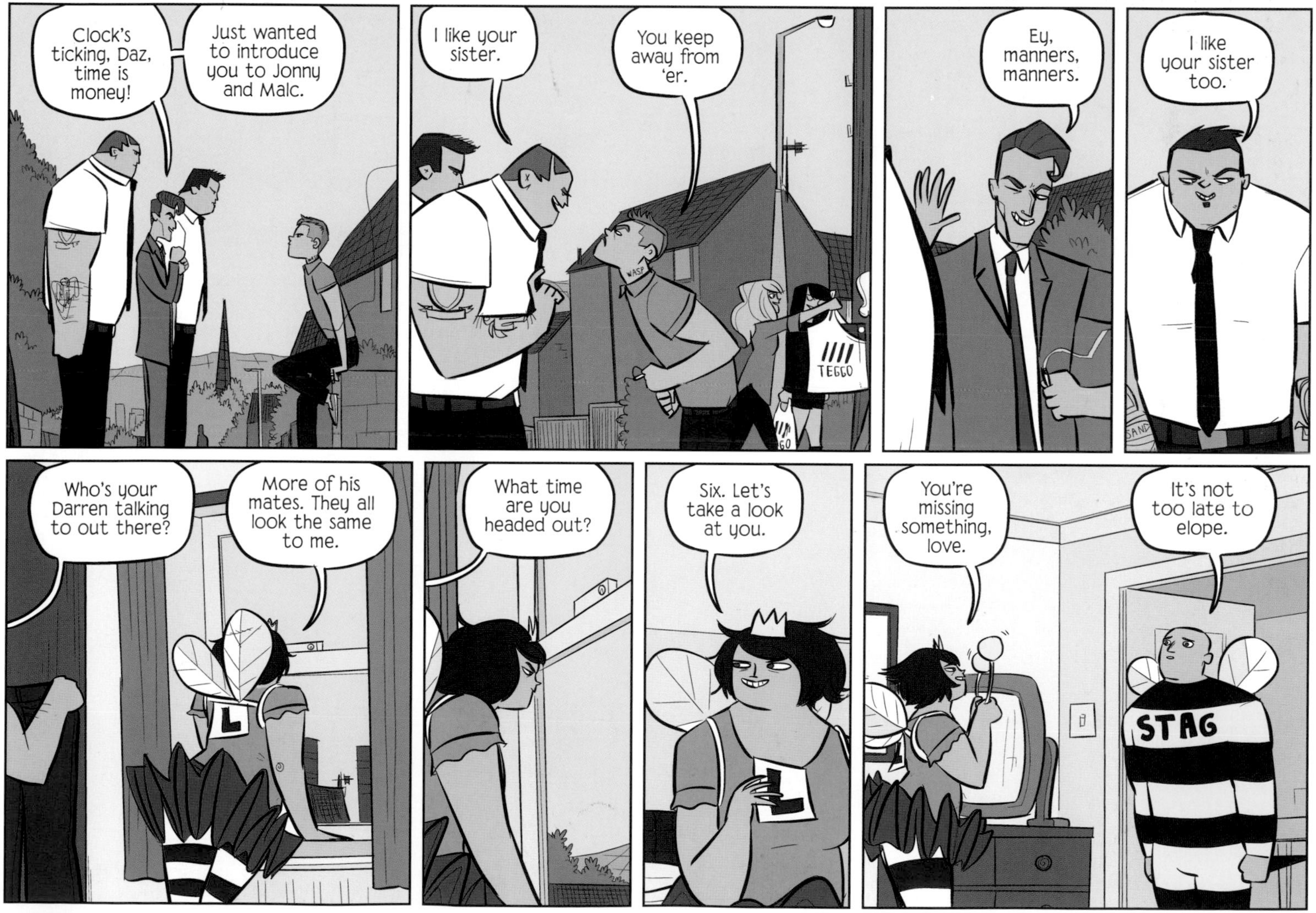
Clock's ticking, Daz, time is money!
Just wanted to introduce you to Jonny and Malc.
WASP
I like your sister.
You keep away from 'er.
TEGGO
Ey, manners, manners.
I like your sister too.
Who's your Darren talking to out there?
More of his mates. They all look the same to me.
What time are you headed out?
Six. Let's take a look at you.
You're missing something, love.
It's not too late to elope.
STAG

Bad Machinery, Volume Nine

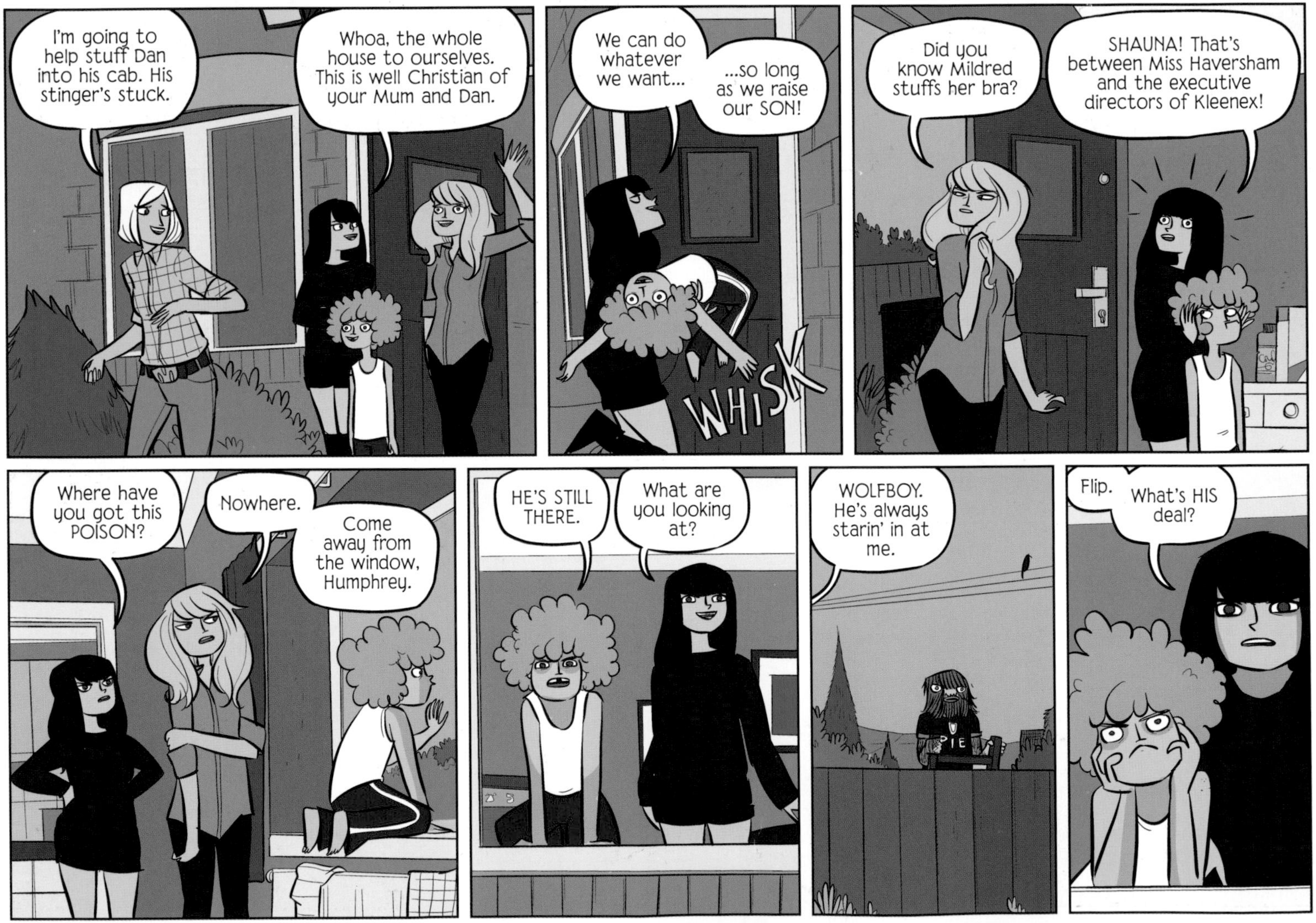
I'm going to help stuff Dan into his cab. His stinger's stuck.
Whoa, the whole house to ourselves. This is well Christian of your Mum and Dan.
We can do whatever we want...
...so long as we raise our SON!
WHISK
Did you know Mildred stuffs her bra?
SHAUNA! That's between Miss Haversham and the executive directors of Kleenex!
Where have you got this POISON?
Nowhere.
Come away from the window, Humphrey.
HE'S STILL THERE.
What are you looking at?
WOLFBOY. He's always starin' in at me.
Flip.
What's HIS deal?

The Case of the Missing Piece

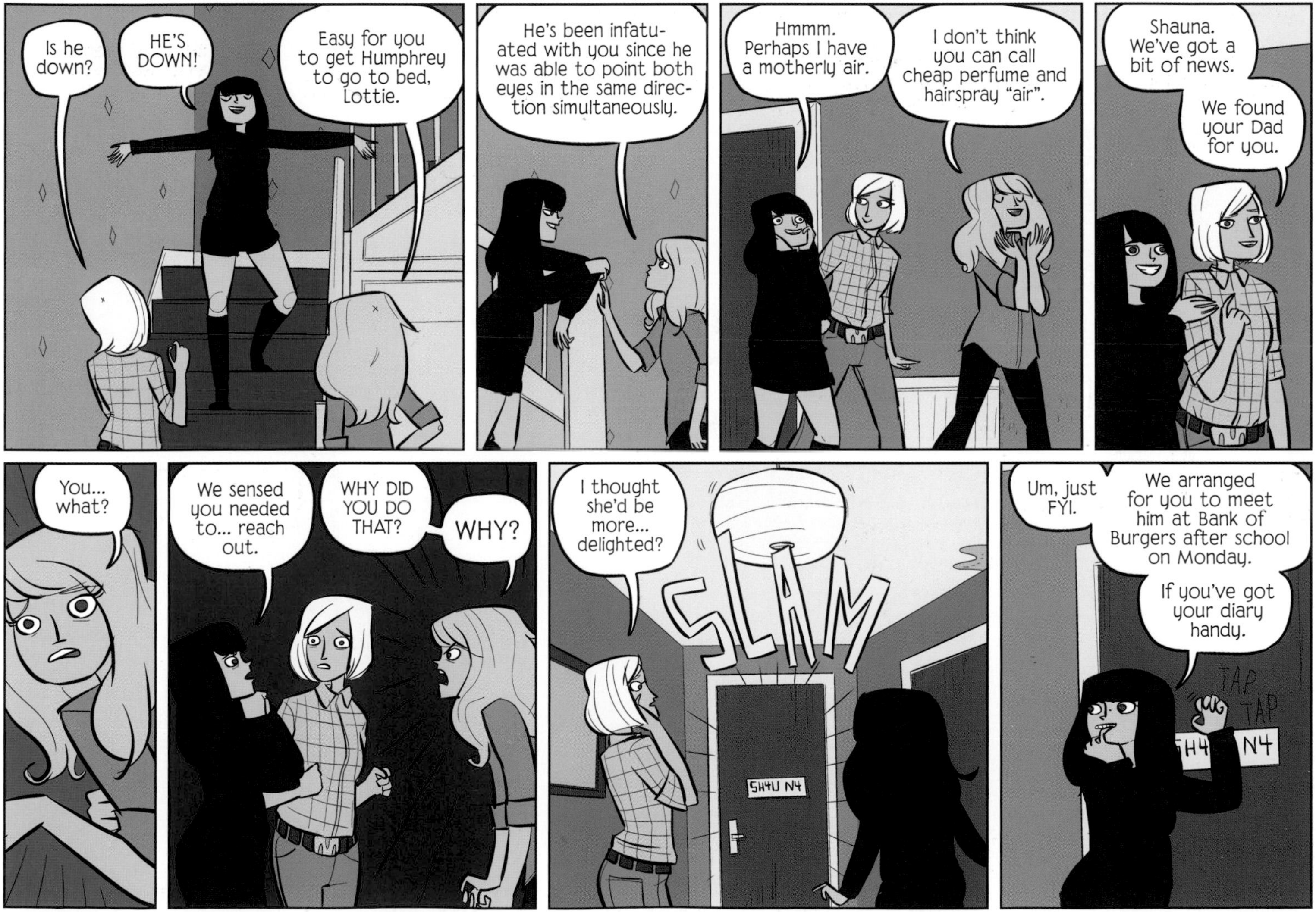

Is he down?
HE'S DOWN!
Easy for you to get Humphrey to go to bed, Lottie.
He's been infatuated with you since he was able to point both eyes in the same direction simultaneously.
Hmmm. Perhaps I have a motherly air.
I don't think you can call cheap perfume and hairspray "air".
Shauna. We've got a bit of news.
We found your Dad for you.
You... what?
We sensed you needed to... reach out.
WHY DID YOU DO THAT?
WHY?
I thought she'd be more... delighted?
SLAM
SH4U N4
Um, just FYI.
We arranged for you to meet him at Bank of Burgers after school on Monday.
If you've got your diary handy.
TAP TAP

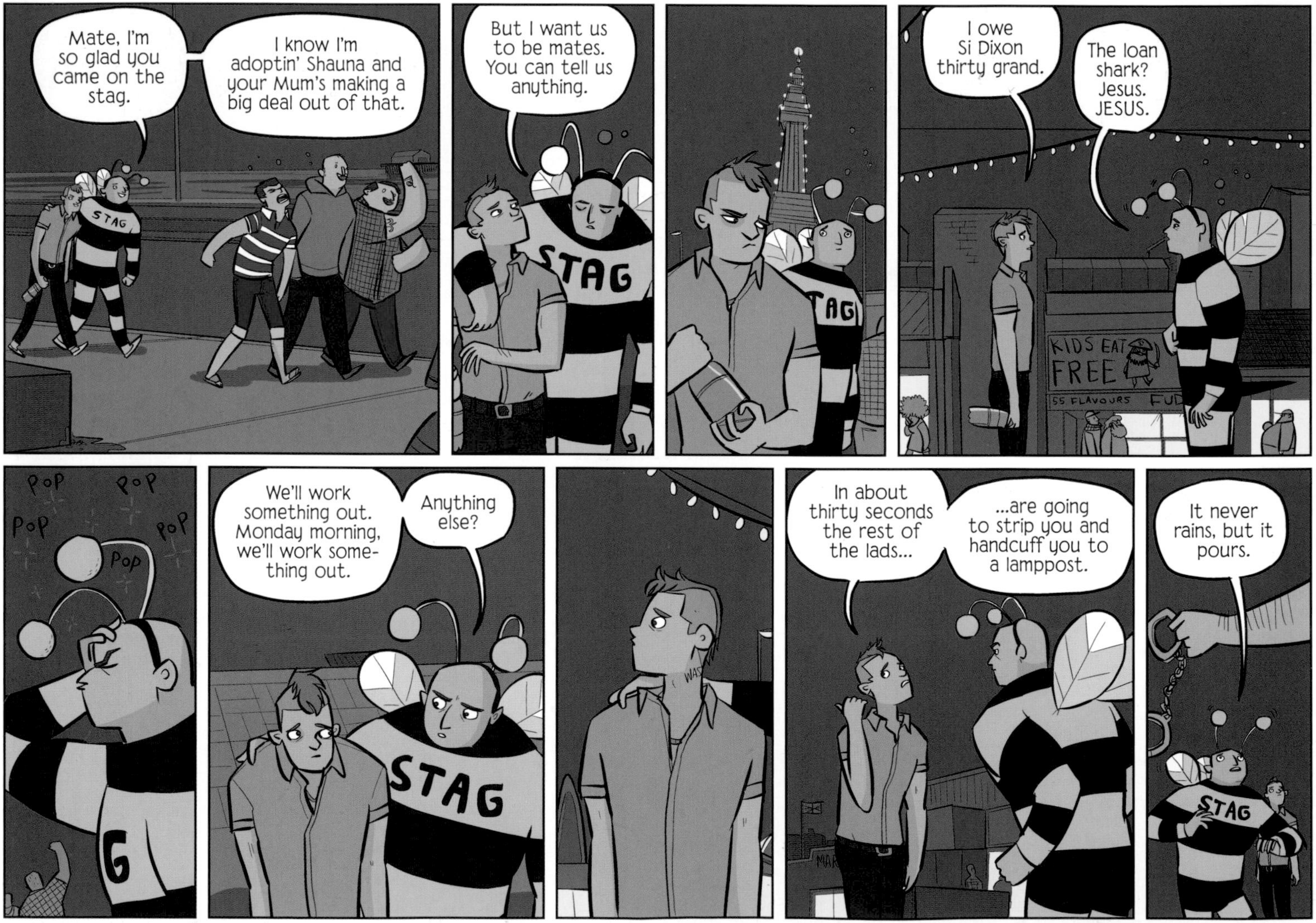
Mate, I'm so glad you came on the stag.
I know I'm adoptin' Shauna and your Mum's making a big deal out of that.
STAG
But I want us to be mates. You can tell us anything.
STAG
I owe Si Dixon thirty grand.
The loan shark? Jesus. JESUS.
KIDS EAT FREE
55 FLAVOURS
POP
POP
POP
POP
POP
We'll work something out. Monday morning, we'll work something out.
Anything else?
STAG
In about thirty seconds the rest of the lads...
...are going to strip you and handcuff you to a lamppost.
It never rains, but it pours.
STAG

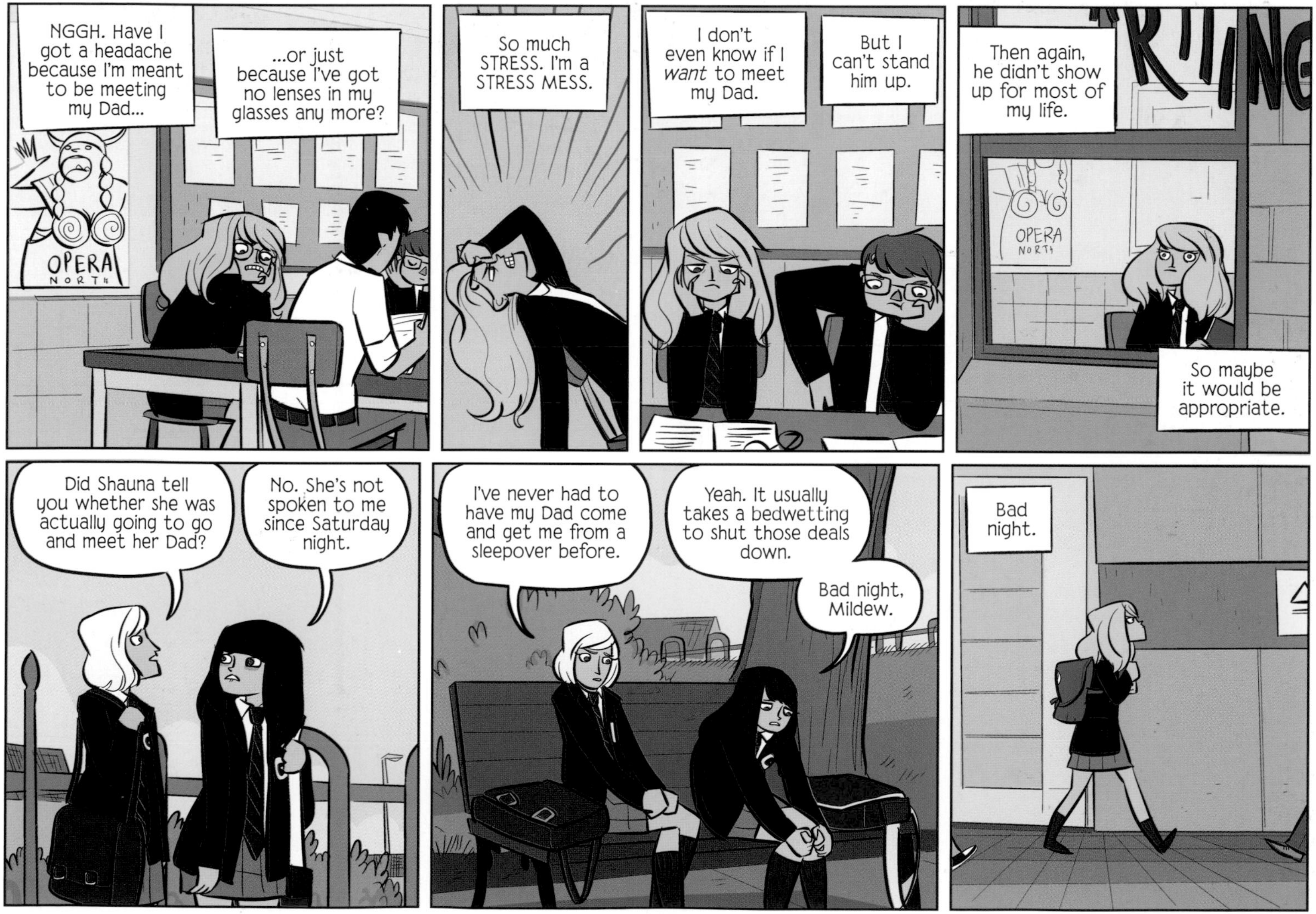

NGGH. Have I got a headache because I'm meant to be meeting my Dad...
...or just because I've got no lenses in my glasses any more?
OPERA NORTH
So much STRESS. I'm a STRESS MESS.
I don't even know if I *want* to meet my Dad.
But I can't stand him up.
Then again, he didn't show up for most of my life.
OPERA NORTH
So maybe it would be appropriate.
Did Shauna tell you whether she was actually going to go and meet her Dad?
No. She's not spoken to me since Saturday night.
I've never had to have my Dad come and get me from a sleepover before.
Yeah. It usually takes a bedwetting to shut those deals down.
Bad night, Mildew.
Bad night.

Bad Machinery, Volume Nine

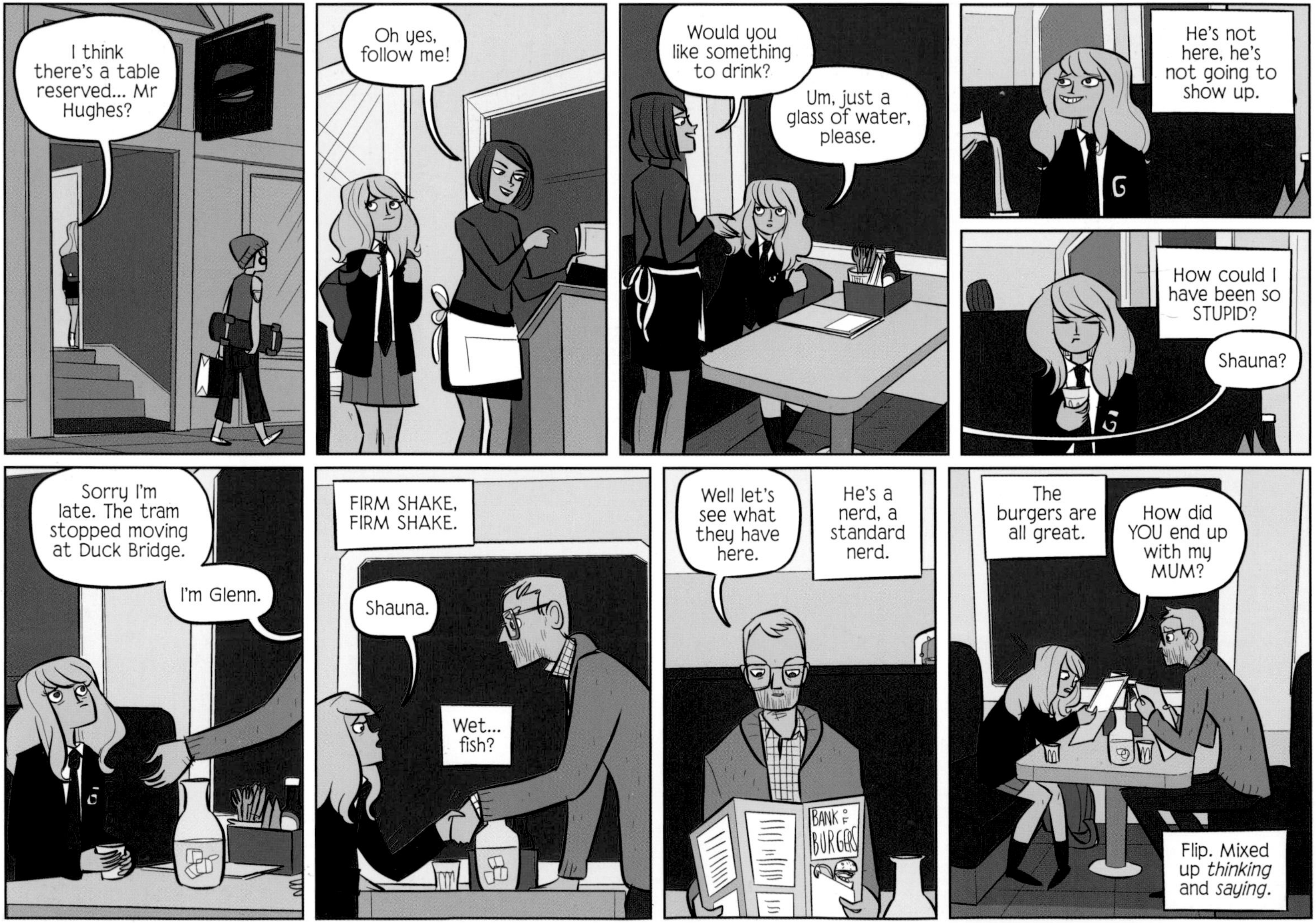
I think there's a table reserved... Mr Hughes?
Oh yes, follow me!
Would you like something to drink?
Um, just a glass of water, please.
He's not here, he's not going to show up.
How could I have been so STUPID?
Shauna?
Sorry I'm late. The tram stopped moving at Duck Bridge.
I'm Glenn.
FIRM SHAKE, FIRM SHAKE.
Shauna.
Wet... fish?
Well let's see what they have here.
He's a nerd, a standard nerd.
BANK OF BURGERS
The burgers are all great.
How did YOU end up with my MUM?
Flip. Mixed up *thinking* and *saying*.

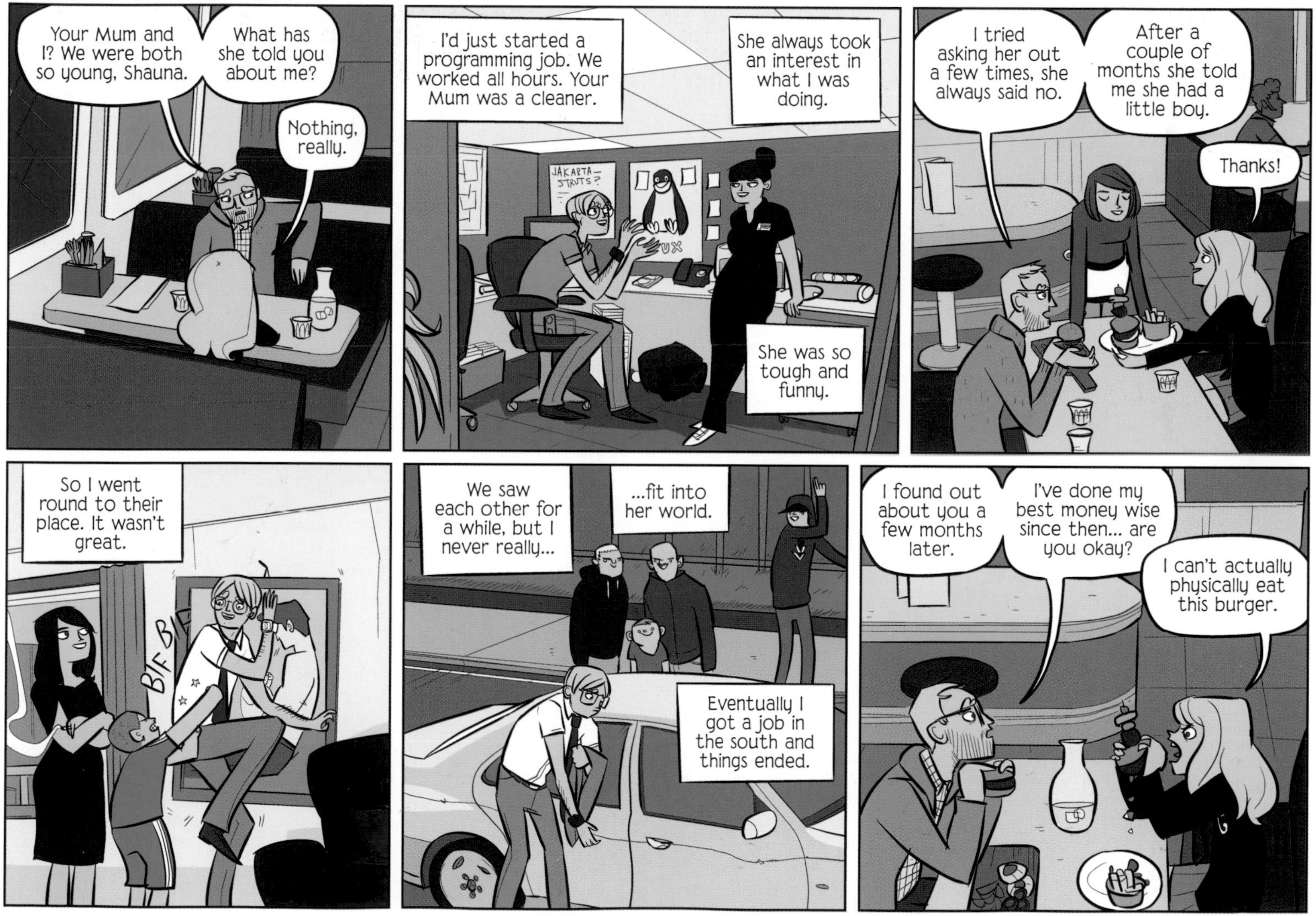

Your Mum and I? We were both so young, Shauna.
What has she told you about me?
Nothing, really.
I'd just started a programming job. We worked all hours. Your Mum was a cleaner.
JAKARTA-STRUTS?
She always took an interest in what I was doing.
She was so tough and funny.
I tried asking her out a few times, she always said no.
After a couple of months she told me she had a little boy.
Thanks!
So I went round to their place. It wasn't great.
BIF BIF
We saw each other for a while, but I never really...
...fit into her world.
Eventually I got a job in the south and things ended.
I found out about you a few months later.
I've done my best money wise since then... are you okay?
I can't actually physically eat this burger.

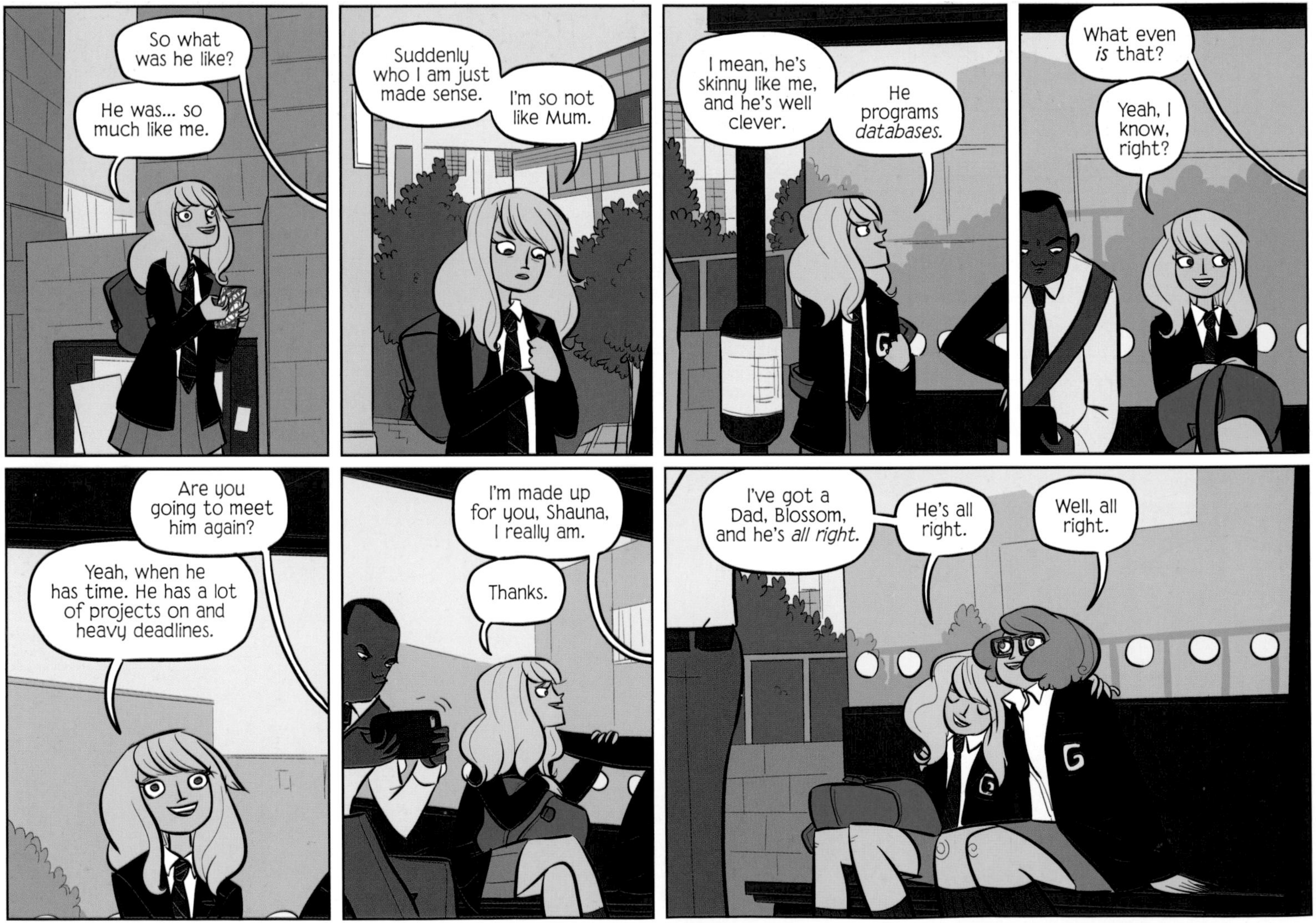
So what was he like?
He was... so much like me.
Suddenly who I am just made sense.
I'm so not like Mum.
I mean, he's skinny like me, and he's well clever.
He programs *databases.*
What even *is* that?
Yeah, I know, right?
Are you going to meet him again?
Yeah, when he has time. He has a lot of projects on and heavy deadlines.
I'm made up for you, Shauna, I really am.
Thanks.
I've got a Dad, Blossom, and he's *all right.*
He's all right.
Well, all right.

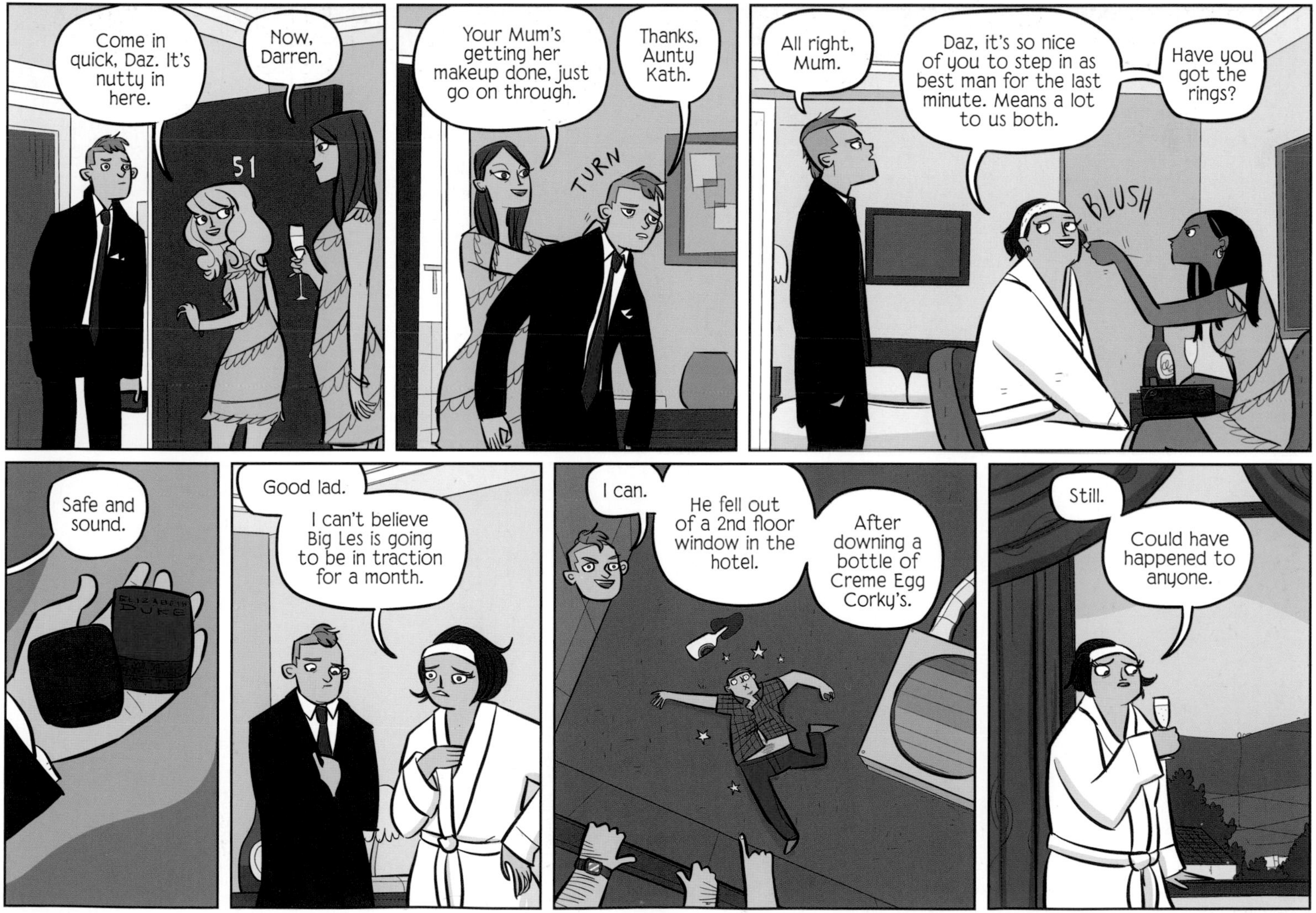
Come in quick, Daz. It's nutty in here.
Now, Darren.
51
Your Mum's getting her makeup done, just go on through.
TURN
Thanks, Aunty Kath.
All right, Mum.
Daz, it's so nice of you to step in as best man for the last minute. Means a lot to us both.
BLUSH
Have you got the rings?
Safe and sound.
ELIZABETH DUKE
Good lad.
I can't believe Big Les is going to be in traction for a month.
I can.
He fell out of a 2nd floor window in the hotel.
After downing a bottle of Creme Egg Corky's.
Still.
Could have happened to anyone.

Bad Machinery, Volume Nine

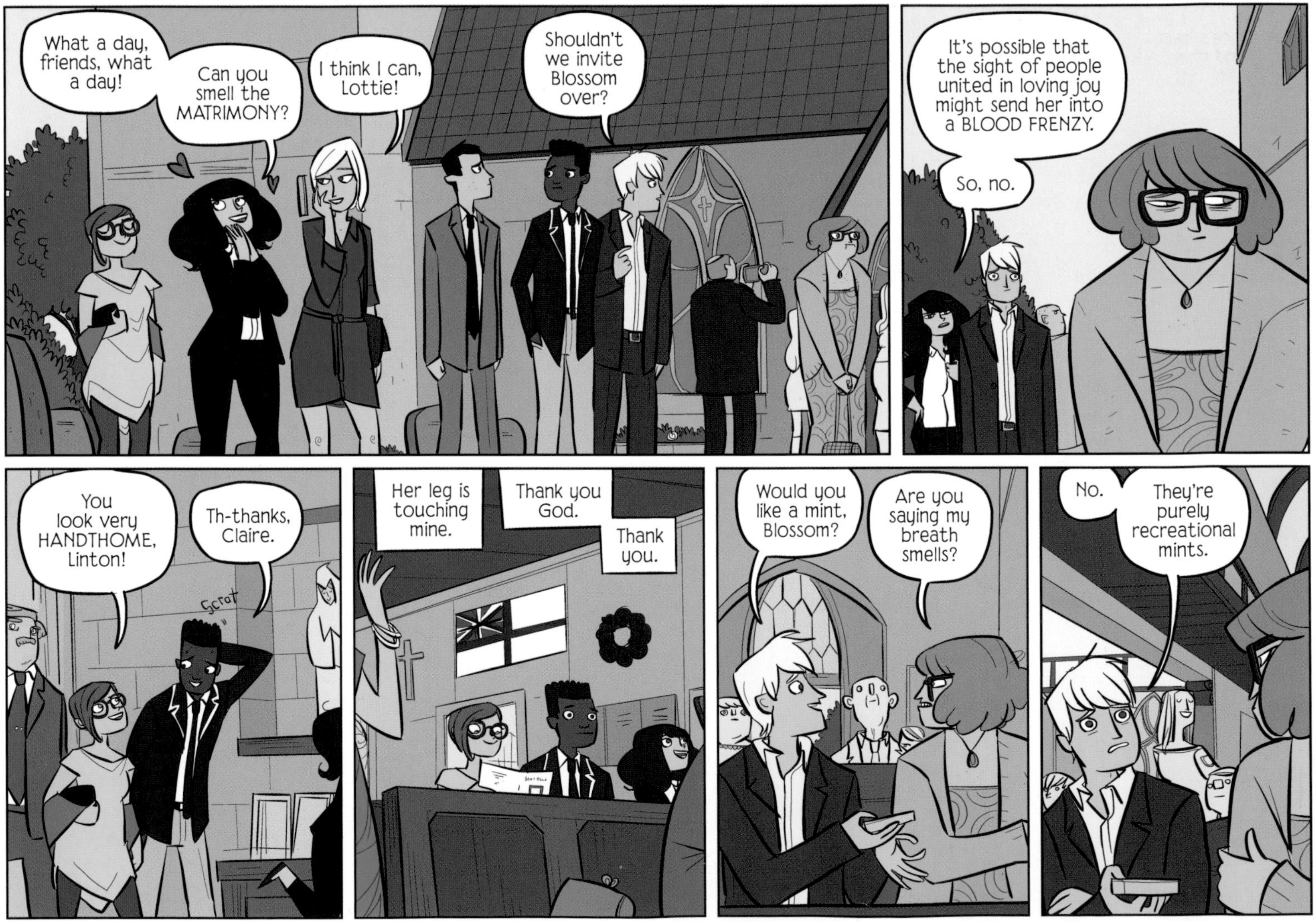
What a day, friends, what a day!
Can you smell the MATRIMONY?
I think I can, Lottie!
Shouldn't we invite Blossom over?
It's possible that the sight of people united in loving joy might send her into a BLOOD FRENZY.
So, no.
You look very HANDTHOME, Linton!
Th-thanks, Claire.
Scrat
Her leg is touching mine.
Thank you God.
Thank you.
Would you like a mint, Blossom?
Are you saying my breath smells?
No.
They're purely recreational mints.

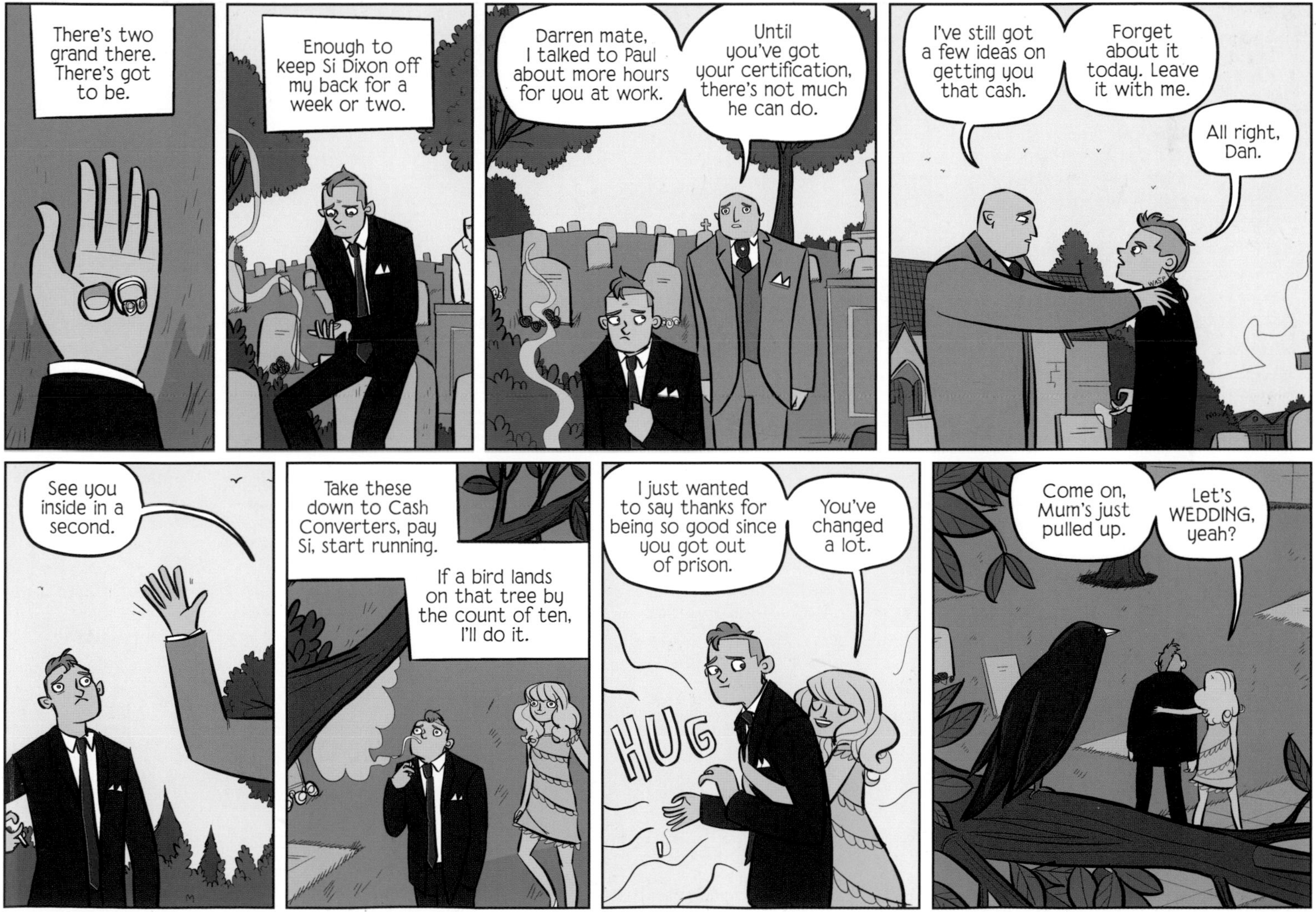

There's two grand there. There's got to be.
Enough to keep Si Dixon off my back for a week or two.
Darren mate, I talked to Paul about more hours for you at work.
Until you've got your certification, there's not much he can do.
I've still got a few ideas on getting you that cash.
Forget about it today. Leave it with me.
All right, Dan.
See you inside in a second.
Take these down to Cash Converters, pay Si, start running.
If a bird lands on that tree by the count of ten, I'll do it.
I just wanted to say thanks for being so good since you got out of prison.
You've changed a lot.
HUG
Come on, Mum's just pulled up.
Let's WEDDING, yeah?

Bad Machinery, Volume Nine

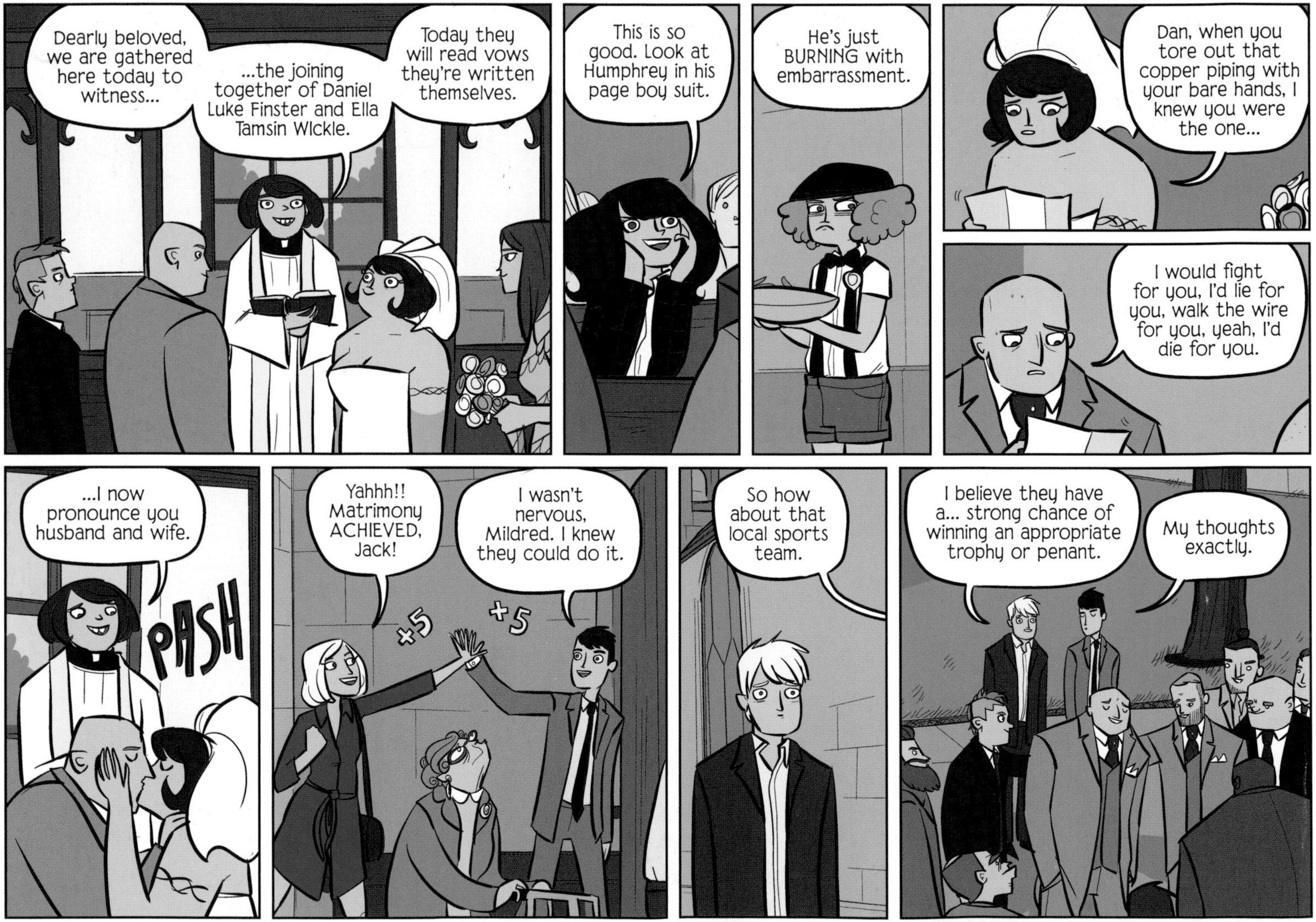
Dearly beloved, we are gathered here today to witness...
...the joining together of Daniel Luke Finster and Ella Tamsin Wickle.
Today they will read vows they're written themselves.
This is so good. Look at Humphrey in his page boy suit.
He's just BURNING with embarrassment.
Dan, when you tore out that copper piping with your bare hands, I knew you were the one...
I would fight for you, I'd lie for you, walk the wire for you, yeah, I'd die for you.
...I now pronounce you husband and wife.
PASH
Yahhh!! Matrimony ACHIEVED, Jack!
+5
+5
I wasn't nervous, Mildred. I knew they could do it.
So how about that local sports team.
I believe they have a... strong chance of winning an appropriate trophy or penant.
My thoughts exactly.

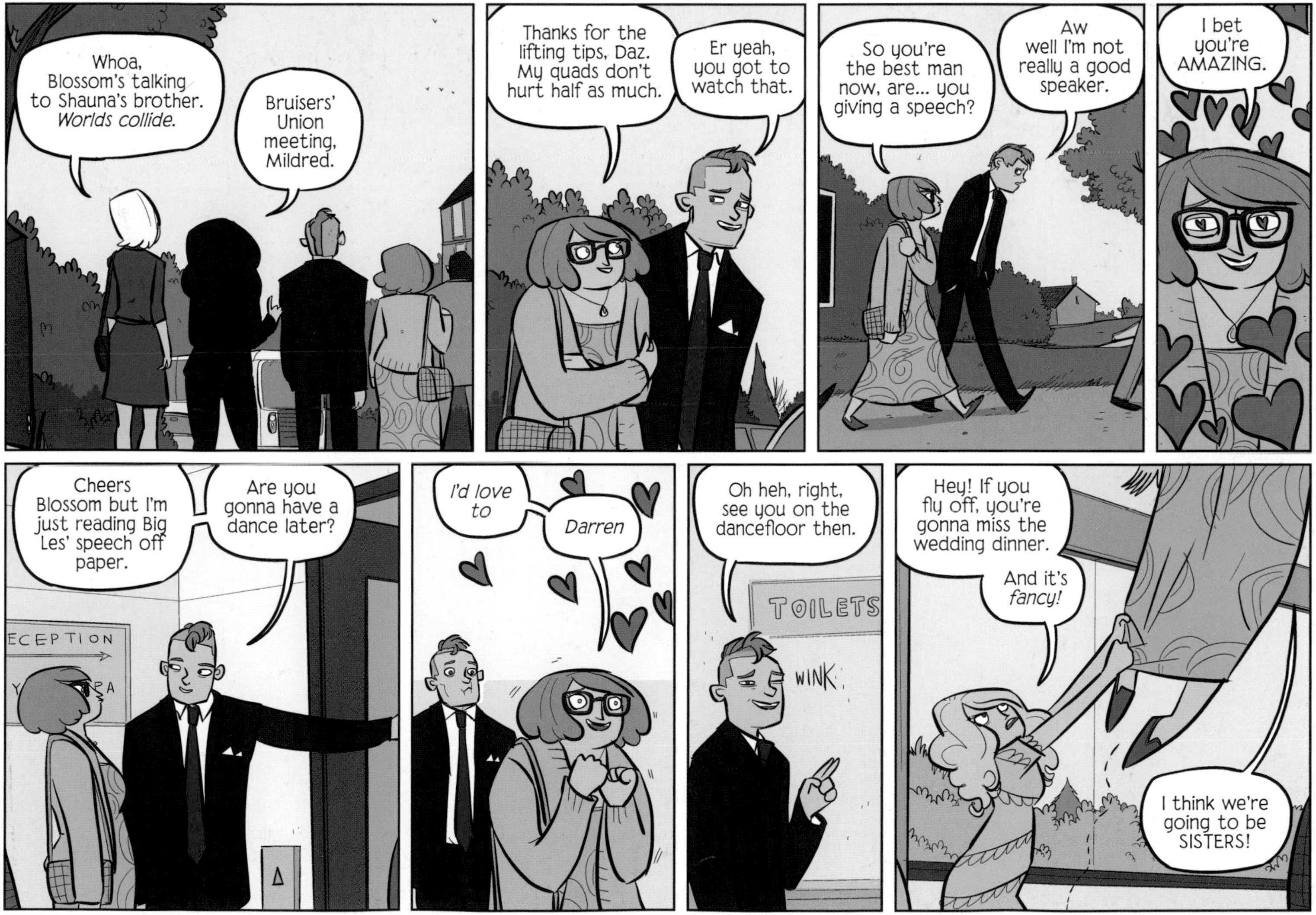

Whoa, Blossom's talking to Shauna's brother. *Worlds collide.*
Bruisers' Union meeting, Mildred.
Thanks for the lifting tips, Daz. My quads don't hurt half as much.
Er yeah, you got to watch that.
So you're the best man now, are... you giving a speech?
Aw well I'm not really a good speaker.
I bet you're AMAZING.
Cheers Blossom but I'm just reading Big Les' speech off paper.
Are you gonna have a dance later?
I'd love to
Darren
Oh heh, right, see you on the dancefloor then.
TOILETS
WINK
Hey! If you fly off, you're gonna miss the wedding dinner.
And it's *fancy!*
I think we're going to be SISTERS!

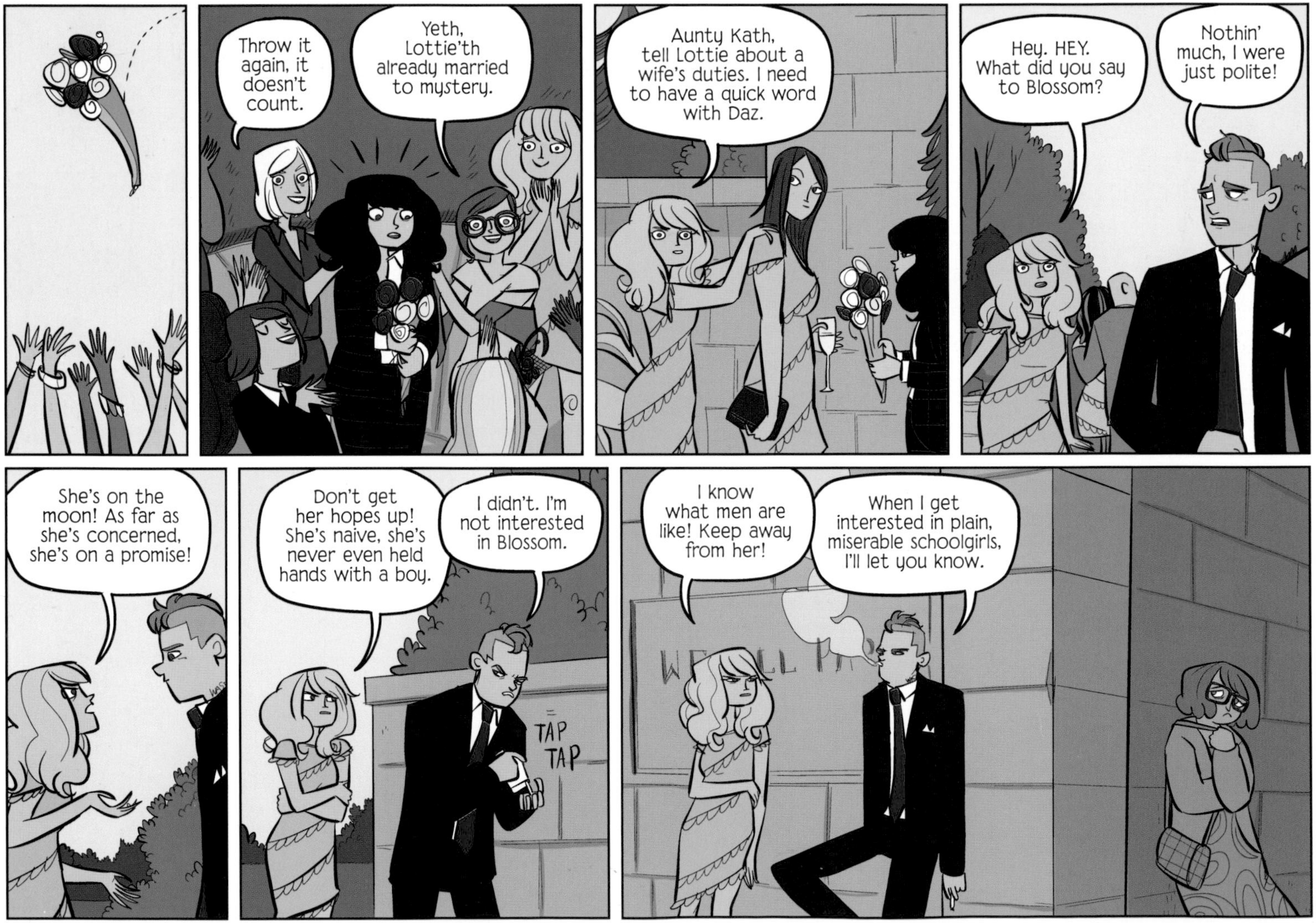

Throw it again, it doesn't count.
Yeth, Lottie'th already married to mystery.
Aunty Kath, tell Lottie about a wife's duties. I need to have a quick word with Daz.
Hey. HEY. What did you say to Blossom?
Nothin' much, I were just polite!
She's on the moon! As far as she's concerned, she's on a promise!
Don't get her hopes up! She's naive, she's never even held hands with a boy.
I didn't. I'm not interested in Blossom.
TAP TAP
I know what men are like! Keep away from her!
When I get interested in plain, miserable schoolgirls, I'll let you know.

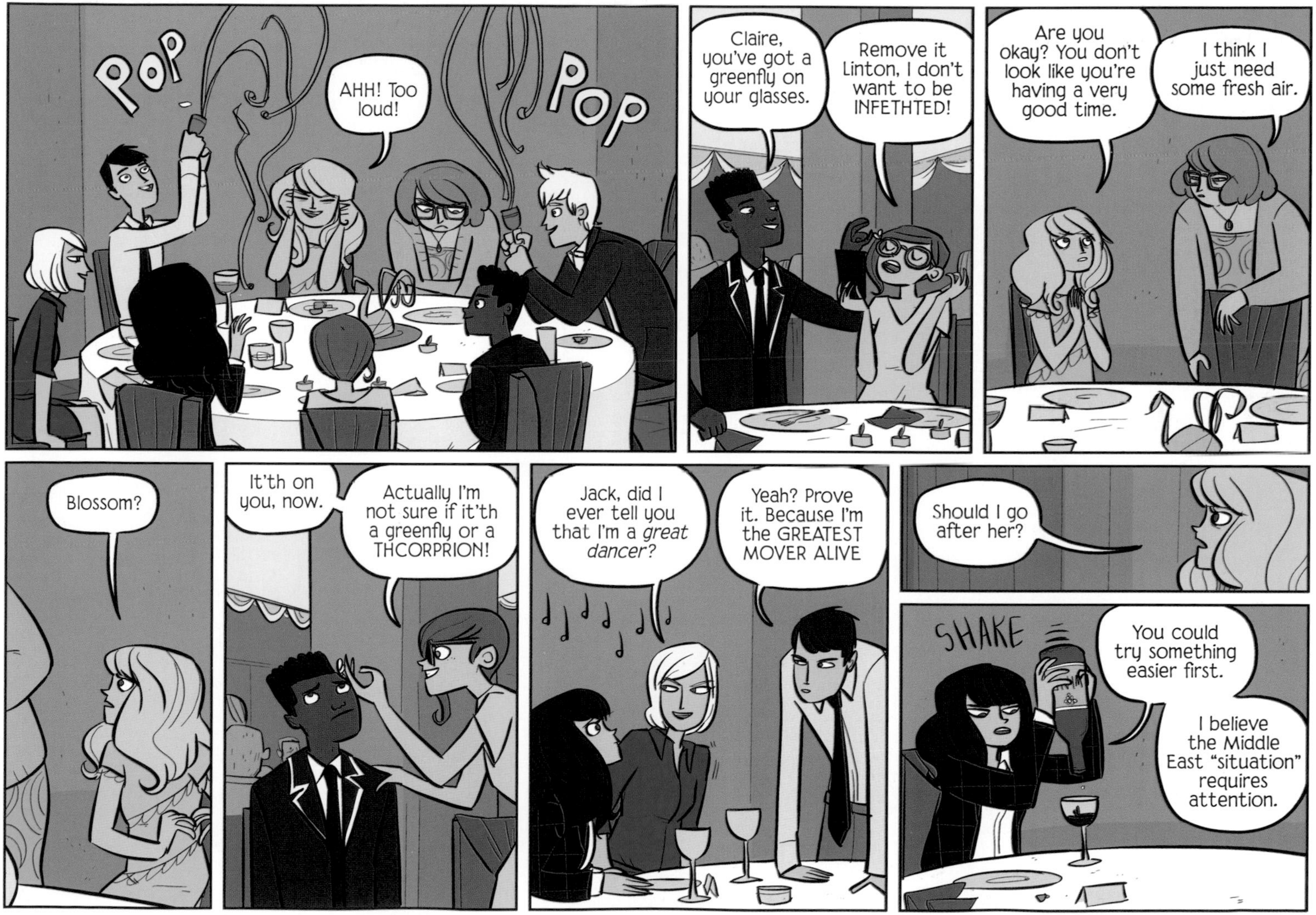

POP
AHH! Too loud!
POP
Claire, you've got a greenfly on your glasses.
Remove it Linton, I don't want to be INFETHTED!
Are you okay? You don't look like you're having a very good time.
I think I just need some fresh air.
Blossom?
It'th on you, now.
Actually I'm not sure if it'th a greenfly or a THCORPRION!
Jack, did I ever tell you that I'm a *great dancer*?
Yeah? Prove it. Because I'm the GREATEST MOVER ALIVE
Should I go after her?
SHAKE
You could try something easier first.
I believe the Middle East "situation" requires attention.

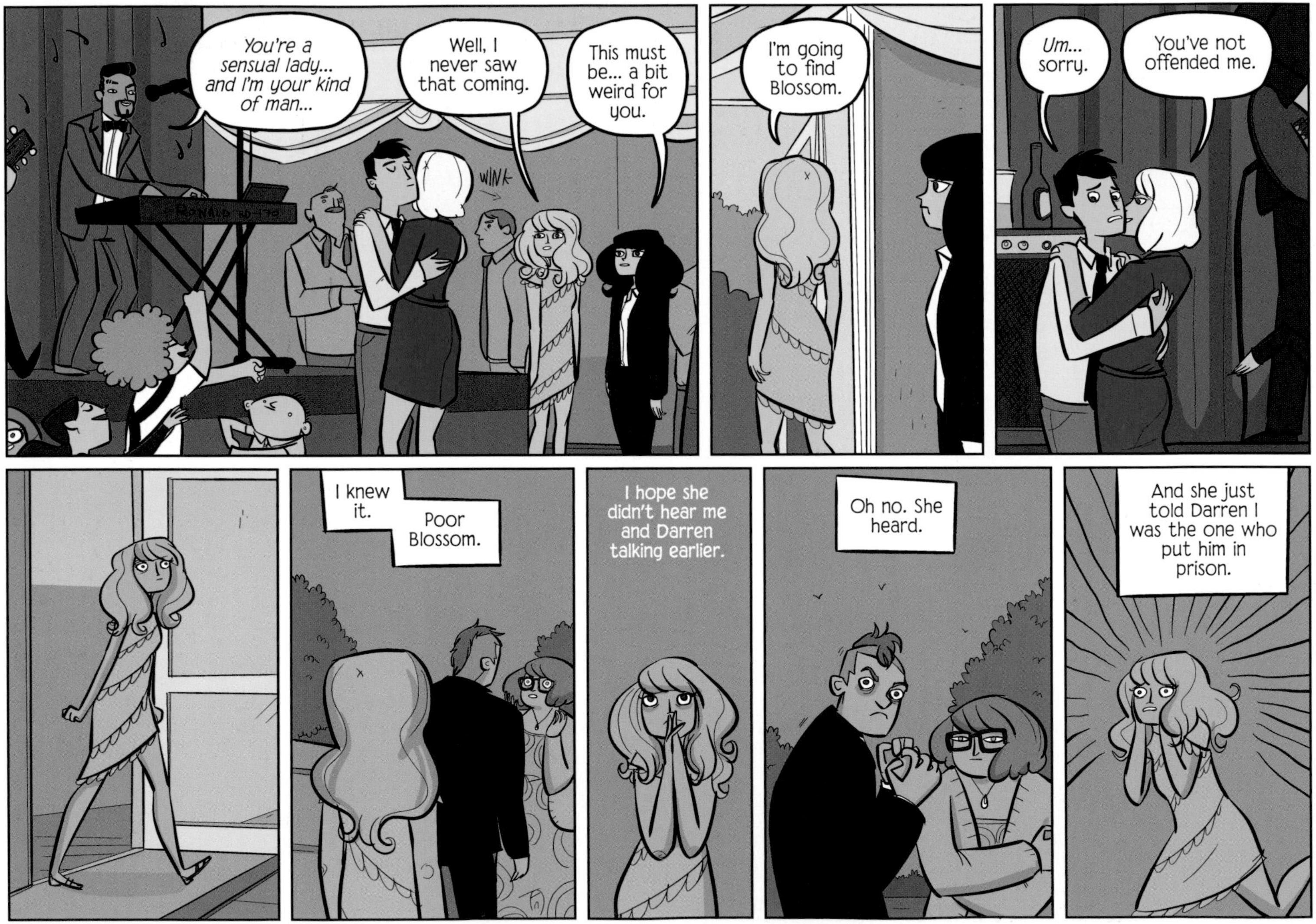
You're a sensual lady... and I'm your kind of man...
Well, I never saw that coming.
WINK
This must be... a bit weird for you.
I'm going to find Blossom.
Um... sorry.
You've not offended me.
I knew it.
Poor Blossom.
I hope she didn't hear me and Darren talking earlier.
Oh no. She heard.
And she just told Darren I was the one who put him in prison.

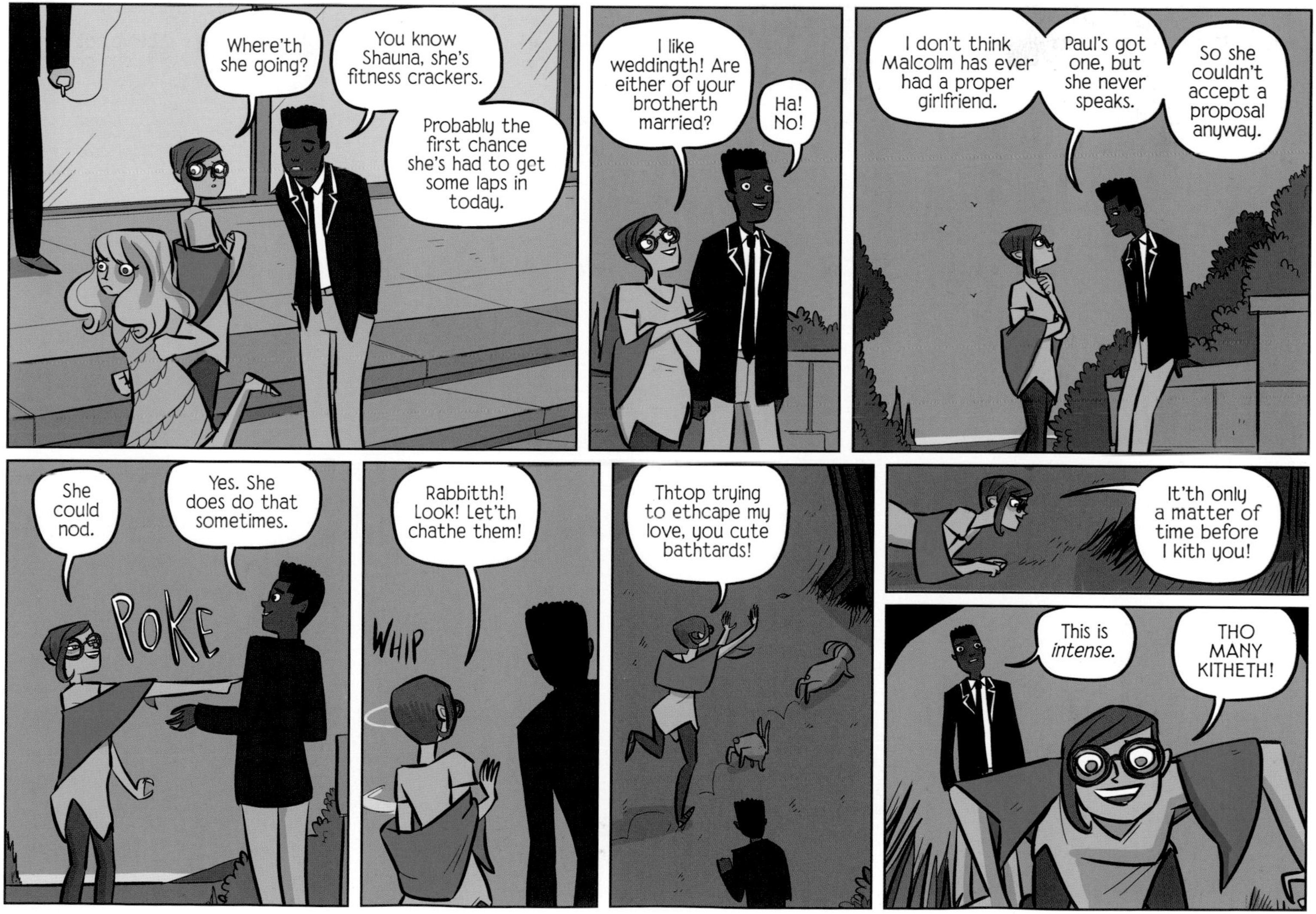
Where'th she going?
You know Shauna, she's fitness crackers.
Probably the first chance she's had to get some laps in today.
I like weddingth! Are either of your brotherth married?
Ha! No!
I don't think Malcolm has ever had a proper girlfriend.
Paul's got one, but she never speaks.
So she couldn't accept a proposal anyway.
She could nod.
Yes. She does do that sometimes.
POKE
Rabbitth! Look! Let'th chathe them!
WHIP
Thtop trying to ethcape my love, you cute bathtards!
It'th only a matter of time before I kith you!
This is *intense.*
THO MANY KITHETH!

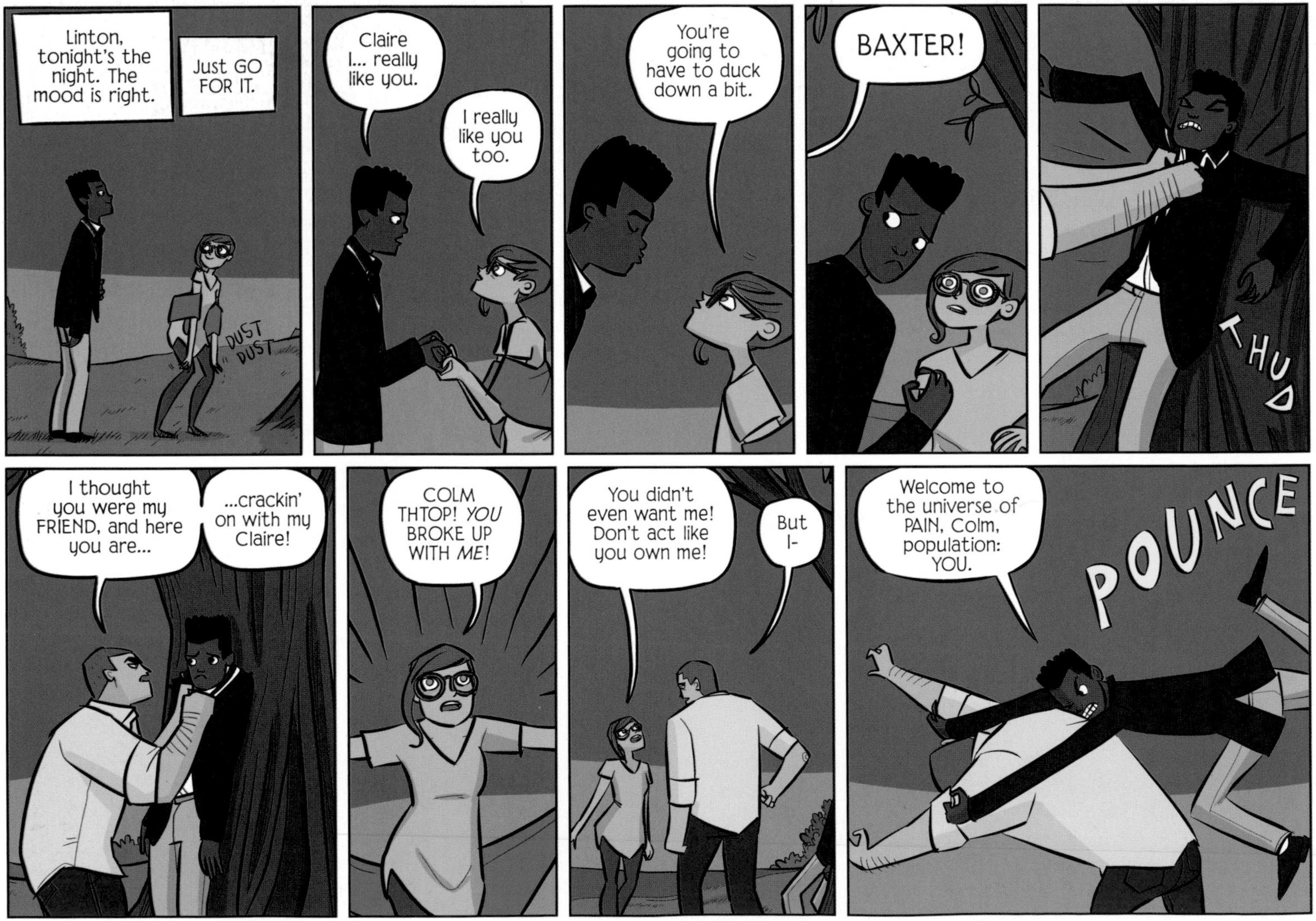
Linton, tonight's the night. The mood is right.
Just GO FOR IT.
DUST DUST
Claire I... really like you.
I really like you too.
You're going to have to duck down a bit.
BAXTER!
THUD
I thought you were my FRIEND, and here you are...
...crackin' on with my Claire!
COLM THTOP! YOU BROKE UP WITH ME!
You didn't even want me! Don't act like you own me!
But I-
Welcome to the universe of PAIN, Colm, population: YOU.
POUNCE

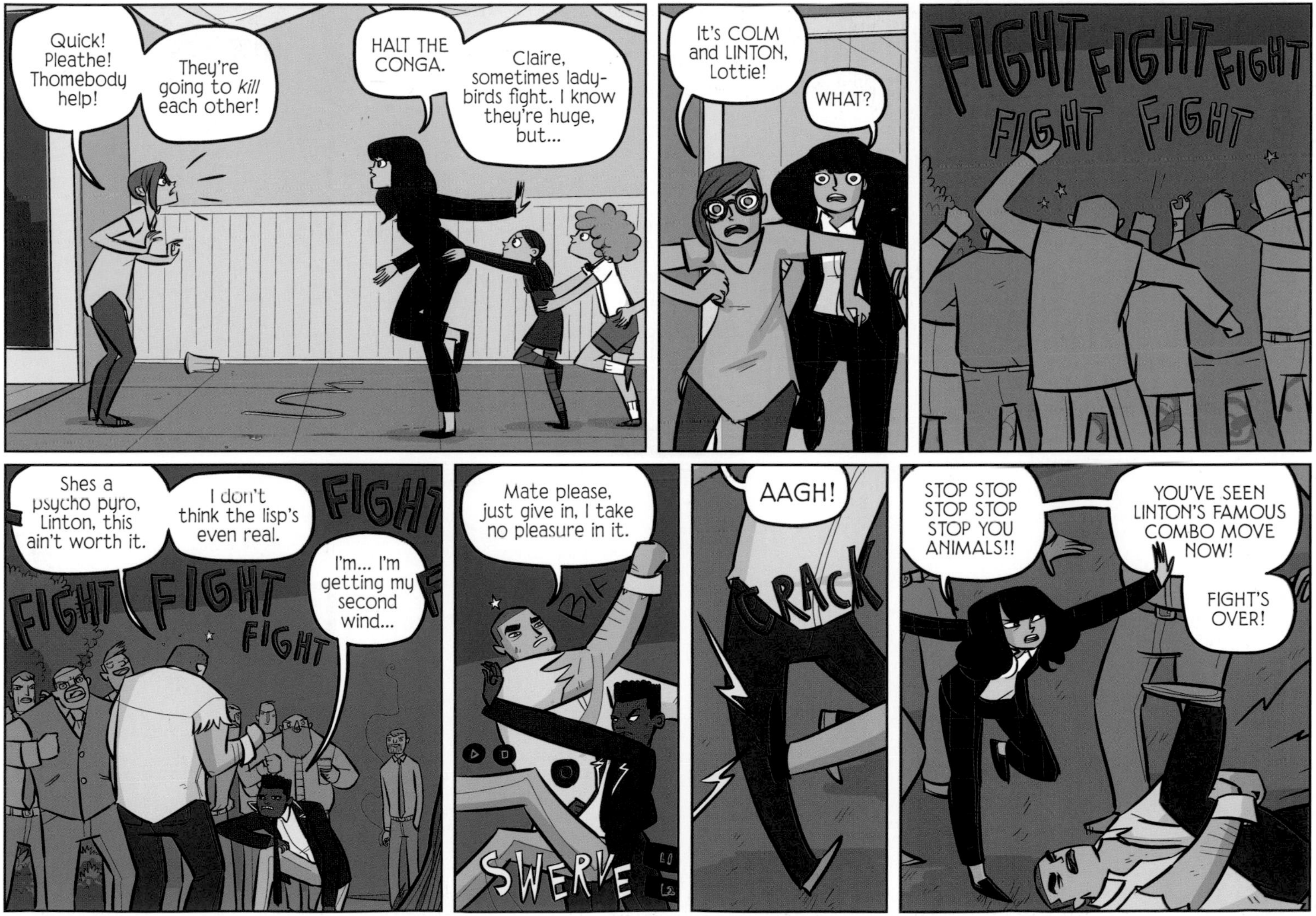
Quick! Pleathe! Thomebody help!
They're going to *kill* each other!
HALT THE CONGA.
Claire, sometimes lady-birds fight. I know they're huge, but...
It's COLM and LINTON, Lottie!
WHAT?
FIGHT FIGHT FIGHT
FIGHT FIGHT
Shes a psycho pyro, Linton, this ain't worth it.
I don't think the lisp's even real.
FIGHT
FIGHT FIGHT
FIGHT
I'm... I'm getting my second wind...
Mate please, just give in, I take no pleasure in it.
BIF
SWERVE
AAGH!
CRACK
STOP STOP STOP STOP STOP YOU ANIMALS!!
YOU'VE SEEN LINTON'S FAMOUS COMBO MOVE NOW!
FIGHT'S OVER!

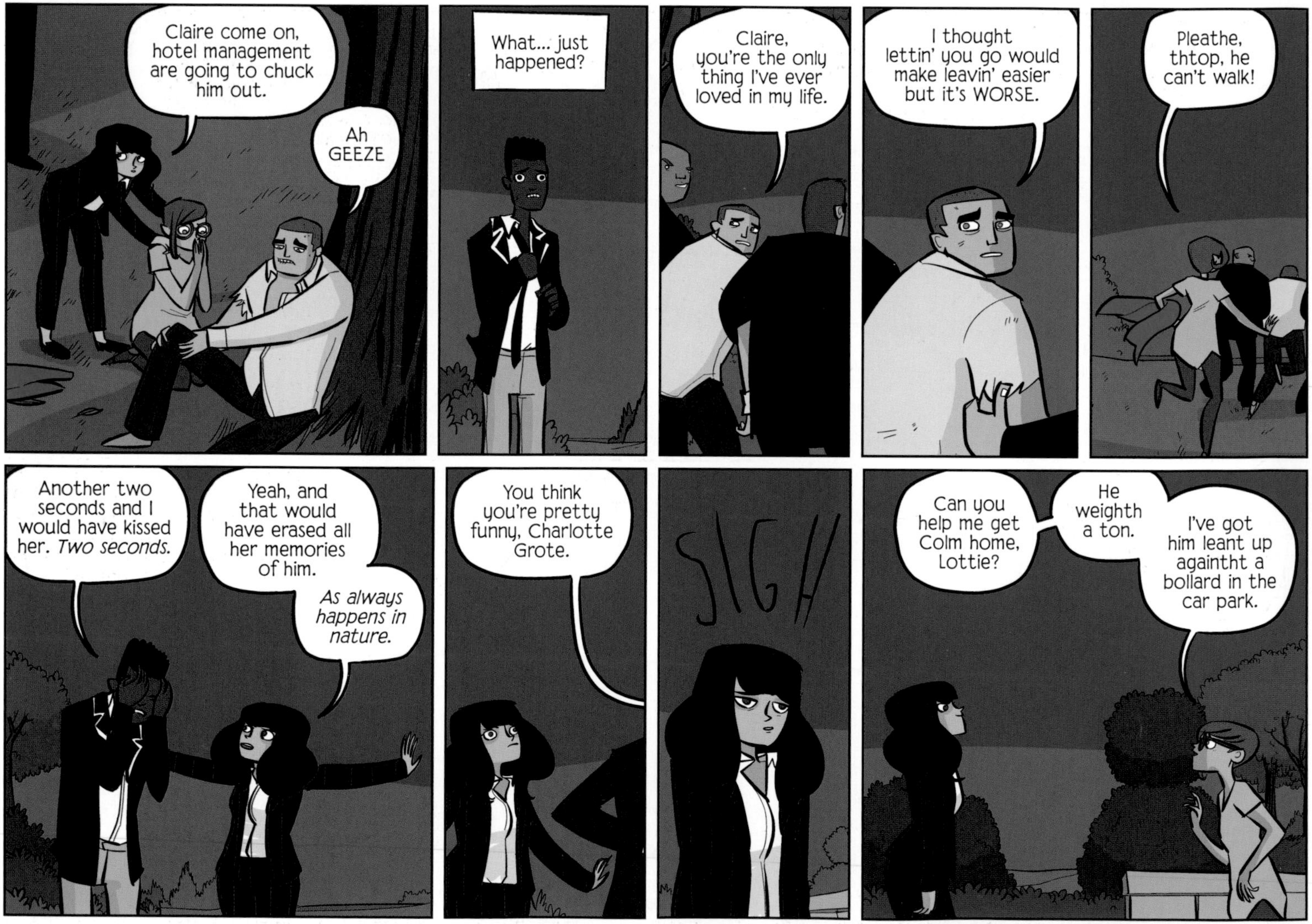
Claire come on, hotel management are going to chuck him out.
Ah GEEZE
What... just happened?
Claire, you're the only thing I've ever loved in my life.
I thought lettin' you go would make leavin' easier but it's WORSE.
Pleathe, thtop, he can't walk!
Another two seconds and I would have kissed her. *Two seconds.*
Yeah, and that would have erased all her memories of him.
As always happens in nature.
You think you're pretty funny, Charlotte Grote.
SIGH
Can you help me get Colm home, Lottie?
He weighth a ton.
I've got him leant up againtht a bollard in the car park.

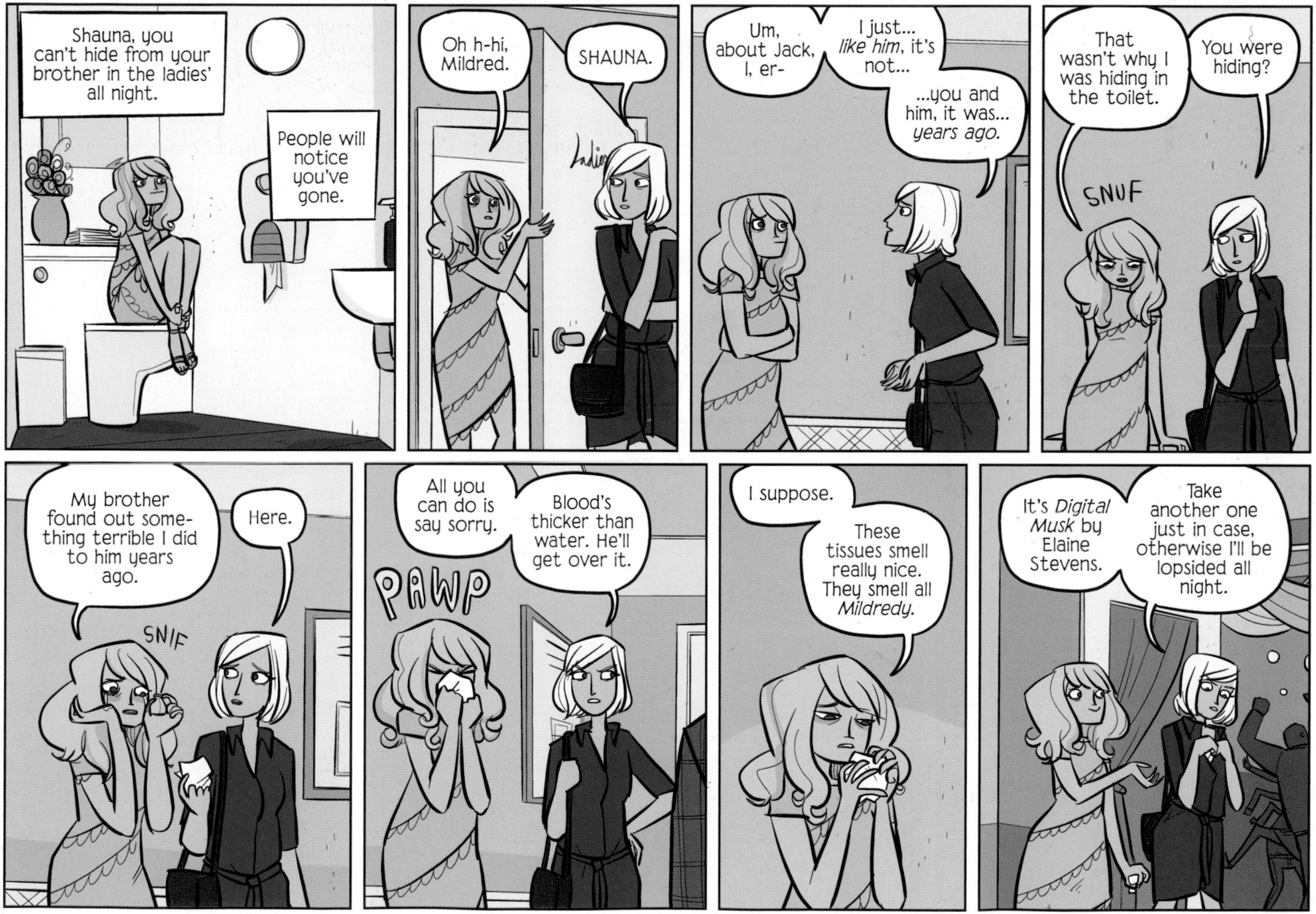

Shauna, you can't hide from your brother in the ladies' all night.
People will notice you've gone.
Oh h-hi, Mildred.
SHAUNA.
Ladies
Um, about Jack, I, er-
I just... *like him*, it's not...
...you and him, it was... *years ago.*
That wasn't why I was hiding in the toilet.
You were hiding?
SNUF
My brother found out some-thing terrible I did to him years ago.
Here.
SNIF
All you can do is say sorry.
Blood's thicker than water. He'll get over it.
PAWP
I suppose.
These tissues smell really nice. They smell all *Mildredy.*
It's *Digital Musk* by Elaine Stevens.
Take another one just in case, otherwise I'll be lopsided all night.

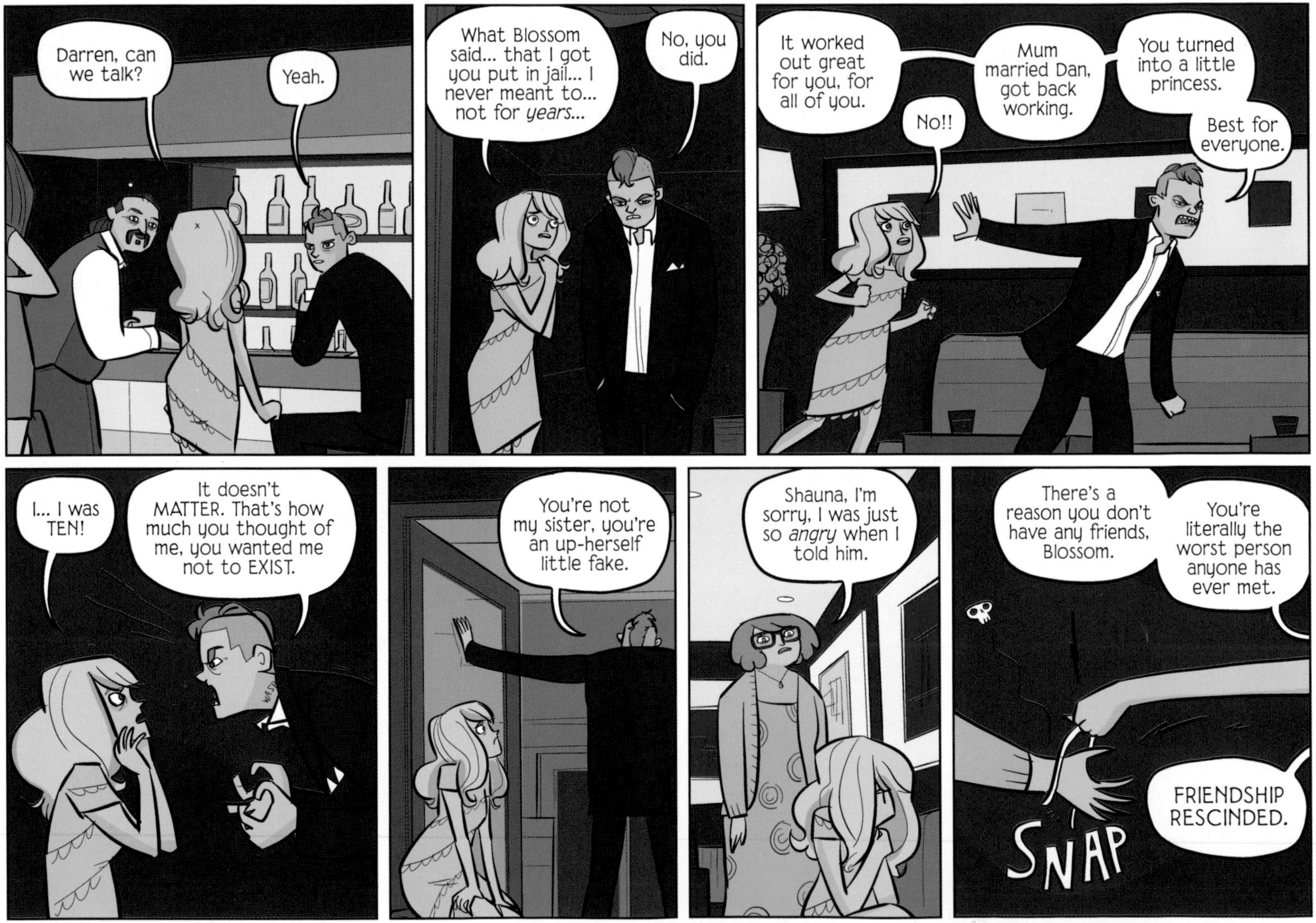
Darren, can we talk?
Yeah.
What Blossom said... that I got you put in jail... I never meant to... not for *years*...
No, you did.
It worked out great for you, for all of you.
Mum married Dan, got back working.
You turned into a little princess.
No!!
Best for everyone.
I... I was TEN!
It doesn't MATTER. That's how much you thought of me, you wanted me not to EXIST.
You're not my sister, you're an up-herself little fake.
Shauna, I'm sorry, I was just so *angry* when I told him.
There's a reason you don't have any friends, Blossom.
You're literally the worst person anyone has ever met.
SNAP
FRIENDSHIP RESCINDED.

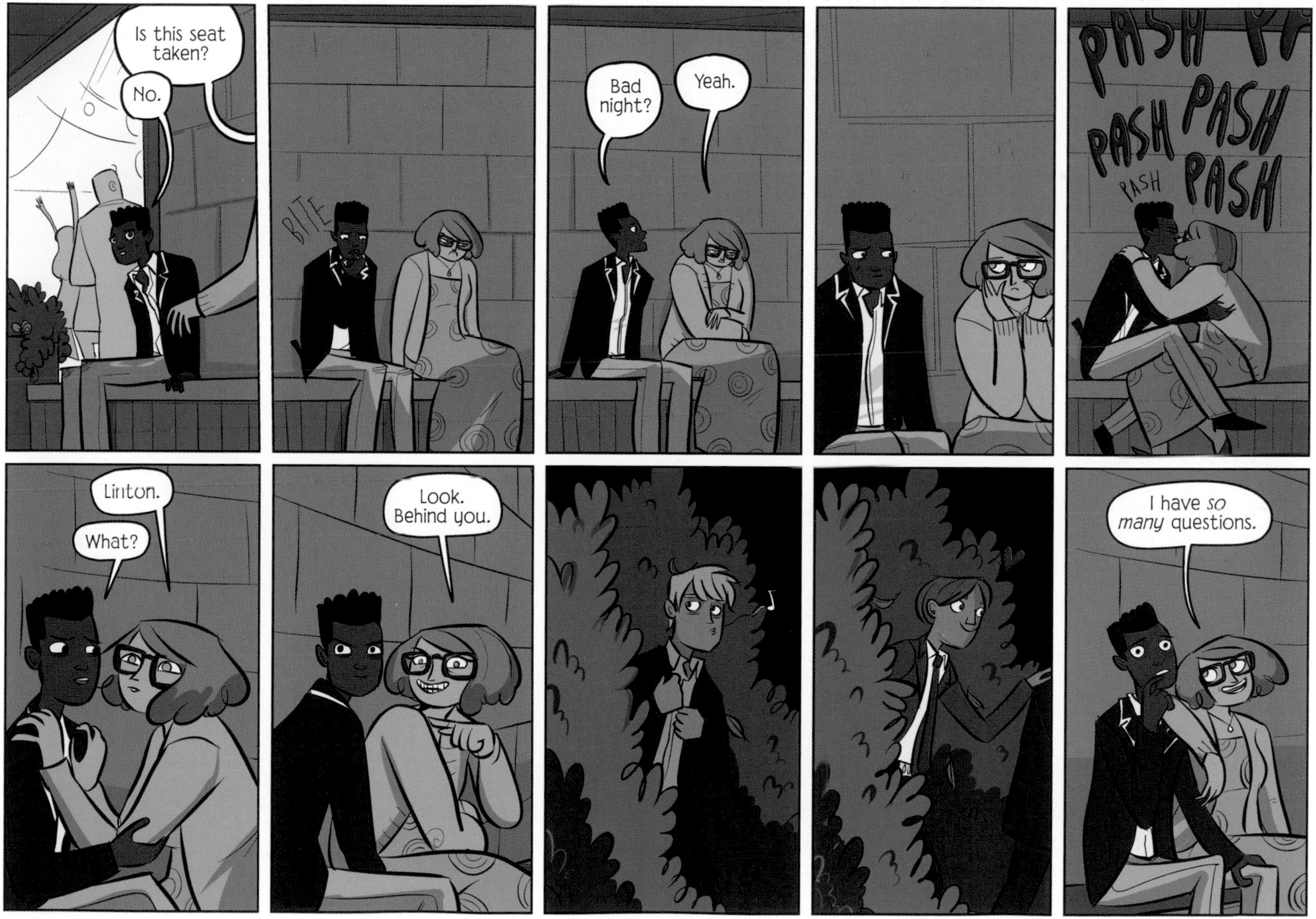

Is this seat taken?
No.
BITE
Bad night?
Yeah.
PASH
PASH PASH
PASH
PASH PASH
Linton.
What?
Look. Behind you.
I have *so many* questions.

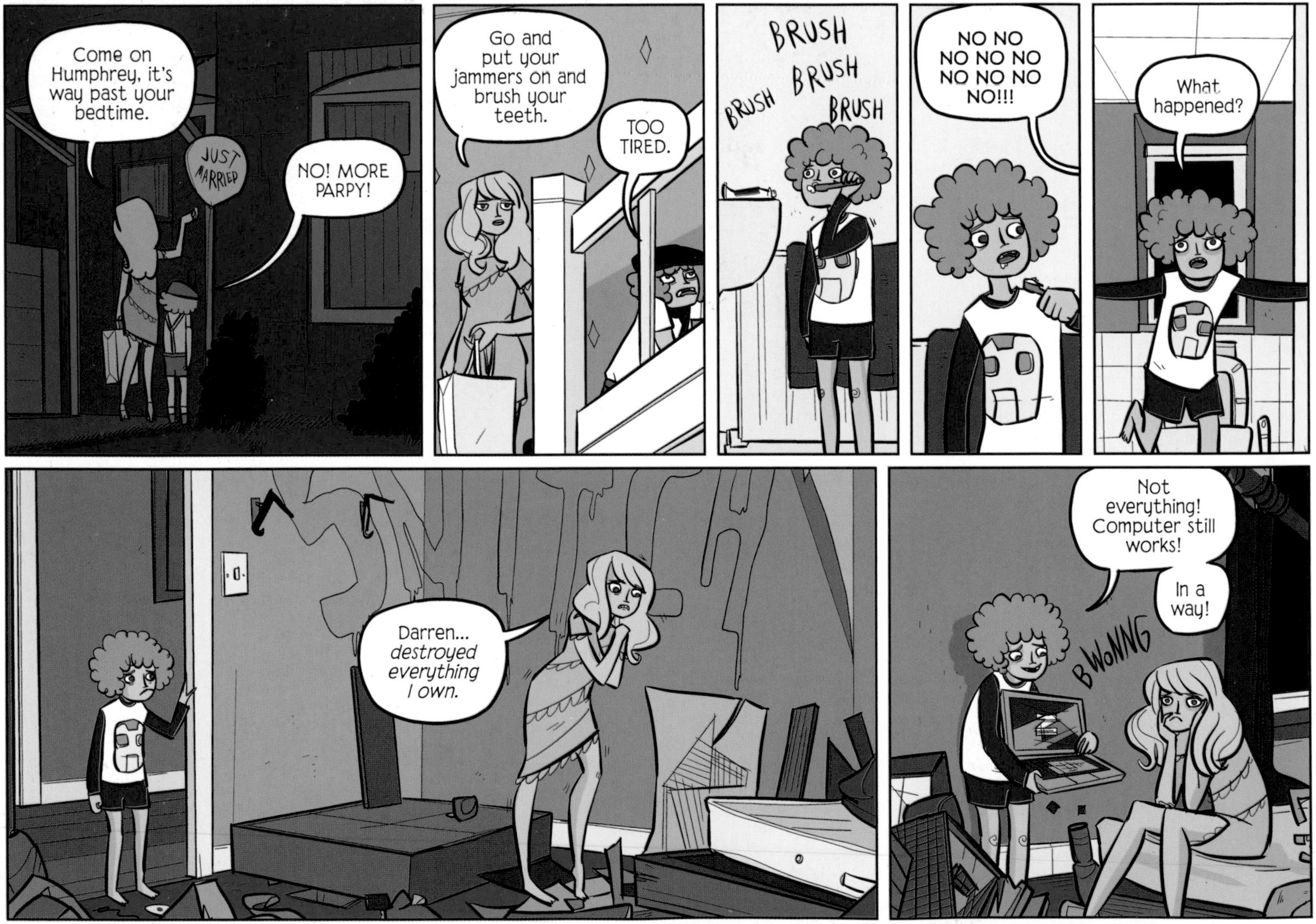
Come on Humphrey, it's way past your bedtime.
JUST MARRIED
NO! MORE PARPY!
Go and put your jammers on and brush your teeth.
TOO TIRED.
BRUSH
BRUSH BRUSH
BRUSH
NO NO NO NO NO NO NO NO NO!!!
What happened?
Darren... *destroyed everything I own.*
Not everything! Computer still works!
BWoNNG
In a way!

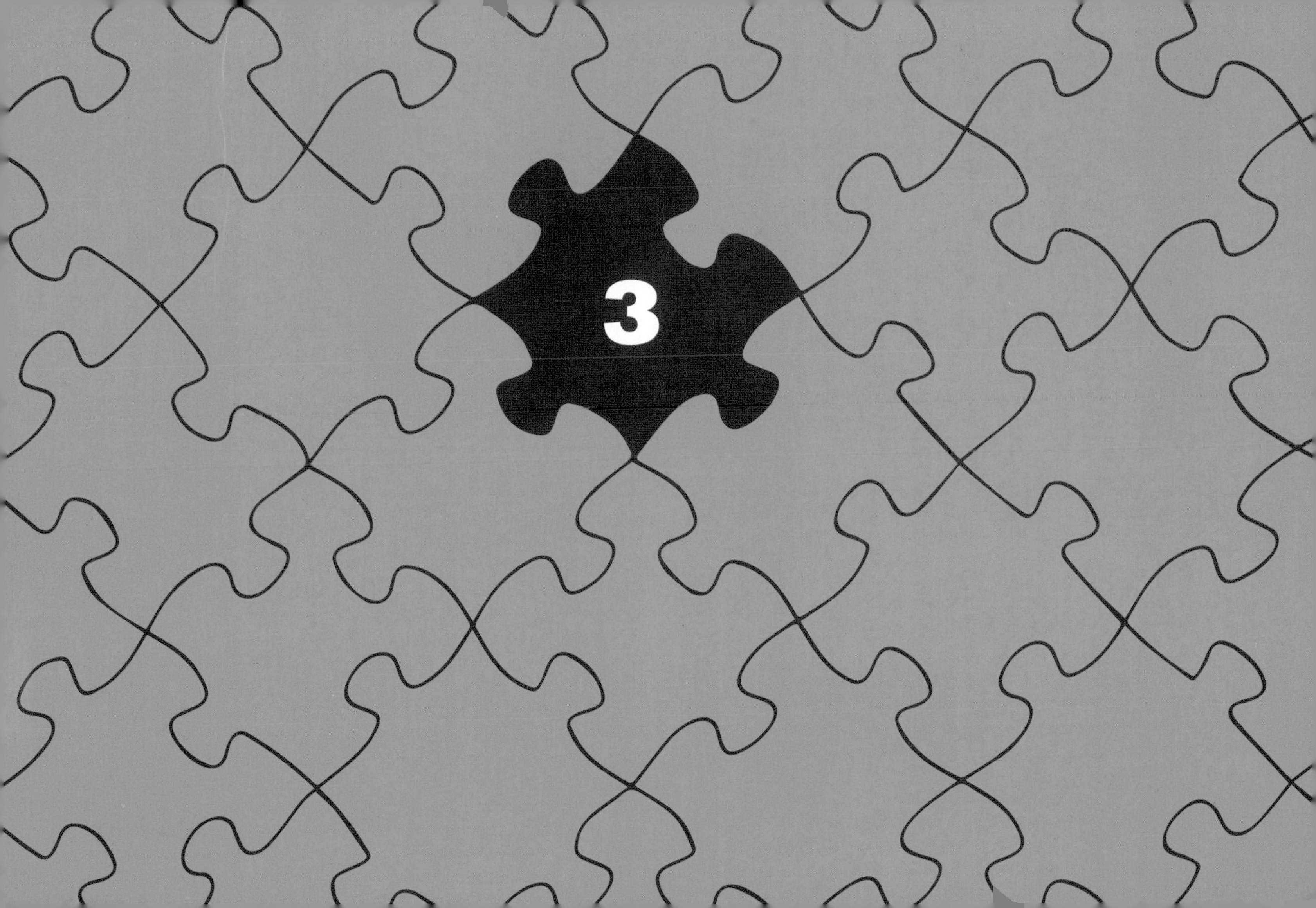
3

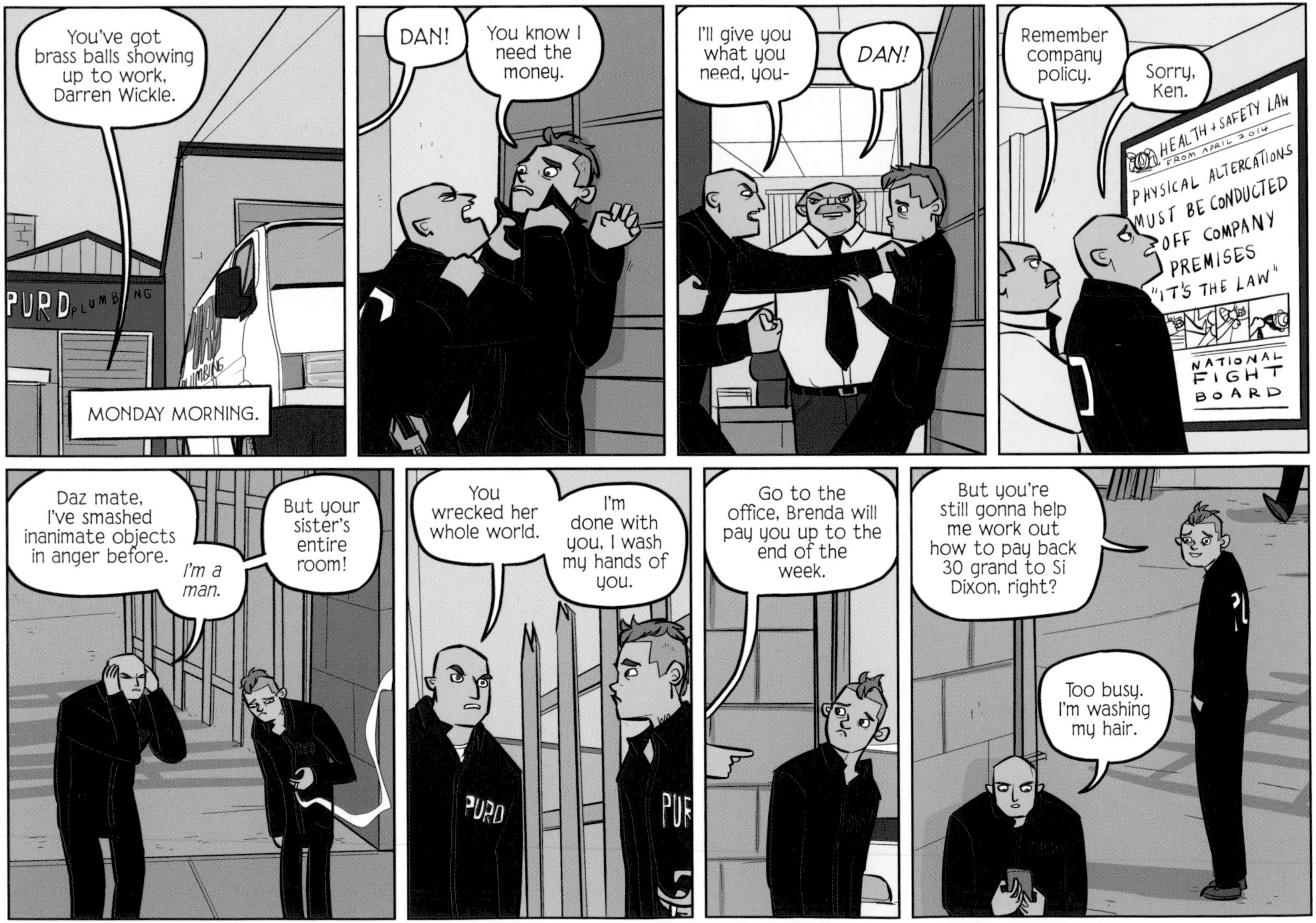
You've got brass balls showing up to work, Darren Wickle.
MONDAY MORNING.
PURD PLUMBING
DAN!
You know I need the money.
I'll give you what you need, you-
DAN!
Remember company policy.
Sorry, Ken.
HEALTH + SAFETY LAW
FROM APRIL 2014
PHYSICAL ALTERCATIONS MUST BE CONDUCTED OFF COMPANY PREMISES
"IT'S THE LAW"
NATIONAL FIGHT BOARD
Daz mate, I've smashed inanimate objects in anger before.
I'm a man.
But your sister's entire room!
You wrecked her whole world.
I'm done with you, I wash my hands of you.
PURD
Go to the office, Brenda will pay you up to the end of the week.
But you're still gonna help me work out how to pay back 30 grand to Si Dixon, right?
Too busy. I'm washing my hair.

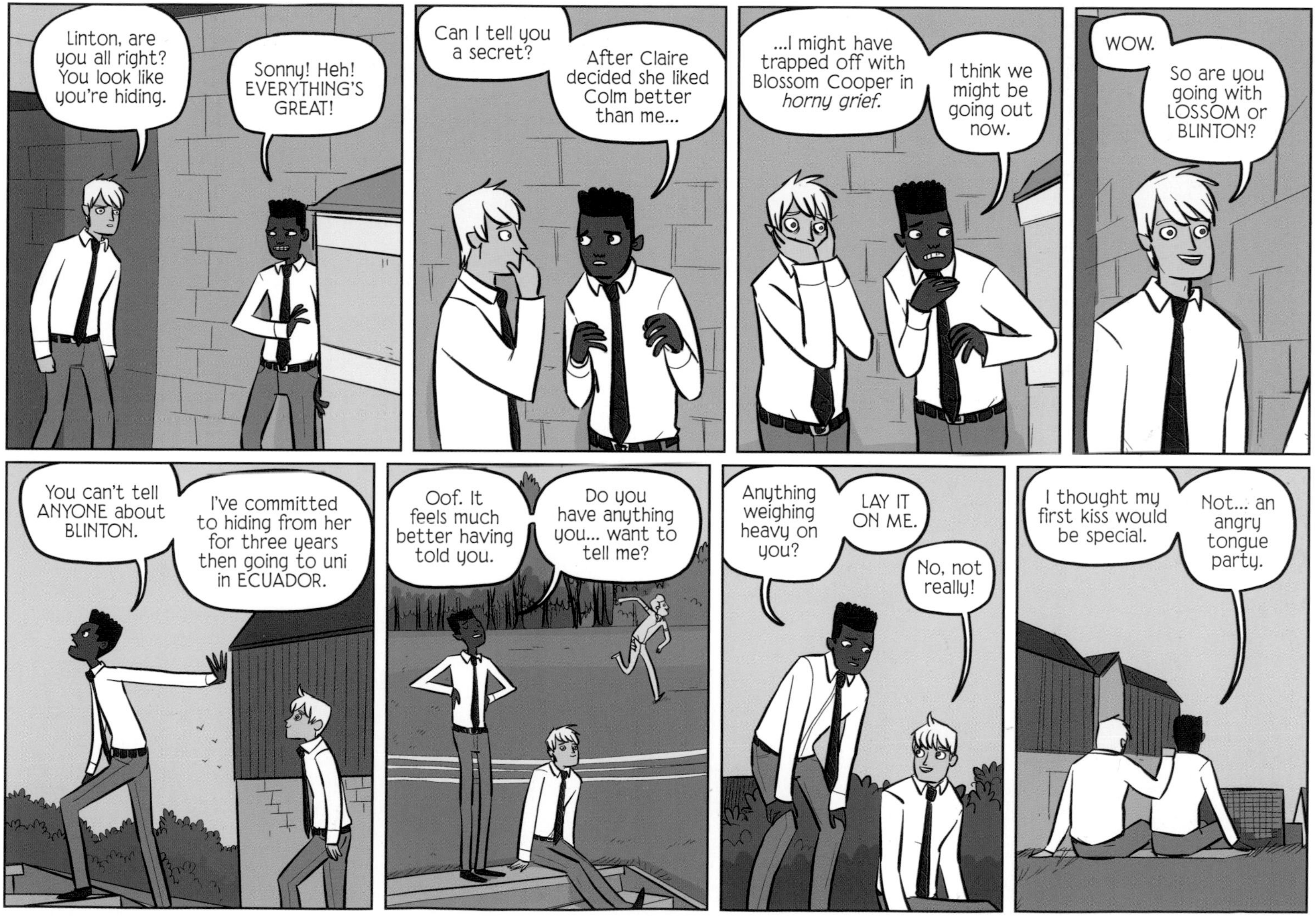

Linton, are you all right? You look like you're hiding.
Sonny! Heh! EVERYTHING'S GREAT!
Can I tell you a secret?
After Claire decided she liked Colm better than me...
...I might have trapped off with Blossom Cooper in *horny grief.*
I think we might be going out now.
WOW.
So are you going with LOSSOM or BLINTON?
You can't tell ANYONE about BLINTON.
I've committed to hiding from her for three years then going to uni in ECUADOR.
Oof. It feels much better having told you.
Do you have anything you... want to tell me?
Anything weighing heavy on you?
LAY IT ON ME.
No, not really!
I thought my first kiss would be special.
Not... an angry tongue party.

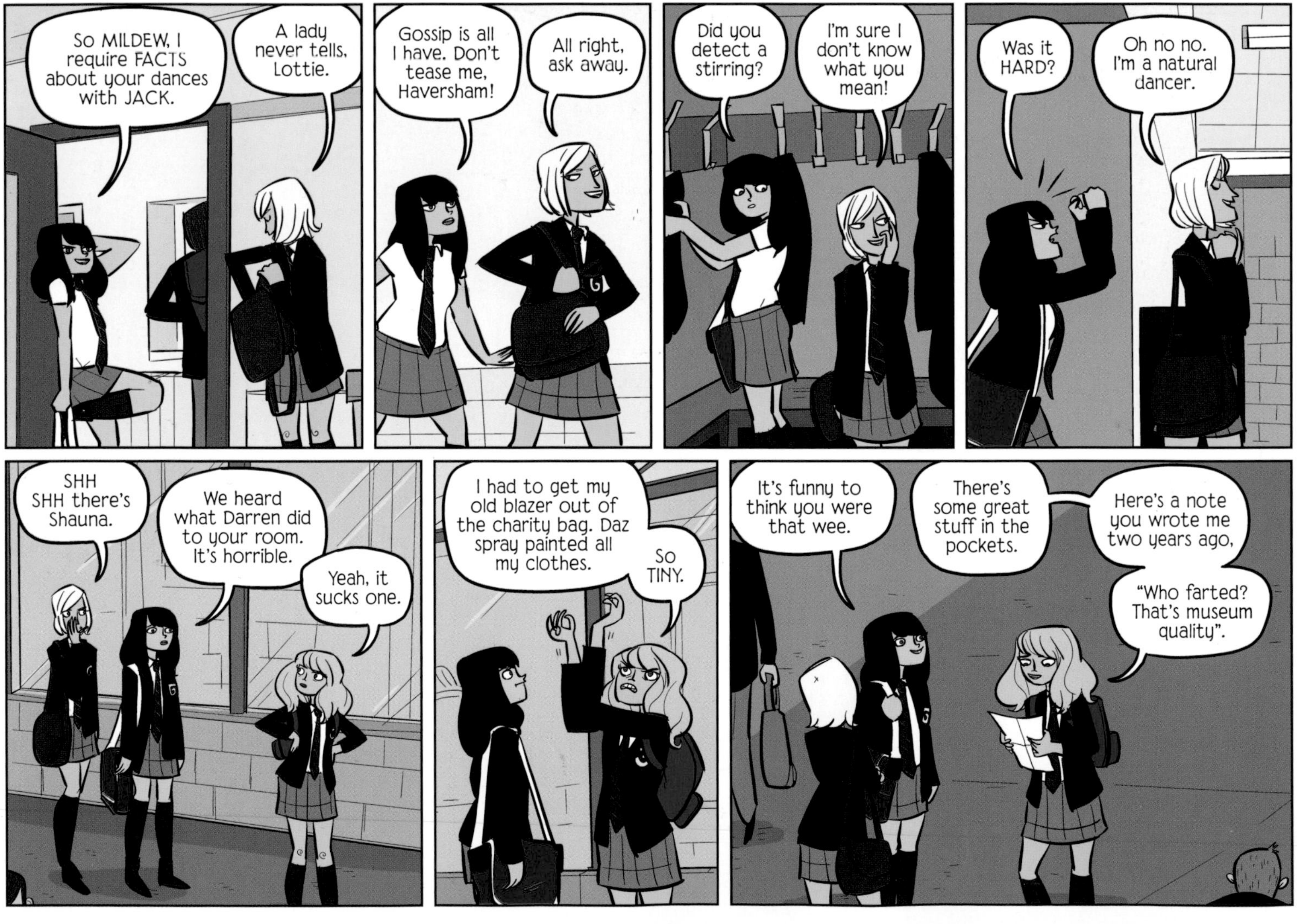
So MILDEW, I require FACTS about your dances with JACK.
A lady never tells, Lottie.
Gossip is all I have. Don't tease me, Haversham!
All right, ask away.
Did you detect a stirring?
I'm sure I don't know what you mean!
Was it HARD?
Oh no no. I'm a natural dancer.
SHH SHH there's Shauna.
We heard what Darren did to your room. It's horrible.
Yeah, it sucks one.
I had to get my old blazer out of the charity bag. Daz spray painted all my clothes.
So TINY.
It's funny to think you were that wee.
There's some great stuff in the pockets.
Here's a note you wrote me two years ago,
"Who farted? That's museum quality".

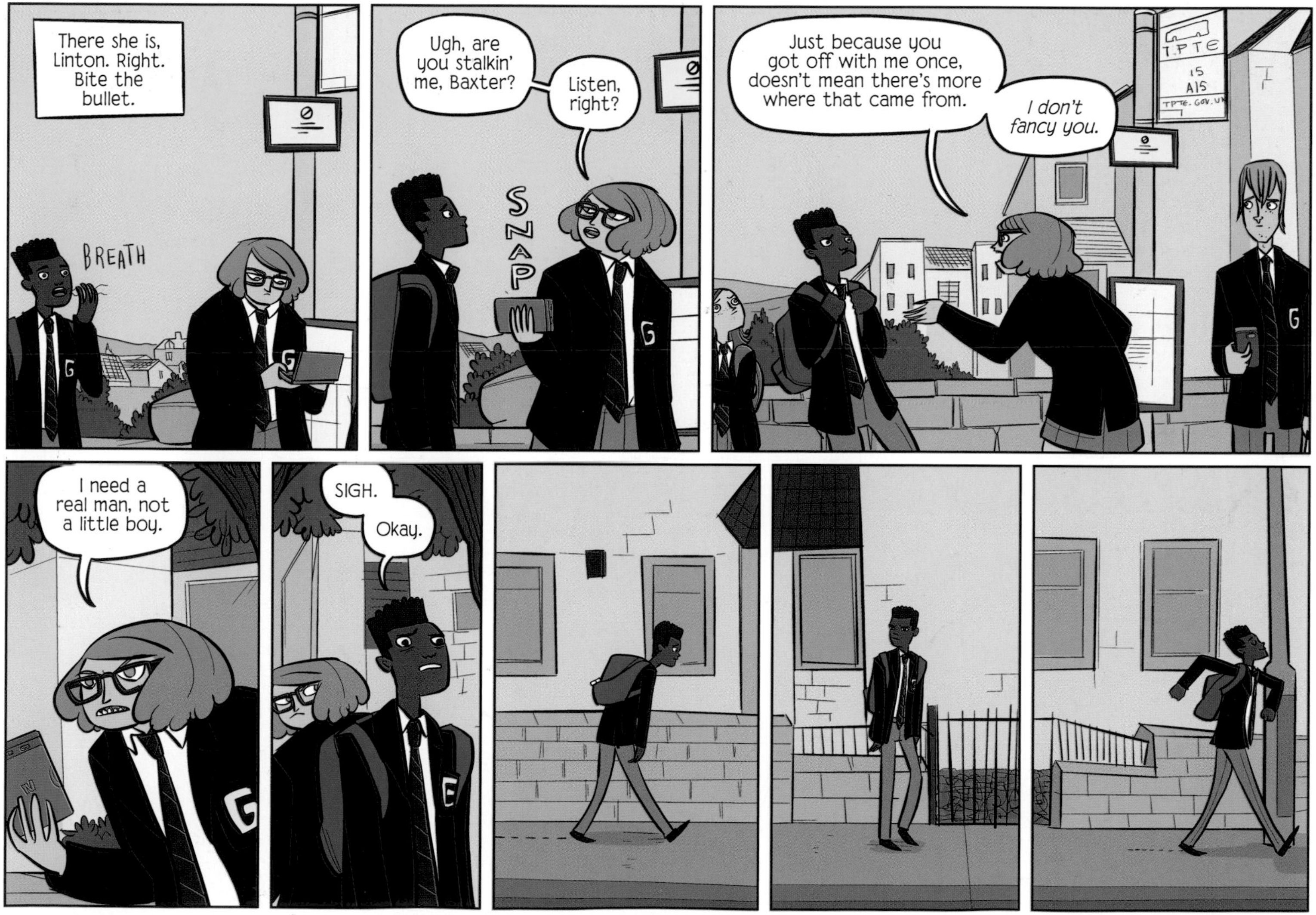
There she is, Linton. Right. Bite the bullet.
BREATH
Ugh, are you stalkin' me, Baxter?
Listen, right?
SNAP
Just because you got off with me once, doesn't mean there's more where that came from.
I don't fancy you.
I need a real man, not a little boy.
SIGH.
Okay.

Bad Machinery, Volume Nine

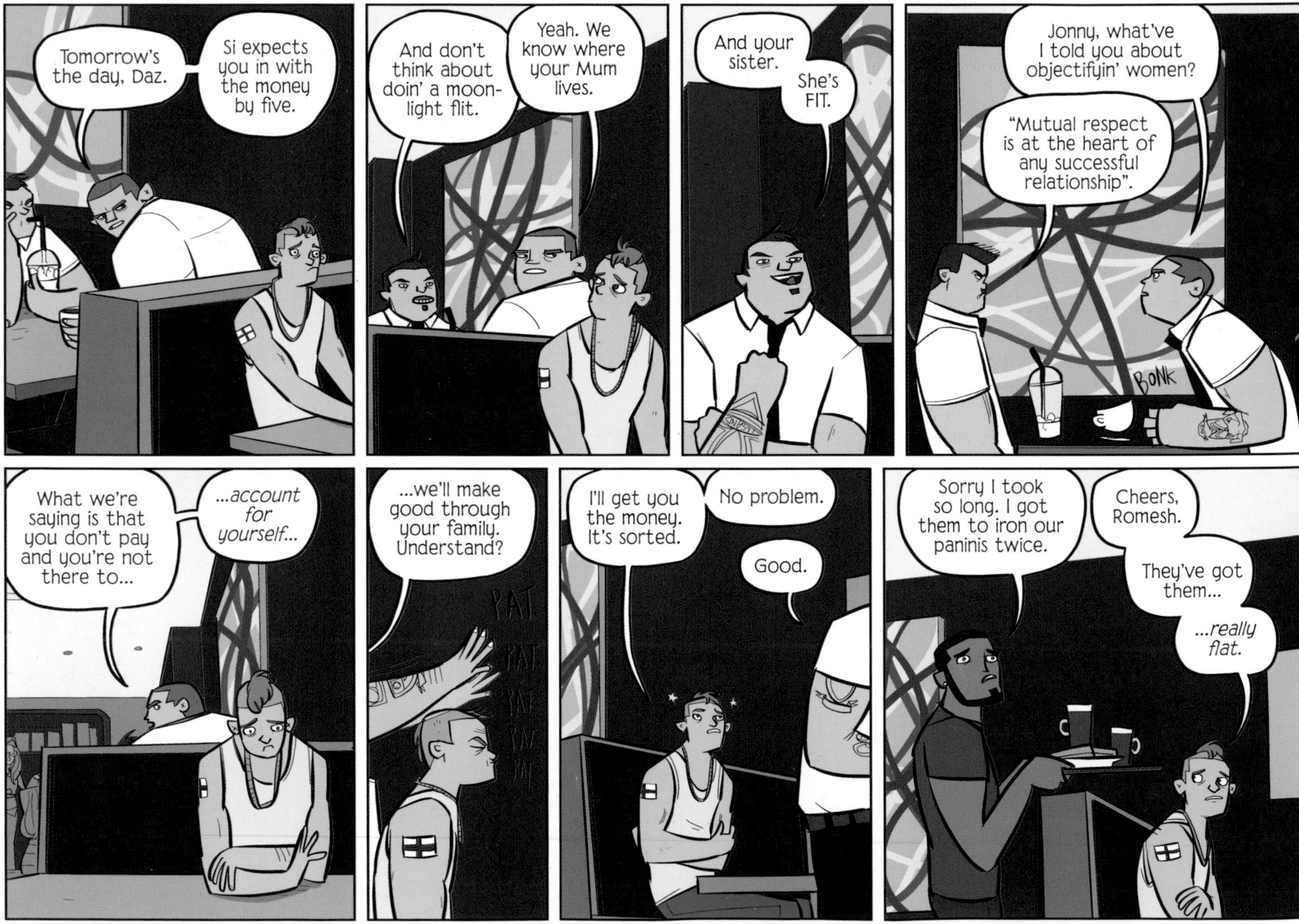
Tomorrow's the day, Daz.
Si expects you in with the money by five.
And don't think about doin' a moon-light flit.
Yeah. We know where your Mum lives.
And your sister.
She's FIT.
Jonny, what've I told you about objectifyin' women?
"Mutual respect is at the heart of any successful relationship".
BONK
What we're saying is that you don't pay and you're not there to...
...*account for yourself*...
...we'll make good through your family. Understand?
PAT PAT PAT PAT PAT PAT
I'll get you the money. It's sorted.
No problem.
Good.
Sorry I took so long. I got them to iron our paninis twice.
Cheers, Romesh.
They've got them...
...*really flat.*

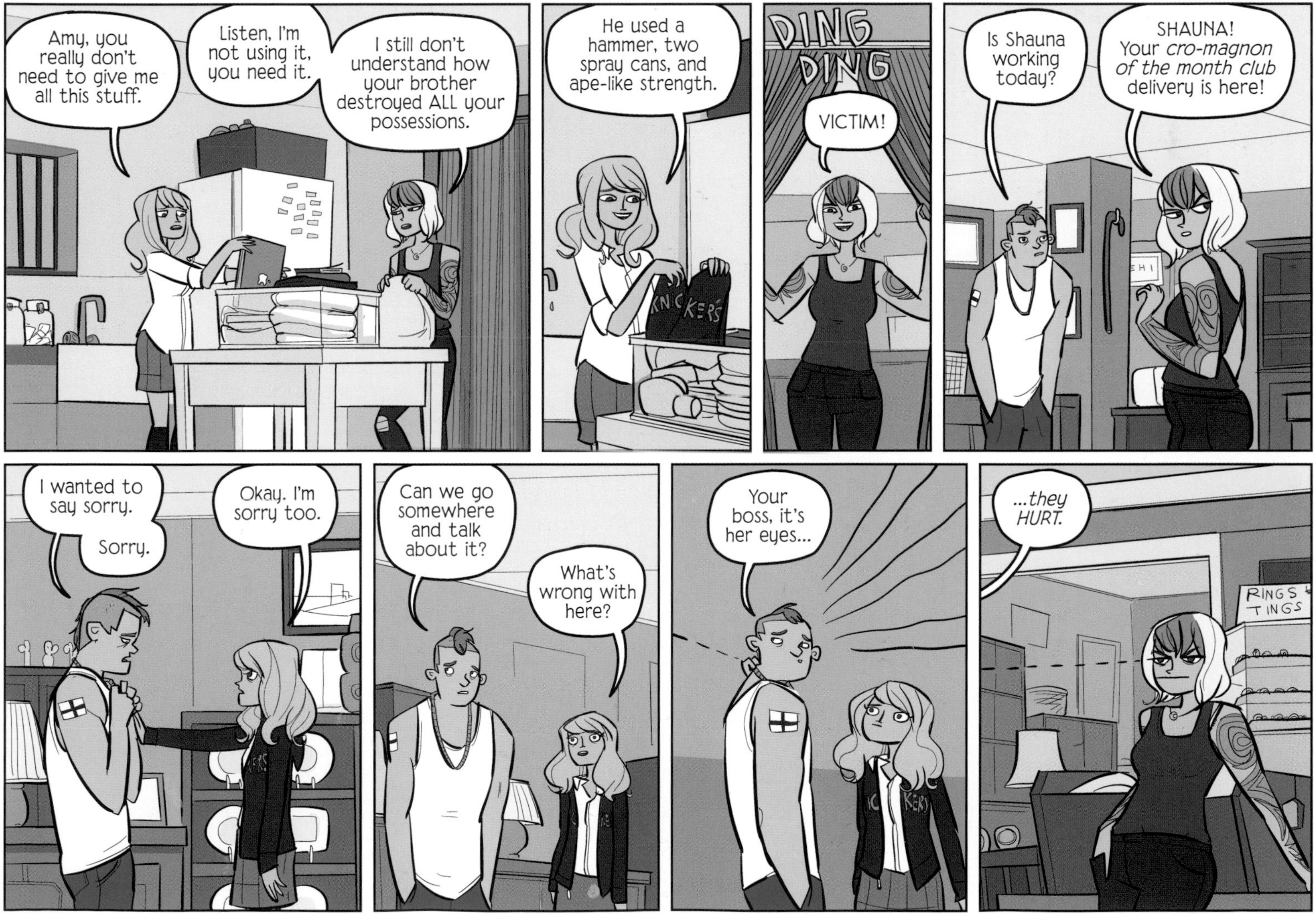
Amy, you really don't need to give me all this stuff.
Listen, I'm not using it, you need it.
I still don't understand how your brother destroyed ALL your possessions.
He used a hammer, two spray cans, and ape-like strength.
KNICKERS
DING DING
VICTIM!
Is Shauna working today?
SHAUNA! Your *cro-magnon of the month club* delivery is here!
I wanted to say sorry.
Sorry.
Okay. I'm sorry too.
Can we go somewhere and talk about it?
What's wrong with here?
Your boss, it's her eyes...
...they HURT.
RINGS & TINGS

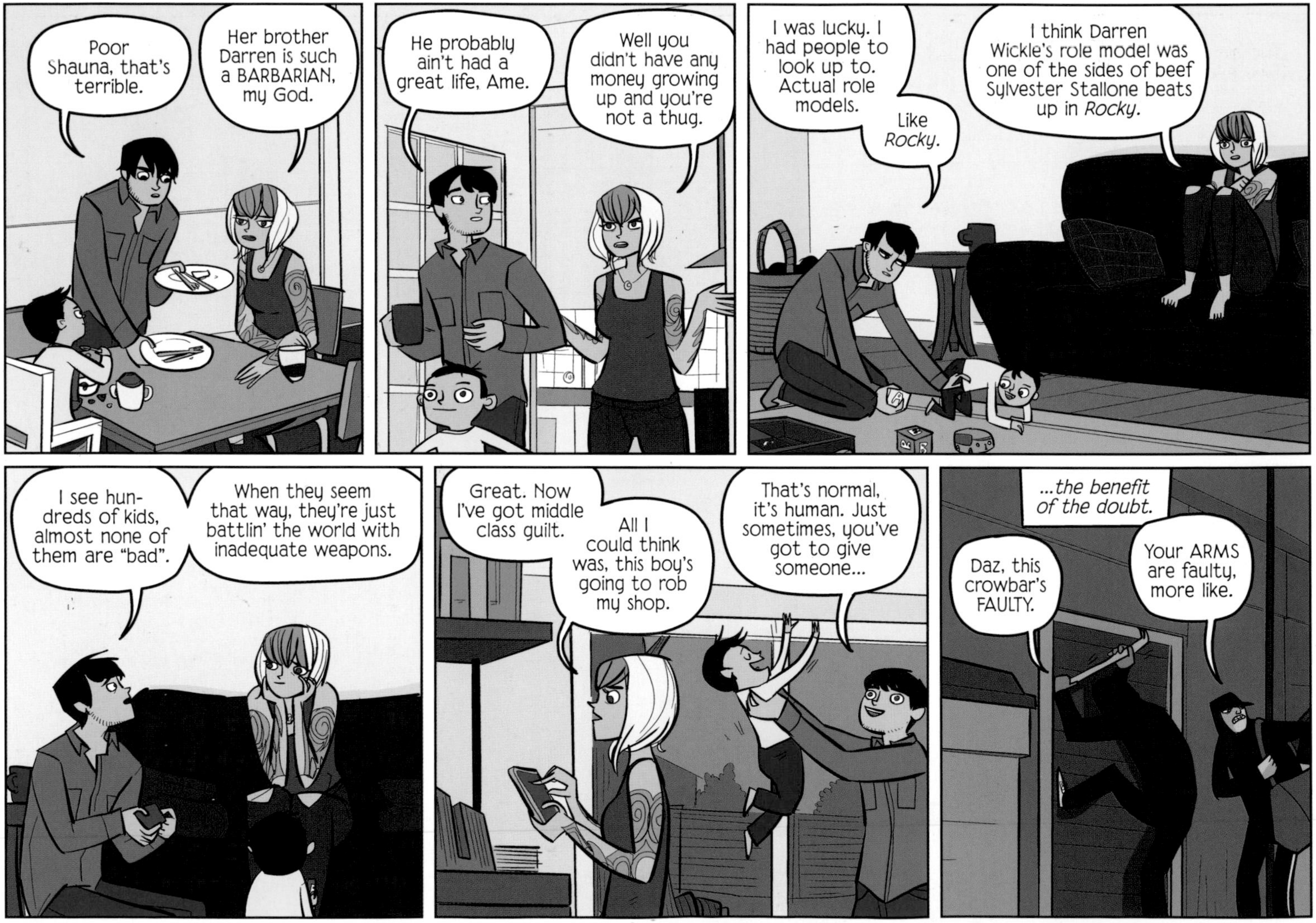
Poor Shauna, that's terrible.
Her brother Darren is such a BARBARIAN, my God.
He probably ain't had a great life, Ame.
Well you didn't have any money growing up and you're not a thug.
I was lucky. I had people to look up to. Actual role models.
Like *Rocky*.
I think Darren Wickle's role model was one of the sides of beef Sylvester Stallone beats up in *Rocky*.
I see hundreds of kids, almost none of them are "bad".
When they seem that way, they're just battlin' the world with inadequate weapons.
Great. Now I've got middle class guilt.
All I could think was, this boy's going to rob my shop.
That's normal, it's human. Just sometimes, you've got to give someone...
...the benefit of the doubt.
Daz, this crowbar's FAULTY.
Your ARMS are faulty, more like.

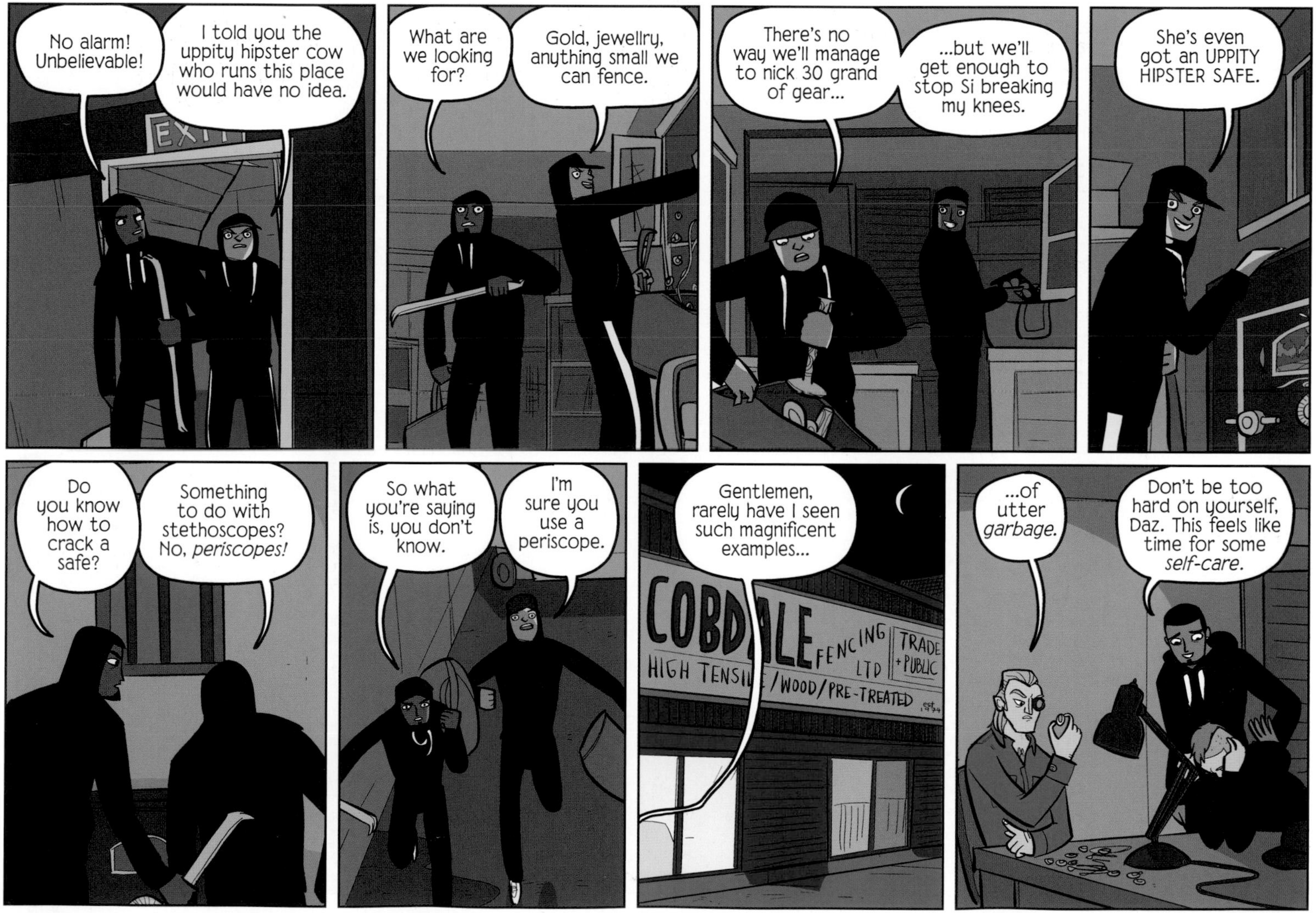

No alarm! Unbelievable!
I told you the uppity hipster cow who runs this place would have no idea.
EXIT
What are we looking for?
Gold, jewellry, anything small we can fence.
There's no way we'll manage to nick 30 grand of gear...
...but we'll get enough to stop Si breaking my knees.
She's even got an UPPITY HIPSTER SAFE.
Do you know how to crack a safe?
Something to do with stethoscopes? No, *periscopes!*
So what you're saying is, you don't know.
I'm sure you use a periscope.
Gentlemen, rarely have I seen such magnificent examples...
COBD LE FENCING LTD
TRADE + PUBLIC
HIGH TENSI /WOOD/PRE-TREATED
...of utter *garbage.*
Don't be too hard on yourself, Daz. This feels like time for some *self-care.*

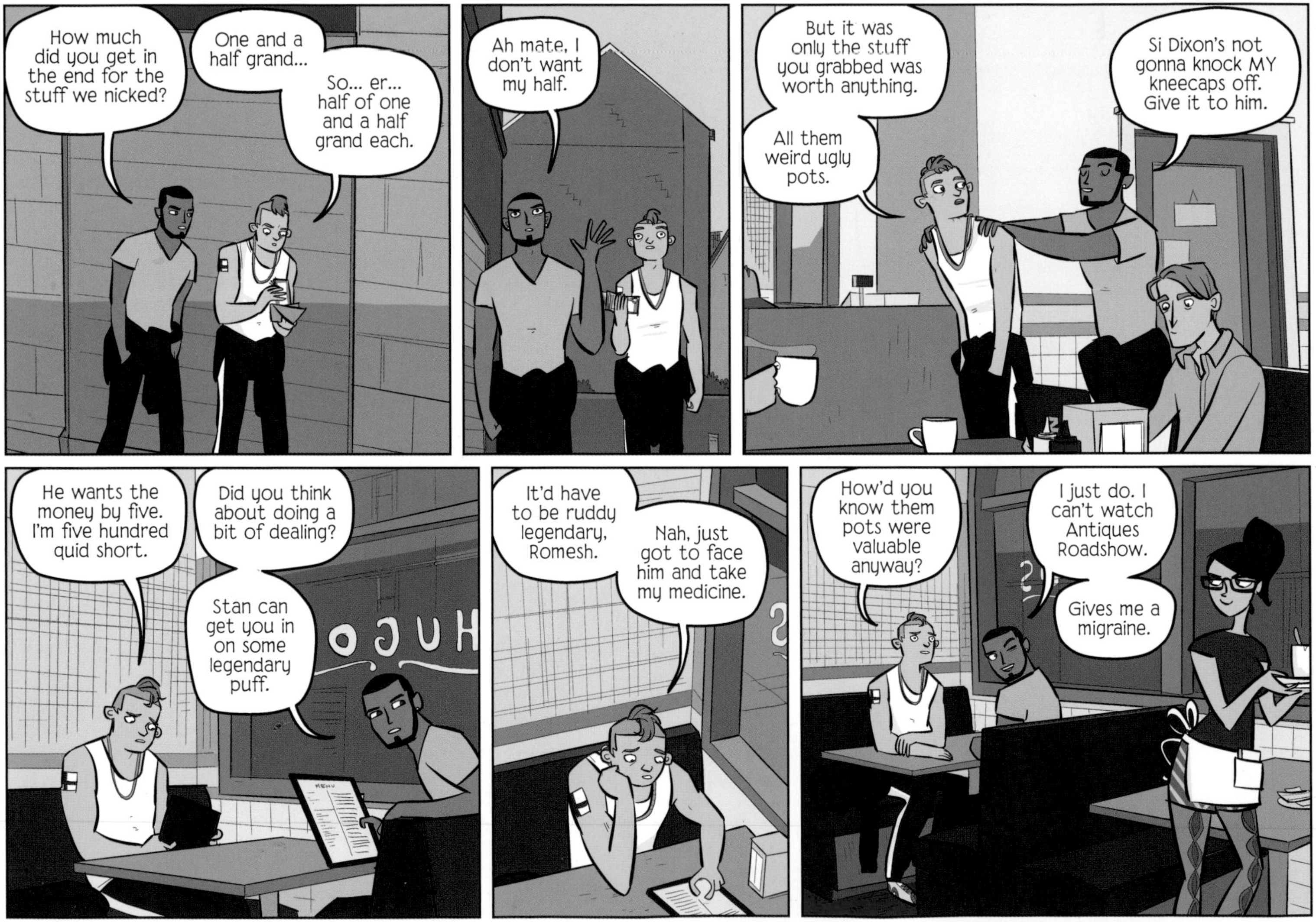
How much did you get in the end for the stuff we nicked?
One and a half grand...
So... er... half of one and a half grand each.
Ah mate, I don't want my half.
But it was only the stuff you grabbed was worth anything.
All them weird ugly pots.
Si Dixon's not gonna knock MY kneecaps off. Give it to him.
He wants the money by five. I'm five hundred quid short.
Did you think about doing a bit of dealing?
Stan can get you in on some legendary puff.
It'd have to be ruddy legendary, Romesh.
Nah, just got to face him and take my medicine.
How'd you know them pots were valuable anyway?
I just do. I can't watch Antiques Roadshow.
Gives me a migraine.

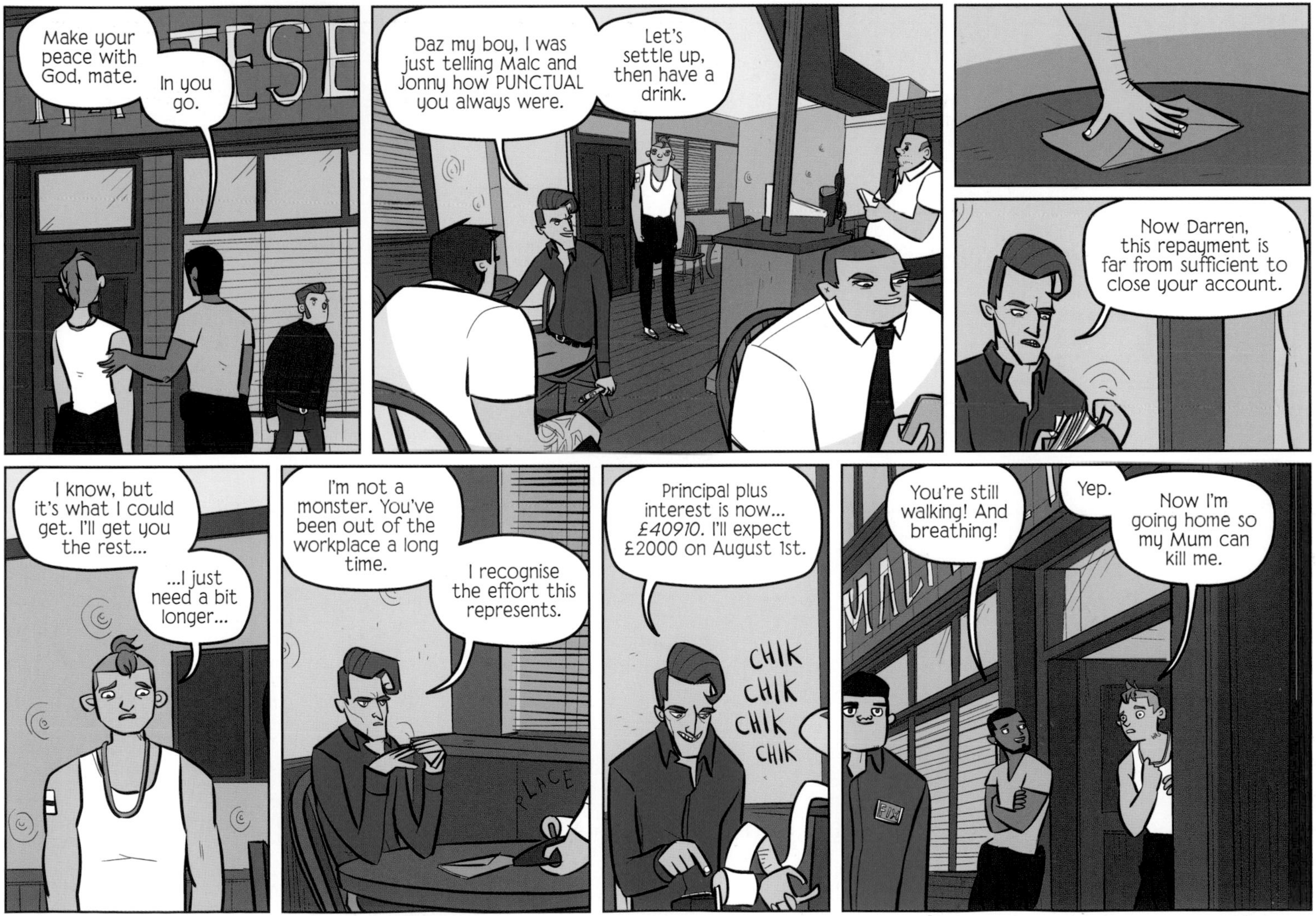

TESE
Make your peace with God, mate.
In you go.
Daz my boy, I was just telling Malc and Jonny how PUNCTUAL you always were.
Let's settle up, then have a drink.
Now Darren, this repayment is far from sufficient to close your account.
I know, but it's what I could get. I'll get you the rest...
...I just need a bit longer...
I'm not a monster. You've been out of the workplace a long time.
I recognise the effort this represents.
PLACE
Principal plus interest is now... *£40910.* I'll expect £2000 on August 1st.
CHIK
CHIK
CHIK
CHIK
You're still walking! And breathing!
Yep.
Now I'm going home so my Mum can kill me.

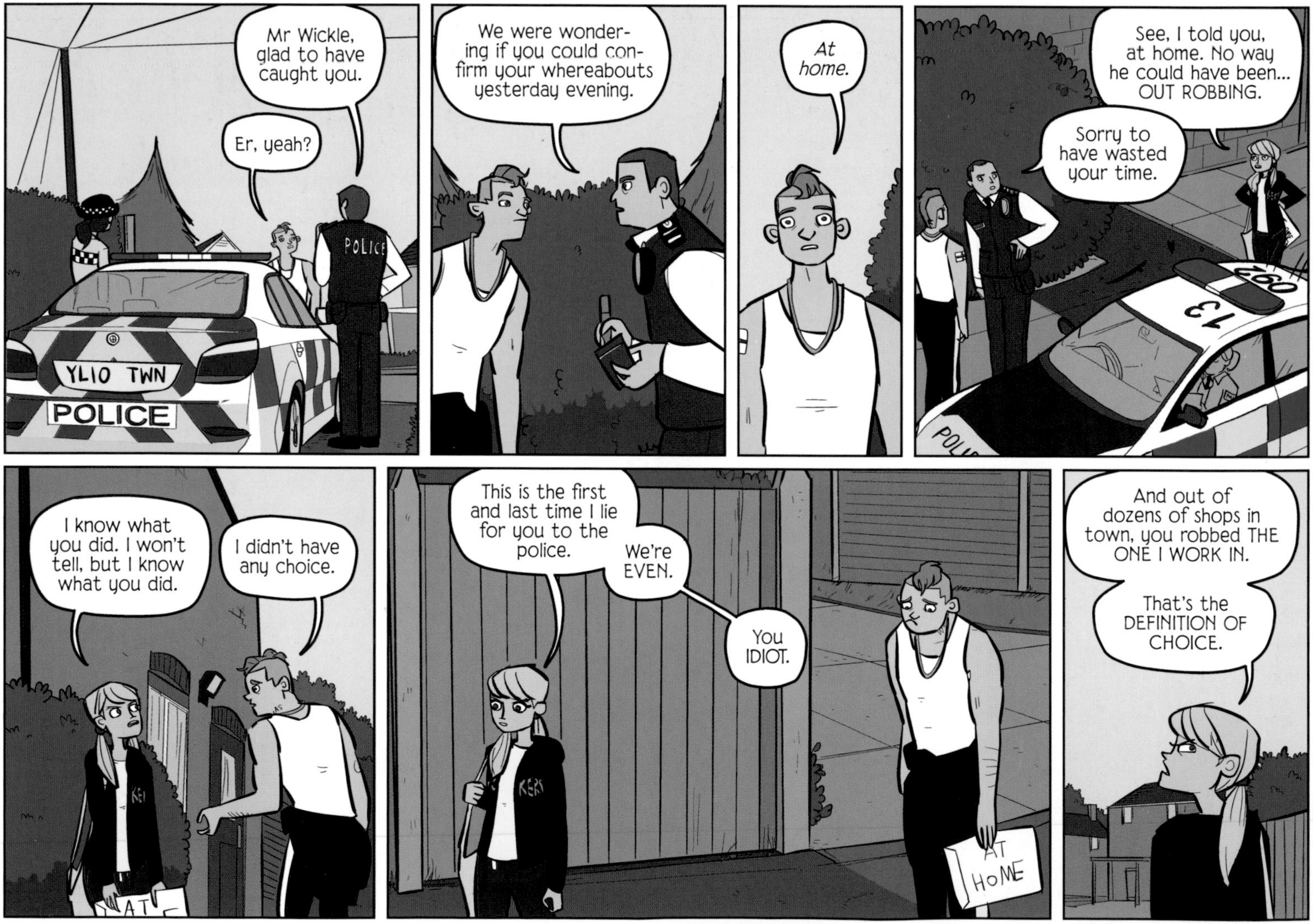
Mr Wickle, glad to have caught you.
Er, yeah?
We were wondering if you could confirm your whereabouts yesterday evening.
YLIO TWN
POLICE
POLICE
At home.
See, I told you, at home. No way he could have been... OUT ROBBING.
Sorry to have wasted your time.
I know what you did. I won't tell, but I know what you did.
I didn't have any choice.
This is the first and last time I lie for you to the police.
We're EVEN.
You IDIOT.
AT HOME
And out of dozens of shops in town, you robbed THE ONE I WORK IN.
That's the DEFINITION OF CHOICE.

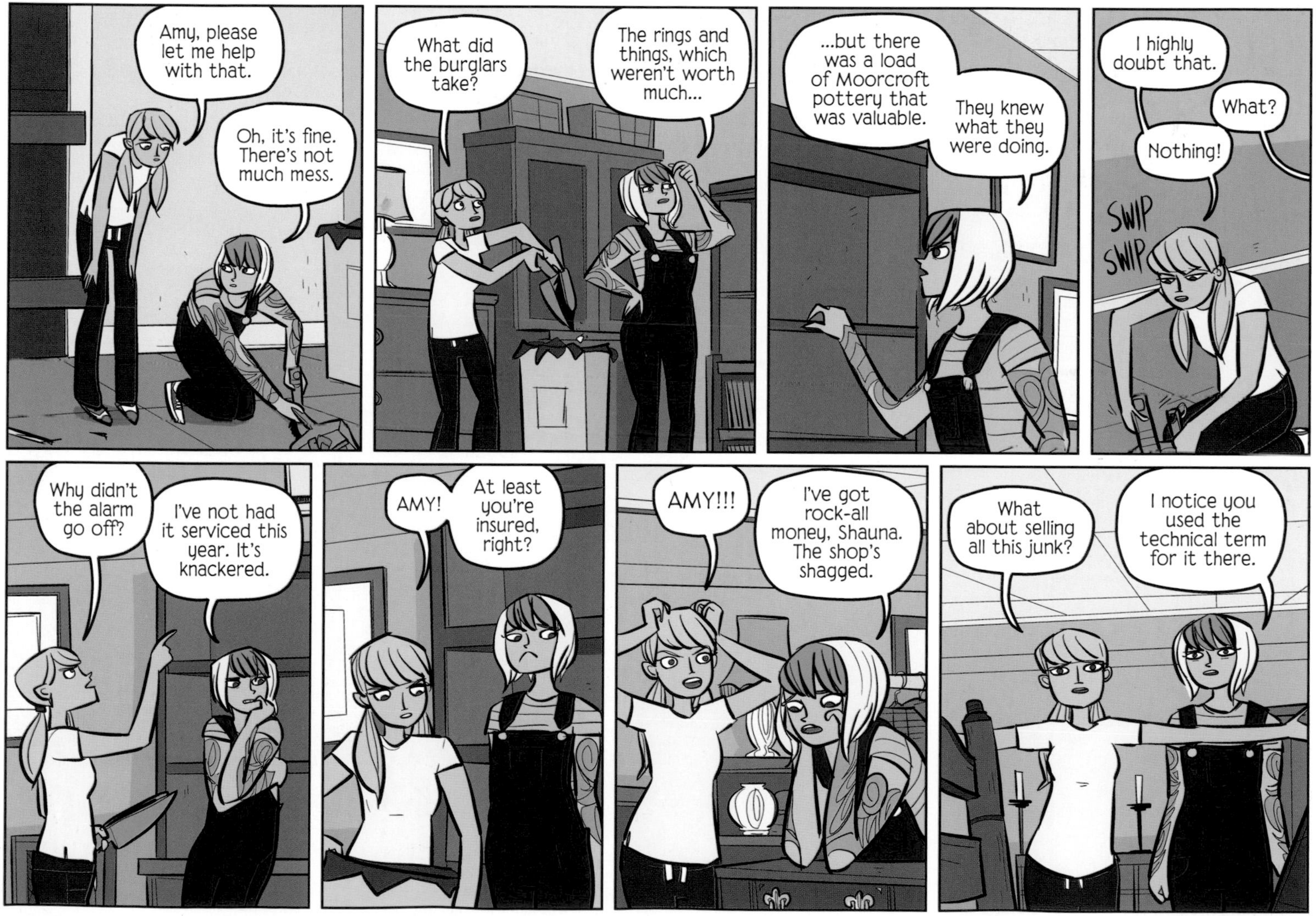

Amy, please let me help with that.
Oh, it's fine. There's not much mess.
What did the burglars take?
The rings and things, which weren't worth much...
...but there was a load of Moorcroft pottery that was valuable.
They knew what they were doing.
I highly doubt that.
Nothing!
What?
SWIP SWIP
Why didn't the alarm go off?
I've not had it serviced this year. It's knackered.
AMY!
At least you're insured, right?
AMY!!!
I've got rock-all money, Shauna. The shop's shagged.
What about selling all this junk?
I notice you used the technical term for it there.

Bad Machinery, Volume Nine

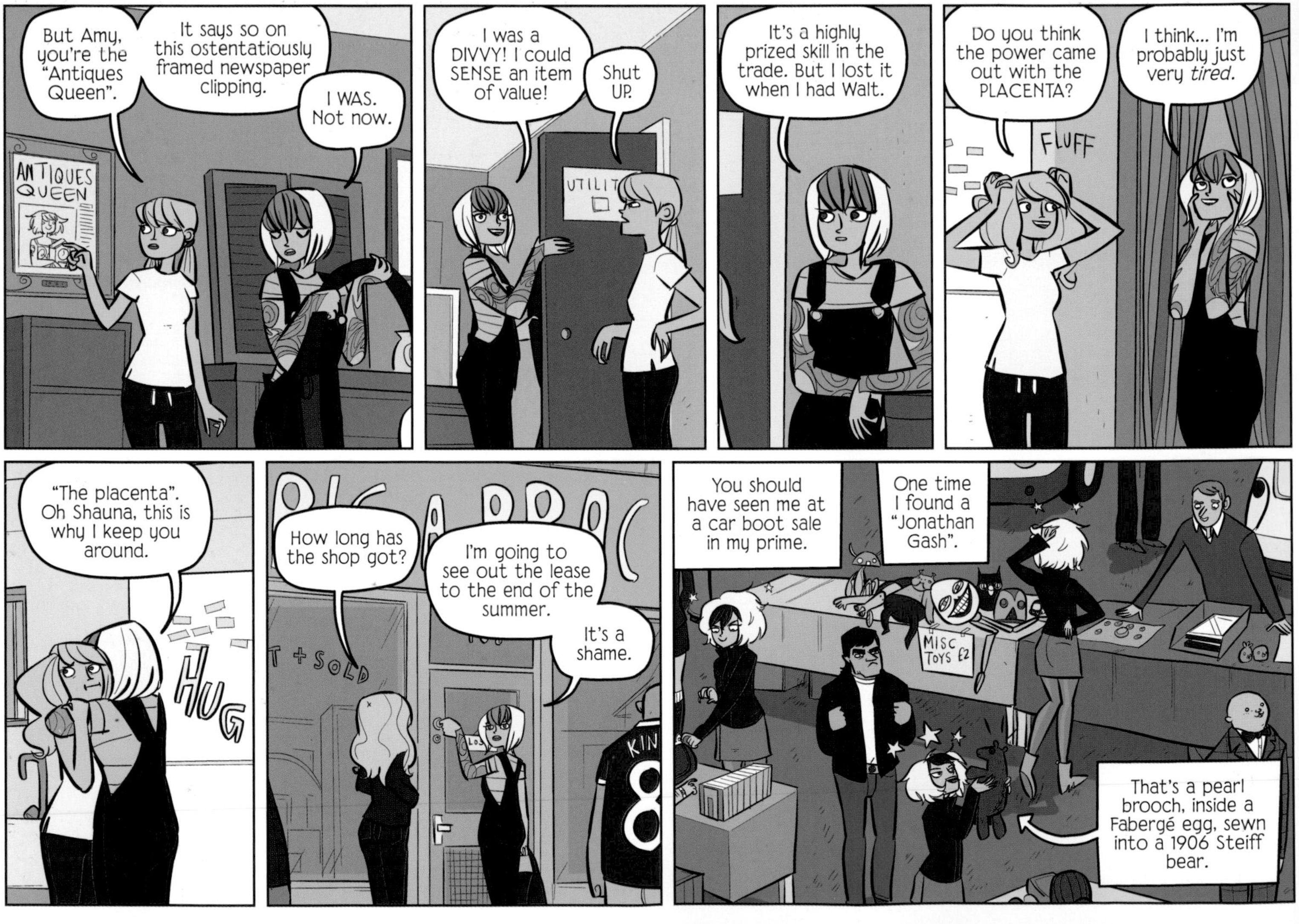

But Amy, you're the "Antiques Queen".
It says so on this ostentatiously framed newspaper clipping.
ANTIQUES QUEEN
I WAS. Not now.
I was a DIVVY! I could SENSE an item of value!
Shut UP.
UTILIT
It's a highly prized skill in the trade. But I lost it when I had Walt.
Do you think the power came out with the PLACENTA?
FLUFF
I think... I'm probably just very *tired.*
"The placenta". Oh Shauna, this is why I keep you around.
HUG
How long has the shop got?
I'm going to see out the lease to the end of the summer.
It's a shame.
T + SOLD
You should have seen me at a car boot sale in my prime.
One time I found a "Jonathan Gash".
MISC TOYS £2
That's a pearl brooch, inside a Fabergé egg, sewn into a 1906 Steiff bear.

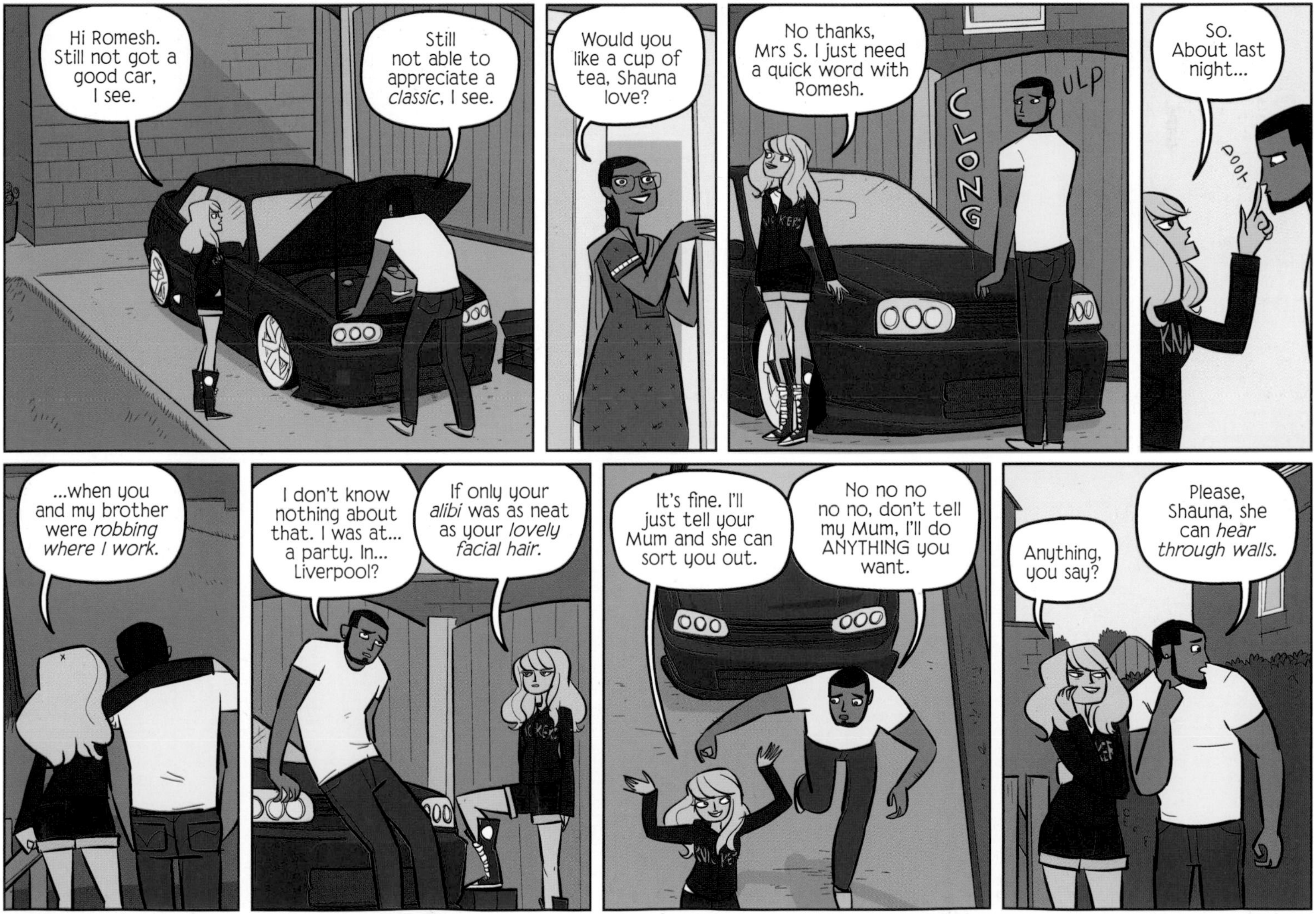
Hi Romesh. Still not got a good car, I see.
Still not able to appreciate a *classic*, I see.
Would you like a cup of tea, Shauna love?
No thanks, Mrs S. I just need a quick word with Romesh.
CLONG
ULP
So. About last night...
DOOT
...when you and my brother were *robbing where I work.*
I don't know nothing about that. I was at... a party. In... Liverpool?
If only your *alibi* was as neat as your *lovely facial hair.*
It's fine. I'll just tell your Mum and she can sort you out.
No no no no no, don't tell my Mum, I'll do ANYTHING you want.
Anything, you say?
Please, Shauna, she can *hear through walls.*

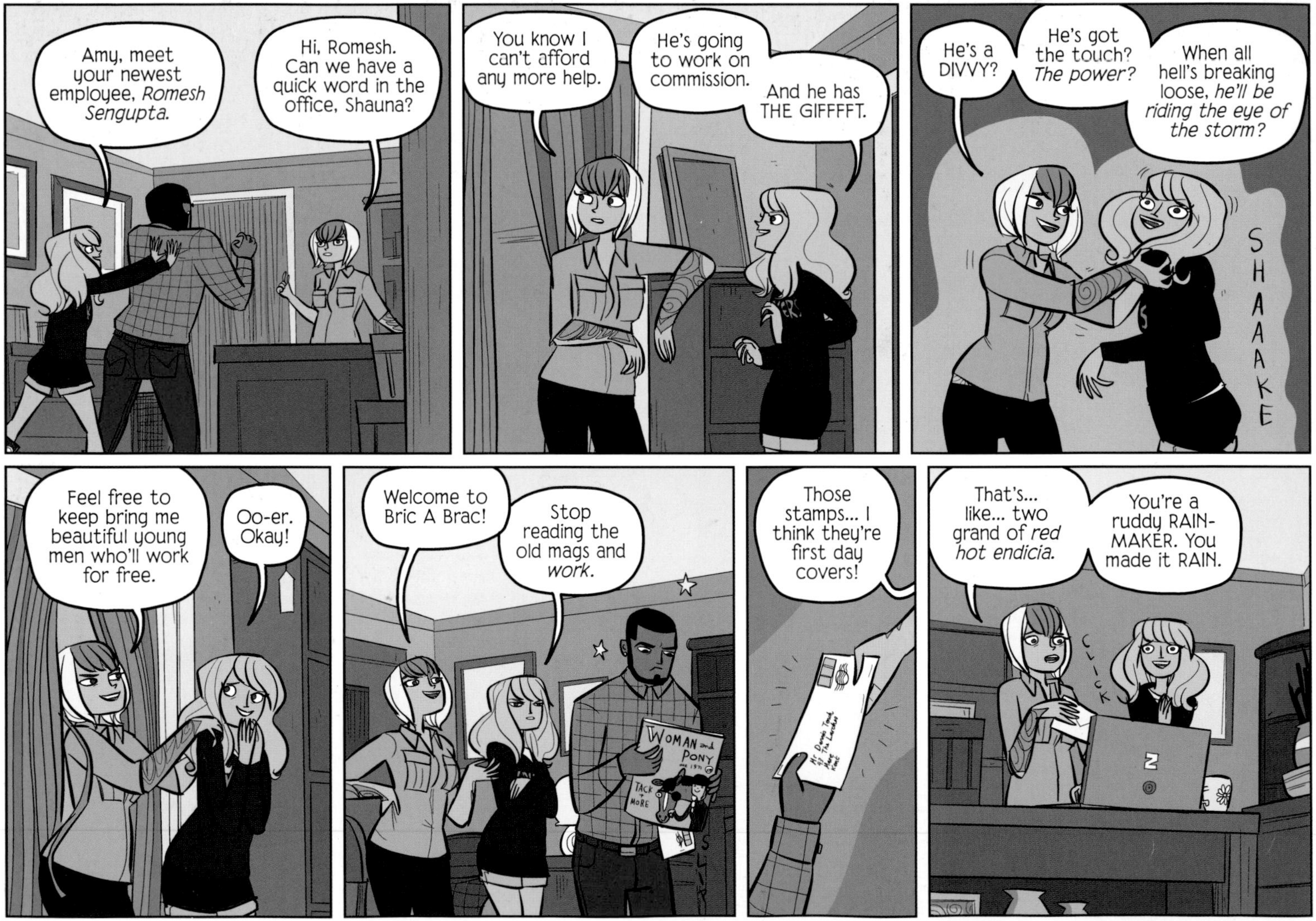
Amy, meet your newest employee, *Romesh Sengupta.*
Hi, Romesh. Can we have a quick word in the office, Shauna?
You know I can't afford any more help.
He's going to work on commission.
And he has THE GIFFFFT.
He's a DIVVY?
He's got the touch? *The power?*
When all hell's breaking loose, *he'll be riding the eye of the storm?*
SHAAAKE
Feel free to keep bring me beautiful young men who'll work for free.
Oo-er. Okay!
Welcome to Bric A Brac!
Stop reading the old mags and *work.*
WOMAN and PONY
TACK + MORE
Those stamps... I think they're first day covers!
That's... like... two grand of *red hot endicia.*
CLICK
You're a ruddy RAIN-MAKER. You made it RAIN.

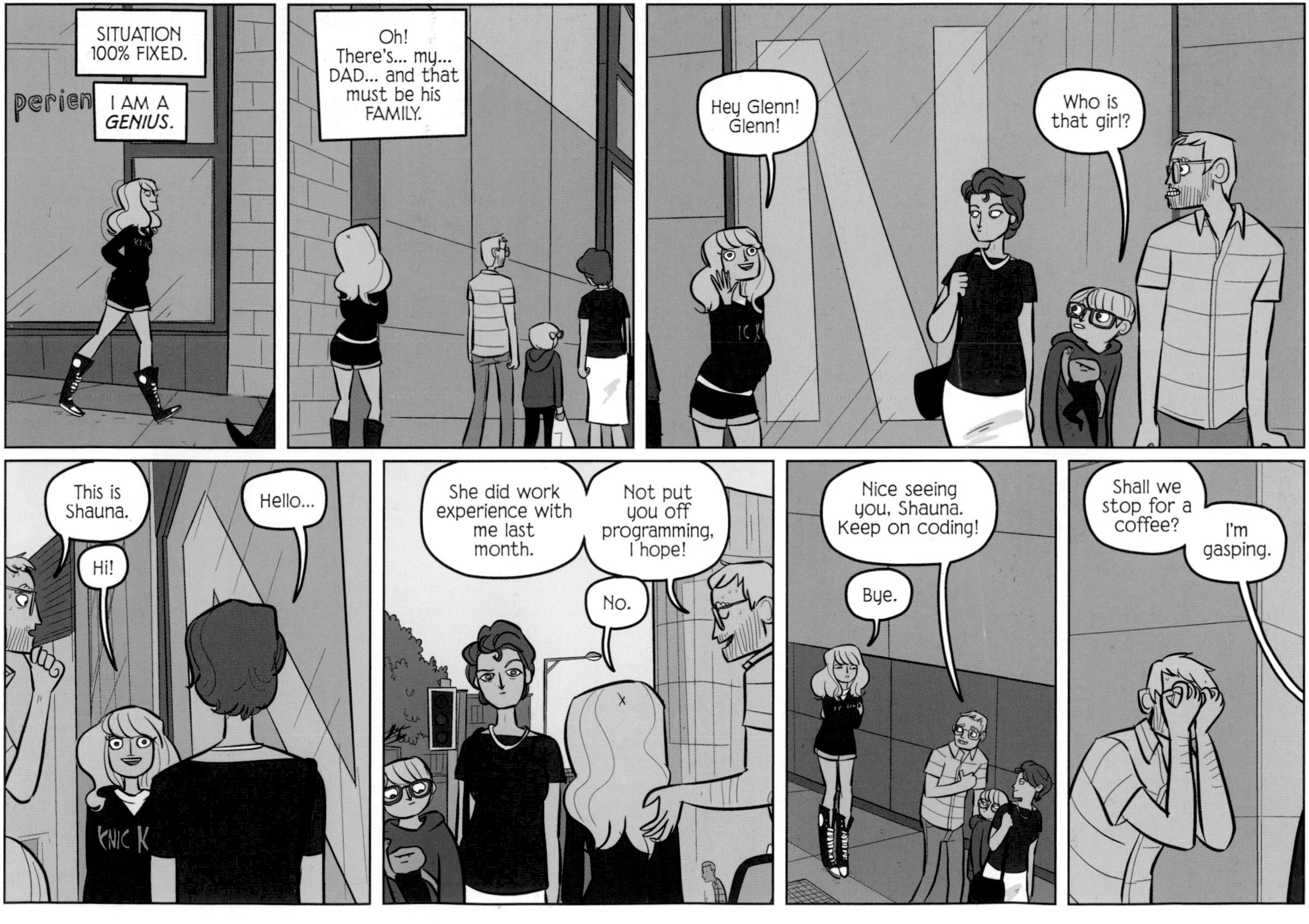

SITUATION 100% FIXED.
I AM A *GENIUS*.
perien
Oh! There's... my... DAD... and that must be his FAMILY.
Hey Glenn! Glenn!
Who is that girl?
This is Shauna.
Hi!
Hello...
She did work experience with me last month.
Not put you off programming, I hope!
No.
Nice seeing you, Shauna. Keep on coding!
Bye.
Shall we stop for a coffee?
I'm gasping.

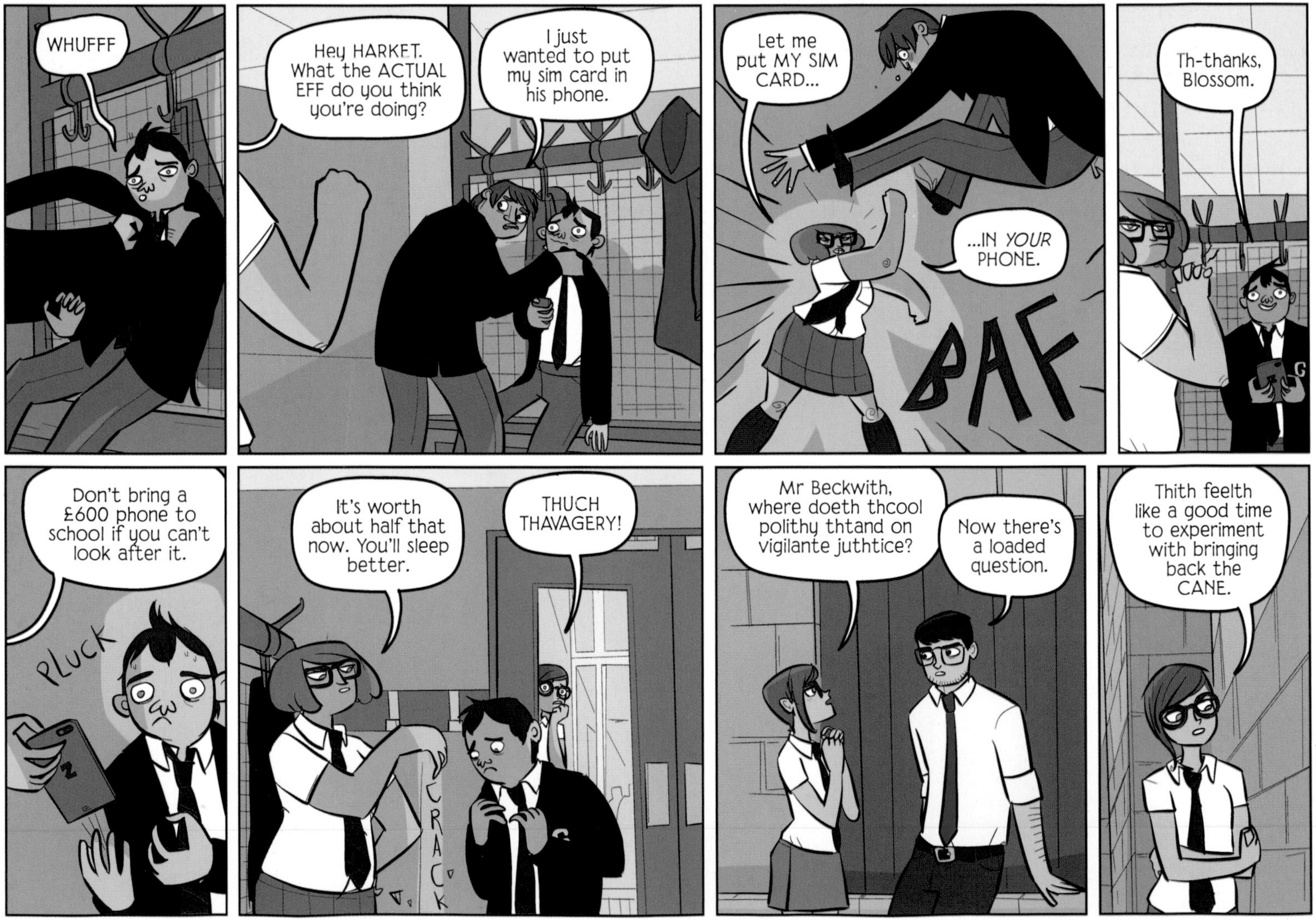

WHUFFF
Hey HARKET. What the ACTUAL EFF do you think you're doing?
I just wanted to put my sim card in his phone.
Let me put MY SIM CARD...
...IN YOUR PHONE.
BAF
Th-thanks, Blossom.
Don't bring a £600 phone to school if you can't look after it.
PLUCK
It's worth about half that now. You'll sleep better.
CRACK
THUCH THAVAGERY!
Mr Beckwith, where doeth thcool polithy thtand on vigilante juthtice?
Now there's a loaded question.
Thith feelth like a good time to experiment with bringing back the CANE.

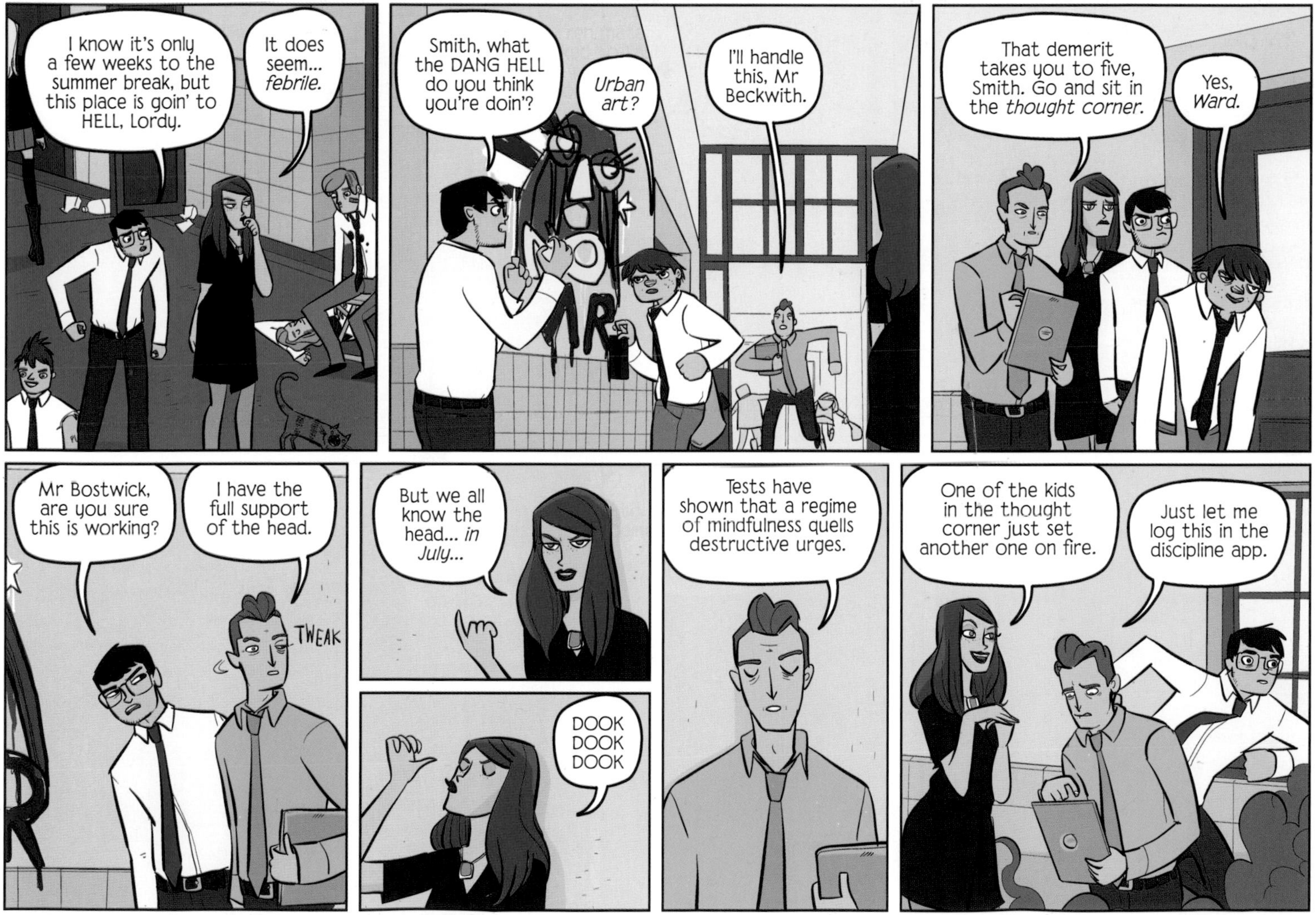

I know it's only a few weeks to the summer break, but this place is goin' to HELL, Lordy.
It does seem... *febrile.*
Smith, what the DANG HELL do you think you're doin'?
Urban art?
I'll handle this, Mr Beckwith.
That demerit takes you to five, Smith. Go and sit in the *thought corner.*
Yes, *Ward.*
Mr Bostwick, are you sure this is working?
I have the full support of the head.
TWEAK
But we all know the head... *in July...*
DOOK DOOK DOOK
Tests have shown that a regime of mindfulness quells destructive urges.
One of the kids in the thought corner just set another one on fire.
Just let me log this in the discipline app.

Bad Machinery, Volume Nine

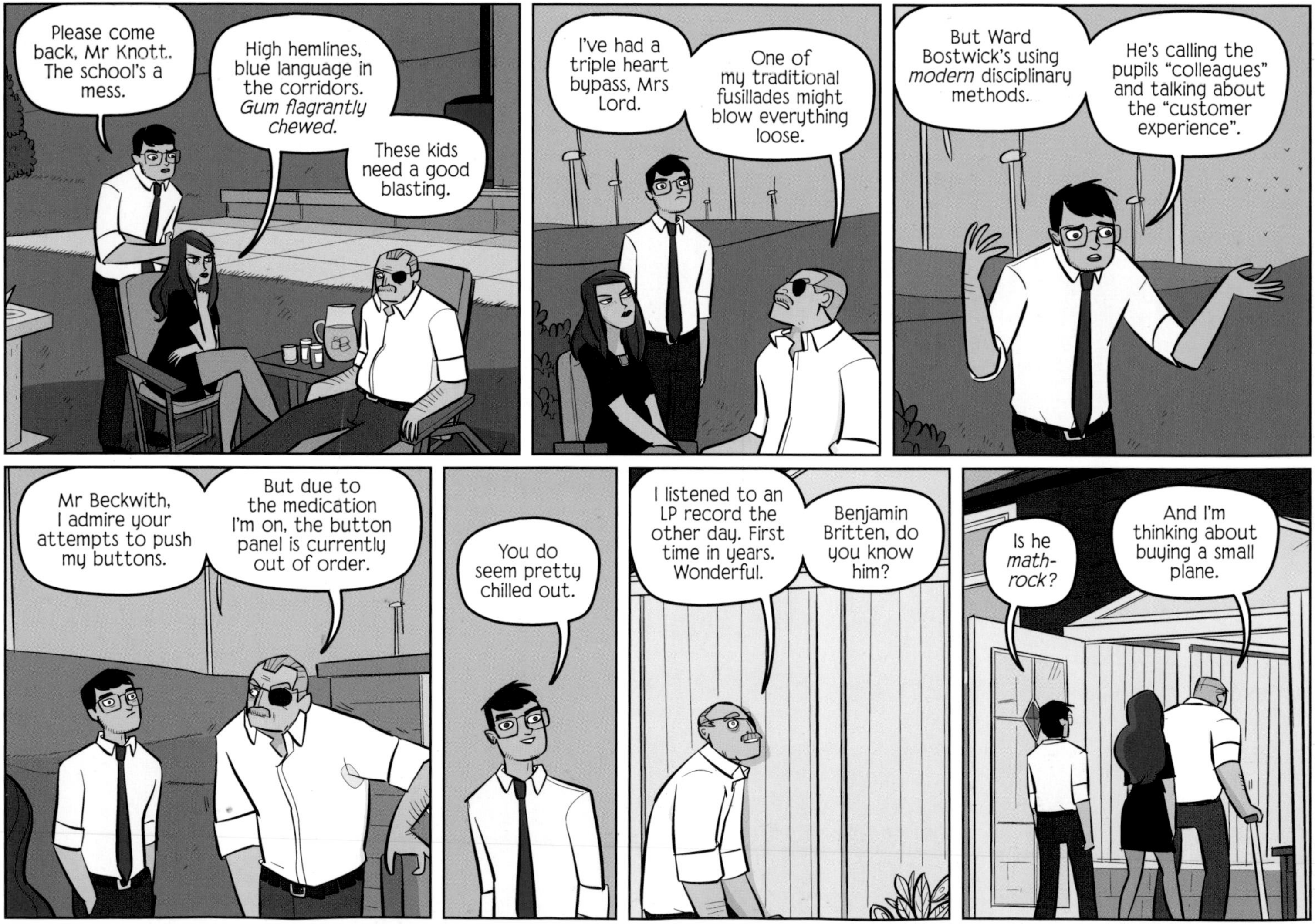
Please come back, Mr Knott. The school's a mess.
High hemlines, blue language in the corridors. *Gum flagrantly chewed.*
These kids need a good blasting.
I've had a triple heart bypass, Mrs Lord.
One of my traditional fusillades might blow everything loose.
But Ward Bostwick's using *modern* disciplinary methods.
He's calling the pupils "colleagues" and talking about the "customer experience".
Mr Beckwith, I admire your attempts to push my buttons.
But due to the medication I'm on, the button panel is currently out of order.
You do seem pretty chilled out.
I listened to an LP record the other day. First time in years. Wonderful.
Benjamin Britten, do you know him?
Is he *math-rock?*
And I'm thinking about buying a small plane.

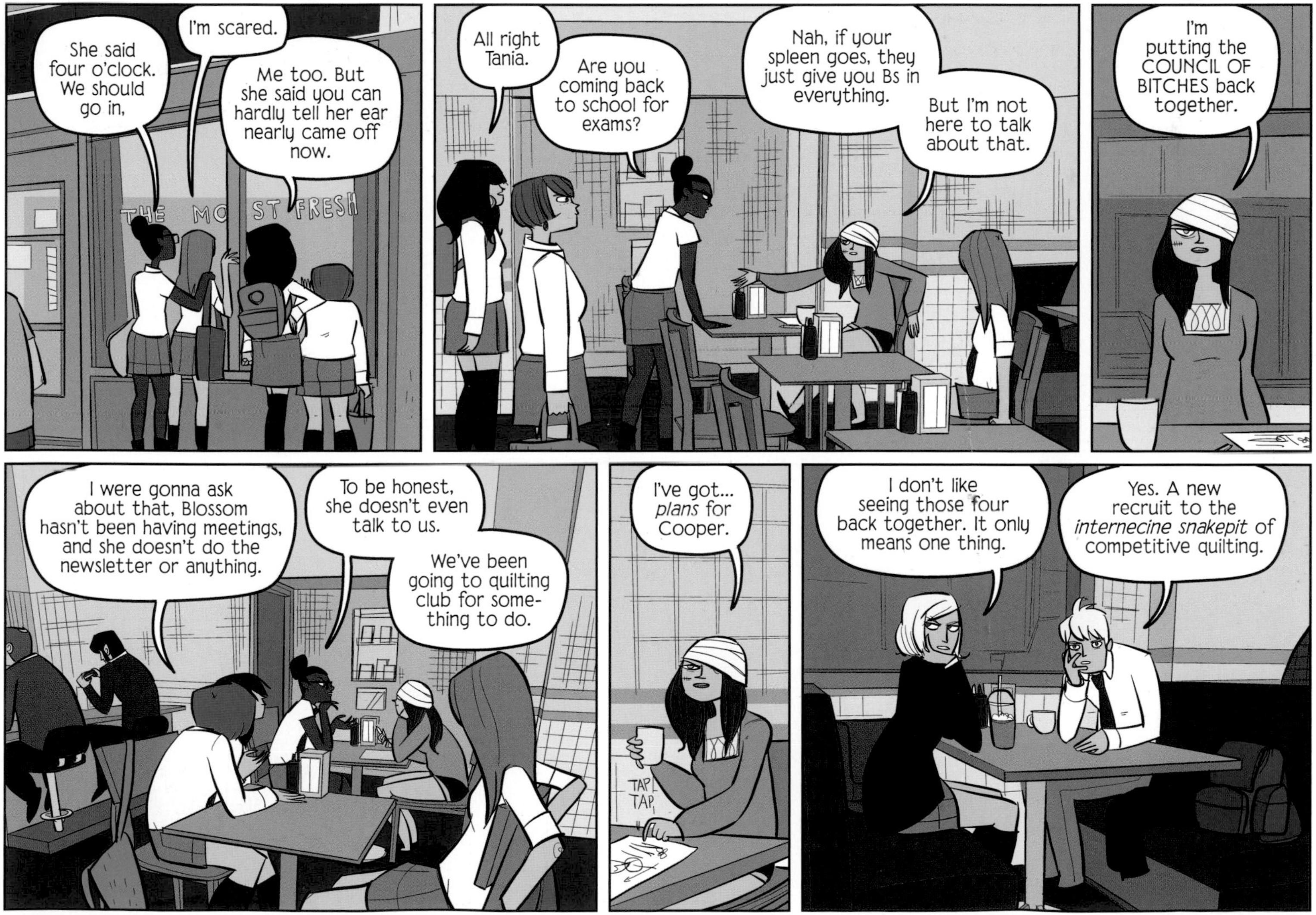
She said four o'clock. We should go in,
I'm scared.
Me too. But she said you can hardly tell her ear nearly came off now.
THE MO ST FRESH
All right Tania.
Are you coming back to school for exams?
Nah, if your spleen goes, they just give you Bs in everything.
But I'm not here to talk about that.
I'm putting the COUNCIL OF BITCHES back together.
I were gonna ask about that, Blossom hasn't been having meetings, and she doesn't do the newsletter or anything.
To be honest, she doesn't even talk to us.
We've been going to quilting club for something to do.
I've got... *plans* for Cooper.
TAP TAP
I don't like seeing those four back together. It only means one thing.
Yes. A new recruit to the *internecine snakepit* of competitive quilting.

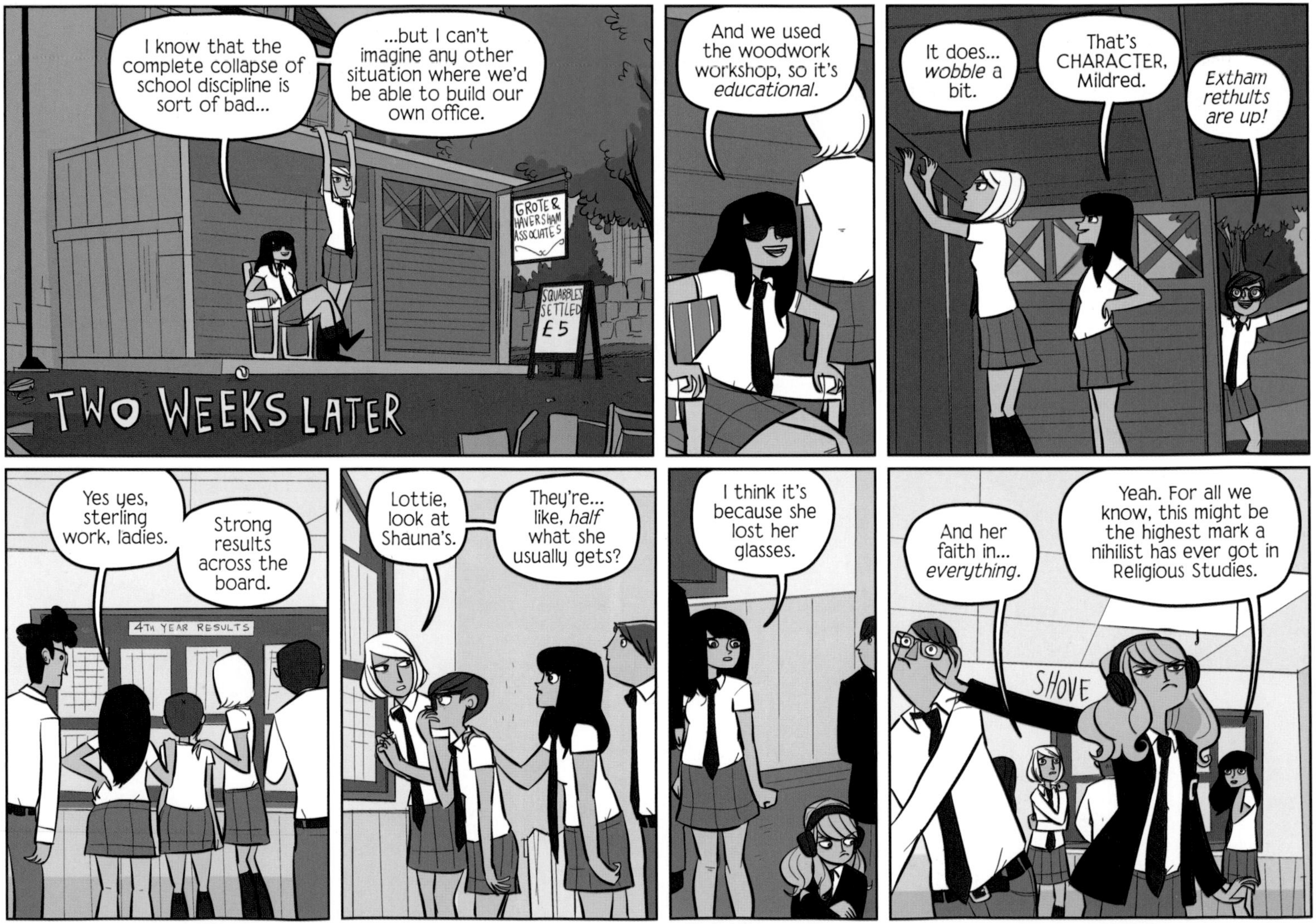
I know that the complete collapse of school discipline is sort of bad...
...but I can't imagine any other situation where we'd be able to build our own office.
GROTE & HAVERSHAM ASSOCIATES
SQUABBLES SETTLED £5
TWO WEEKS LATER
And we used the woodwork workshop, so it's *educational.*
It does... *wobble* a bit.
That's CHARACTER, Mildred.
Extham rethults are up!
Yes yes, sterling work, ladies.
Strong results across the board.
4TH YEAR RESULTS
Lottie, look at Shauna's.
They're... like, *half* what she usually gets?
I think it's because she lost her glasses.
And her faith in... *everything.*
Yeah. For all we know, this might be the highest mark a nihilist has ever got in Religious Studies.
SHOVE

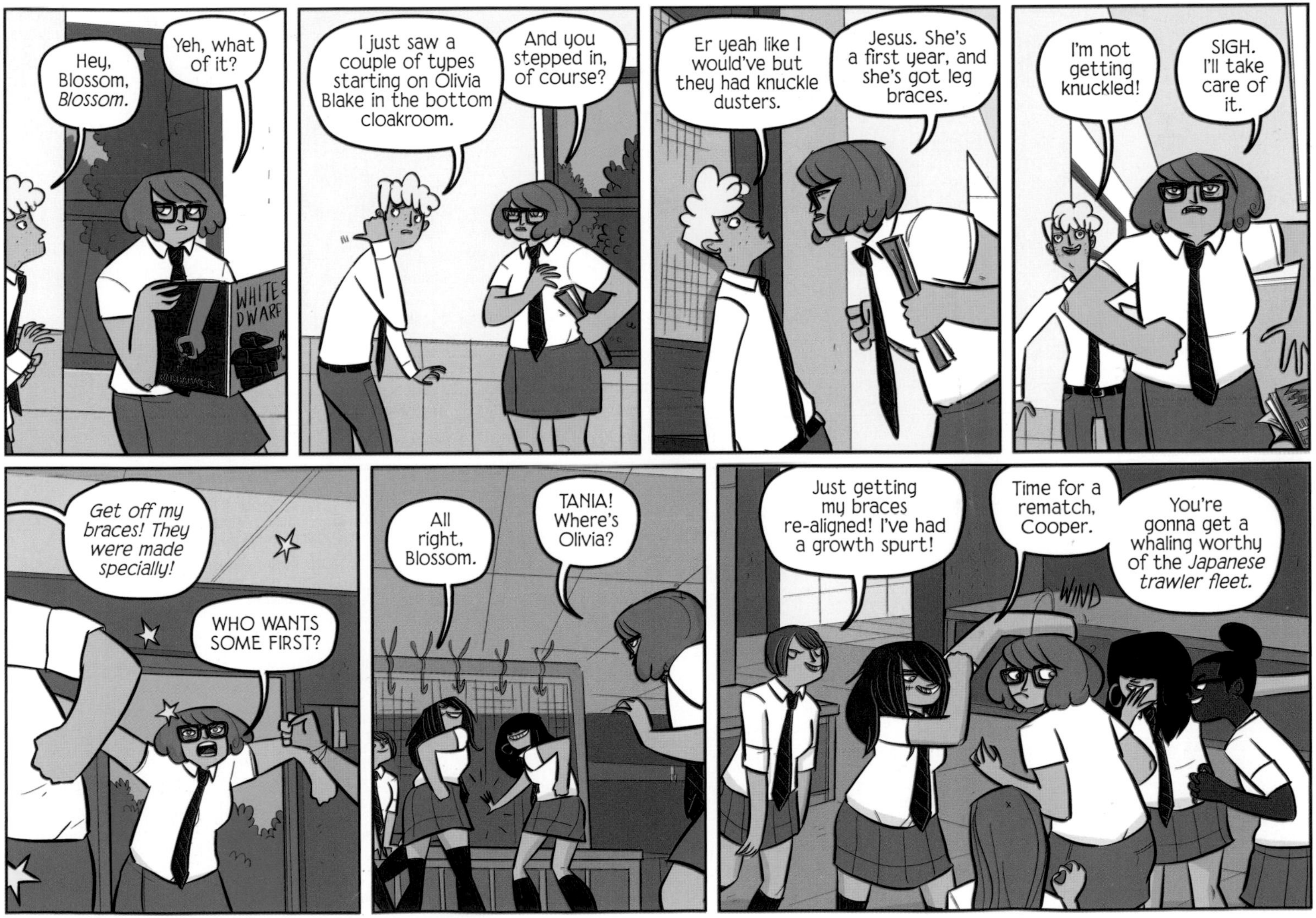

Hey, Blossom, *Blossom*.
Yeh, what of it?
I just saw a couple of types starting on Olivia Blake in the bottom cloakroom.
And you stepped in, of course?
Er yeah like I would've but they had knuckle dusters.
Jesus. She's a first year, and she's got leg braces.
I'm not getting knuckled!
SIGH. I'll take care of it.
Get off my braces! They were made specially!
WHO WANTS SOME FIRST?
All right, Blossom.
TANIA! Where's Olivia?
Just getting my braces re-aligned! I've had a growth spurt!
Time for a rematch, Cooper.
WIND
You're gonna get a whaling worthy of the *Japanese trawler fleet.*

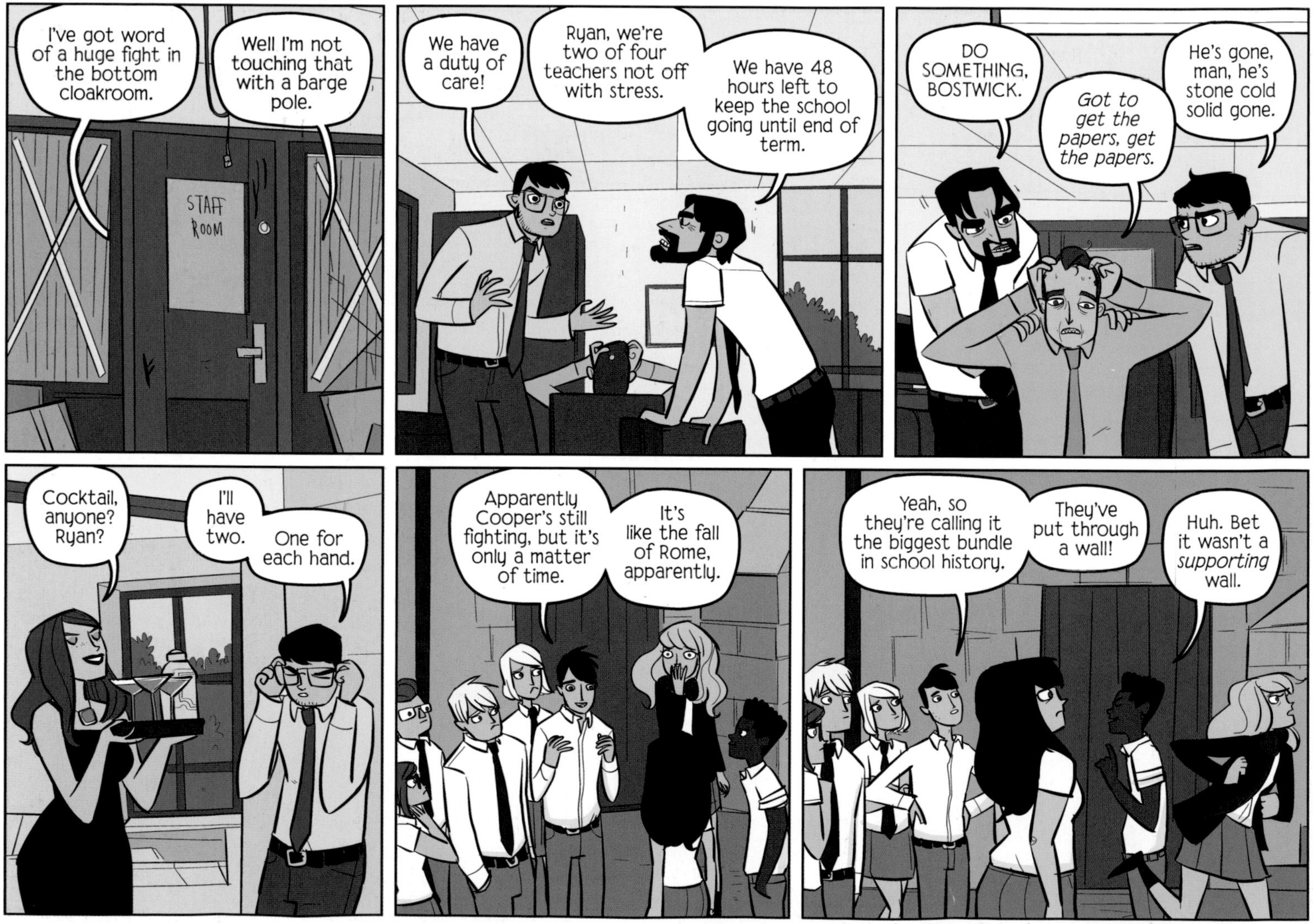

I've got word of a huge fight in the bottom cloakroom.
Well I'm not touching that with a barge pole.
STAFF ROOM
We have a duty of care!
Ryan, we're two of four teachers not off with stress.
We have 48 hours left to keep the school going until end of term.
DO SOMETHING, BOSTWICK.
Got to get the papers, get the papers.
He's gone, man, he's stone cold solid gone.
Cocktail, anyone? Ryan?
I'll have two.
One for each hand.
Apparently Cooper's still fighting, but it's only a matter of time.
It's like the fall of Rome, apparently.
Yeah, so they're calling it the biggest bundle in school history.
They've put through a wall!
Huh. Bet it wasn't a *supporting* wall.

The Case of the Missing Piece

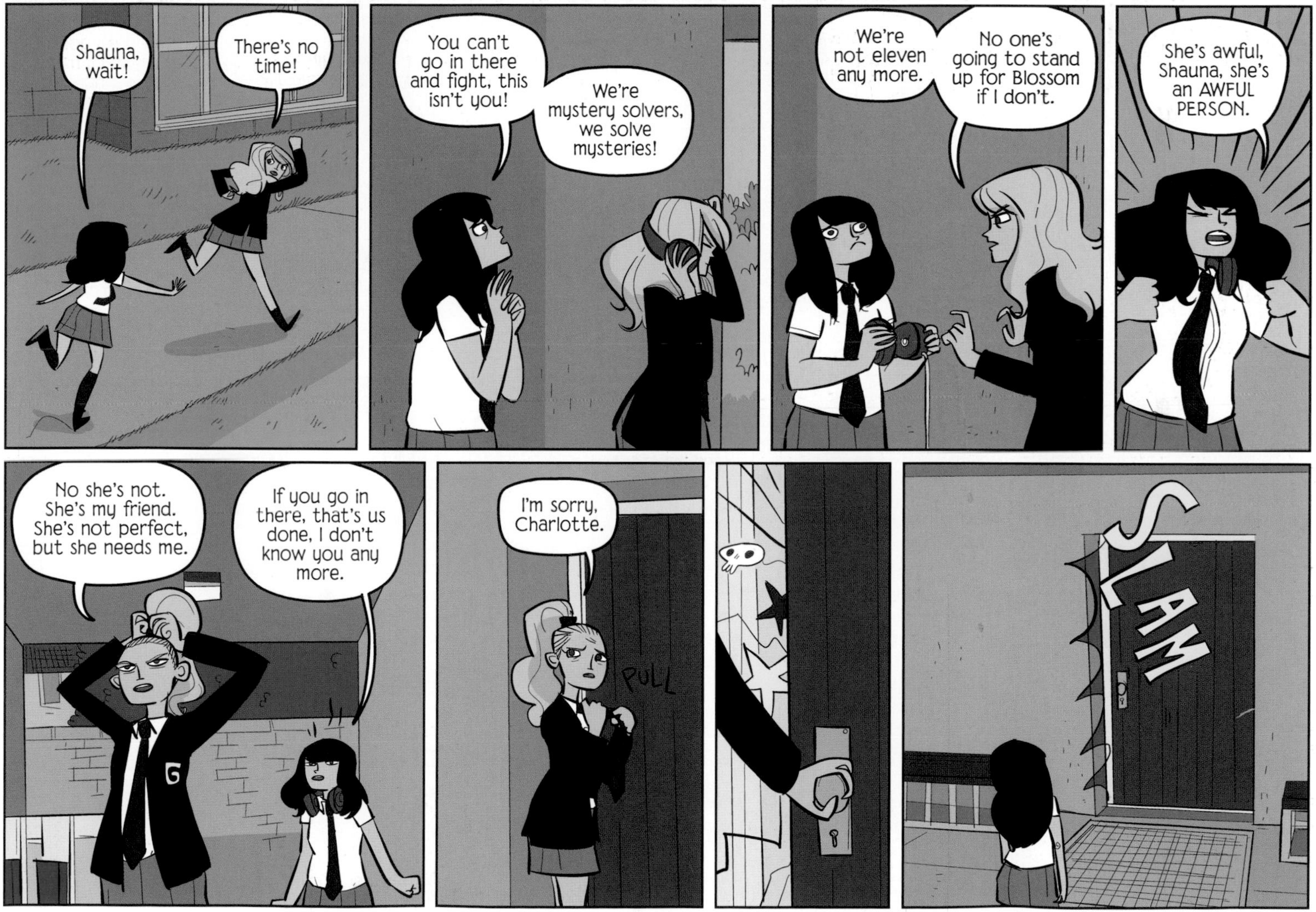
Shauna, wait!
There's no time!
You can't go in there and fight, this isn't you!
We're mystery solvers, we solve mysteries!
We're not eleven any more.
No one's going to stand up for Blossom if I don't.
She's awful, Shauna, she's an AWFUL PERSON.
No she's not. She's my friend. She's not perfect, but she needs me.
If you go in there, that's us done, I don't know you any more.
I'm sorry, Charlotte.
PULL
SLAM

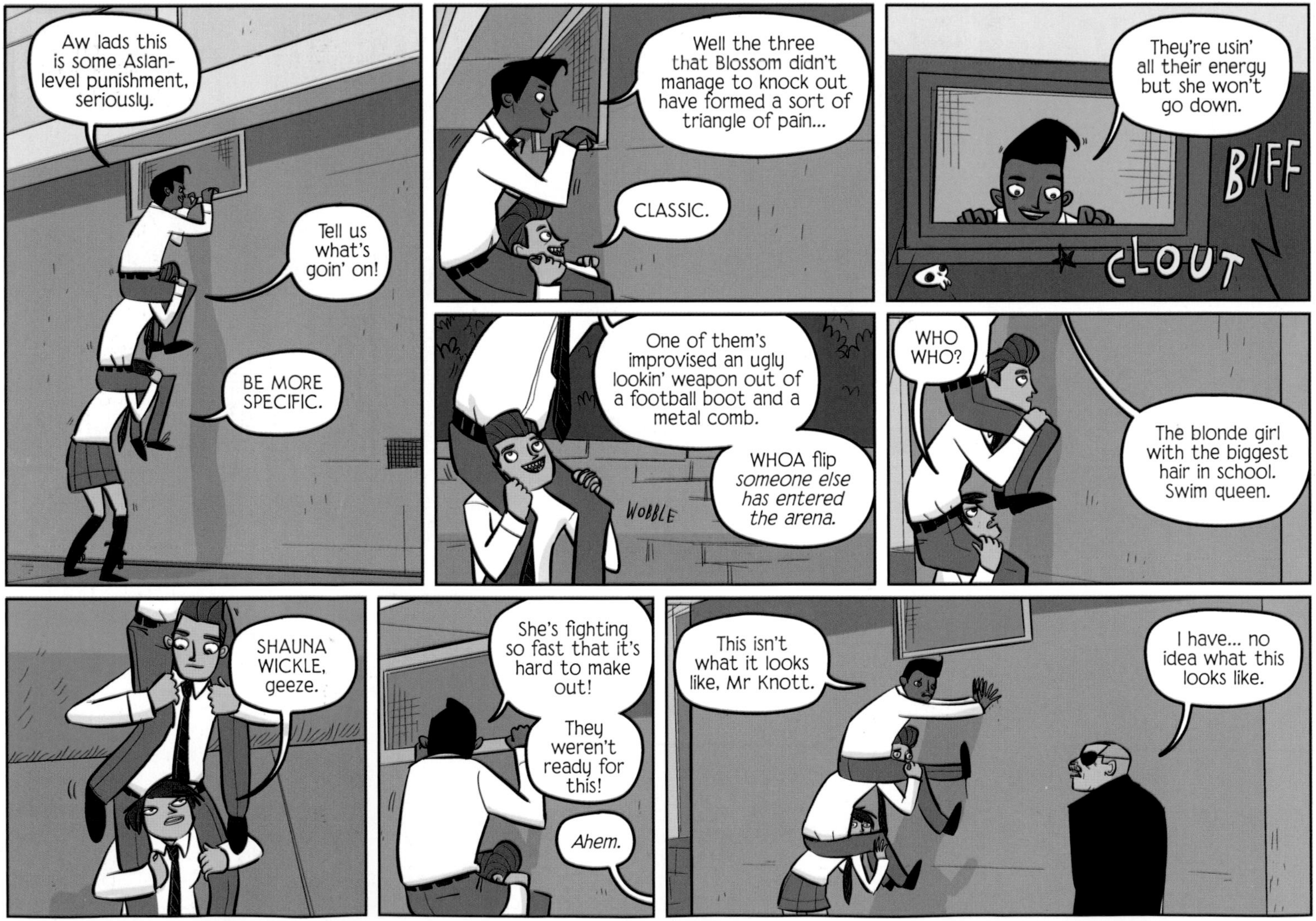

Aw lads this is some Aslan-level punishment, seriously.
Tell us what's goin' on!
BE MORE SPECIFIC.
Well the three that Blossom didn't manage to knock out have formed a sort of triangle of pain...
CLASSIC.
They're usin' all their energy but she won't go down.
BIFF
CLOUT
One of them's improvised an ugly lookin' weapon out of a football boot and a metal comb.
WHOA flip *someone else has entered the arena.*
WOBBLE
WHO WHO?
The blonde girl with the biggest hair in school. Swim queen.
SHAUNA WICKLE, geeze.
She's fighting so fast that it's hard to make out!
They weren't ready for this!
Ahem.
This isn't what it looks like, Mr Knott.
I have... no idea what this looks like.

The Case of the Missing Piece

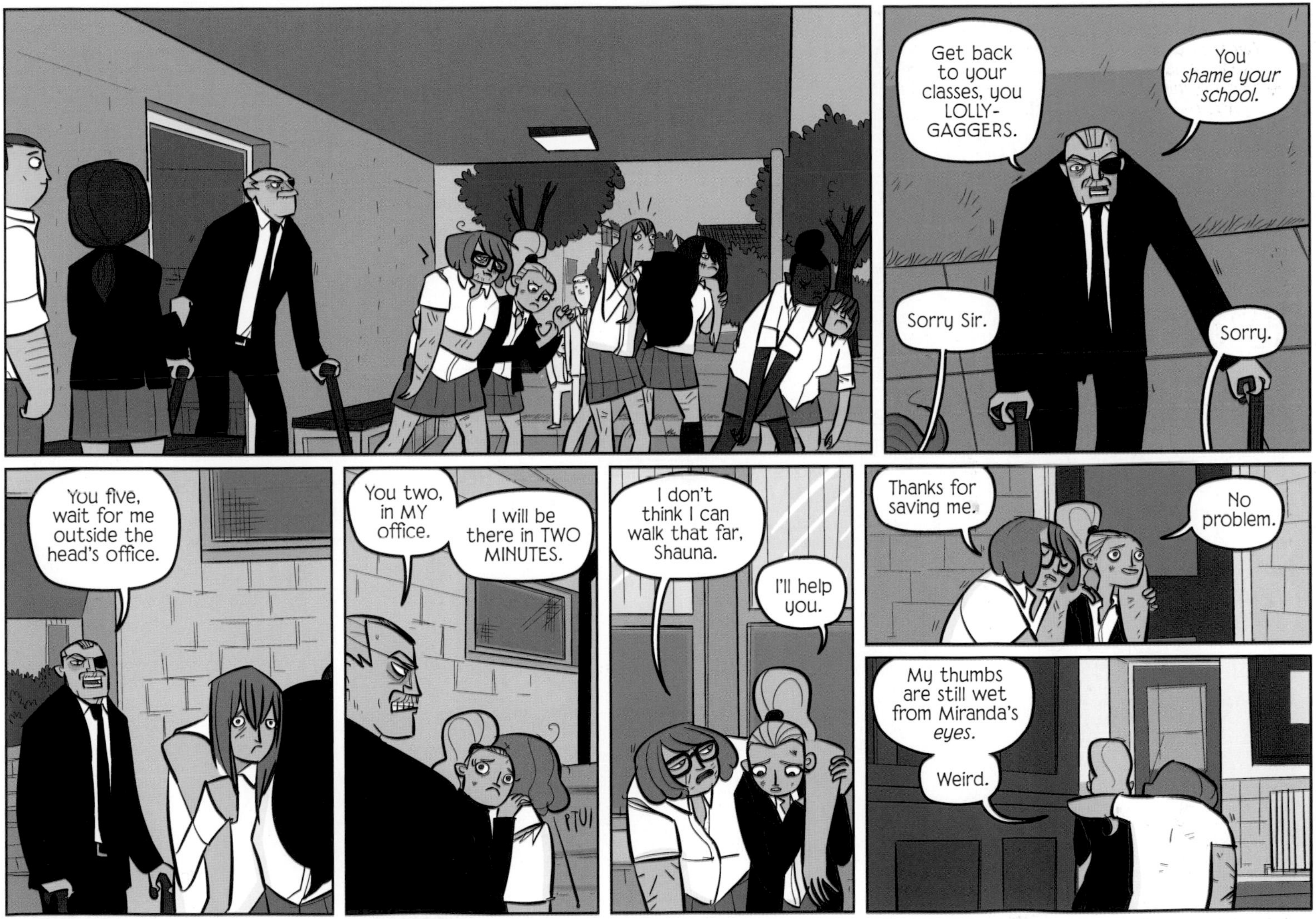
Get back to your classes, you LOLLY-GAGGERS.
You *shame your school.*
Sorry Sir.
Sorry.
You five, wait for me outside the head's office.
You two, in MY office.
I will be there in TWO MINUTES.
PTUI
I don't think I can walk that far, Shauna.
I'll help you.
Thanks for saving me.
No problem.
My thumbs are still wet from Miranda's *eyes.*
Weird.

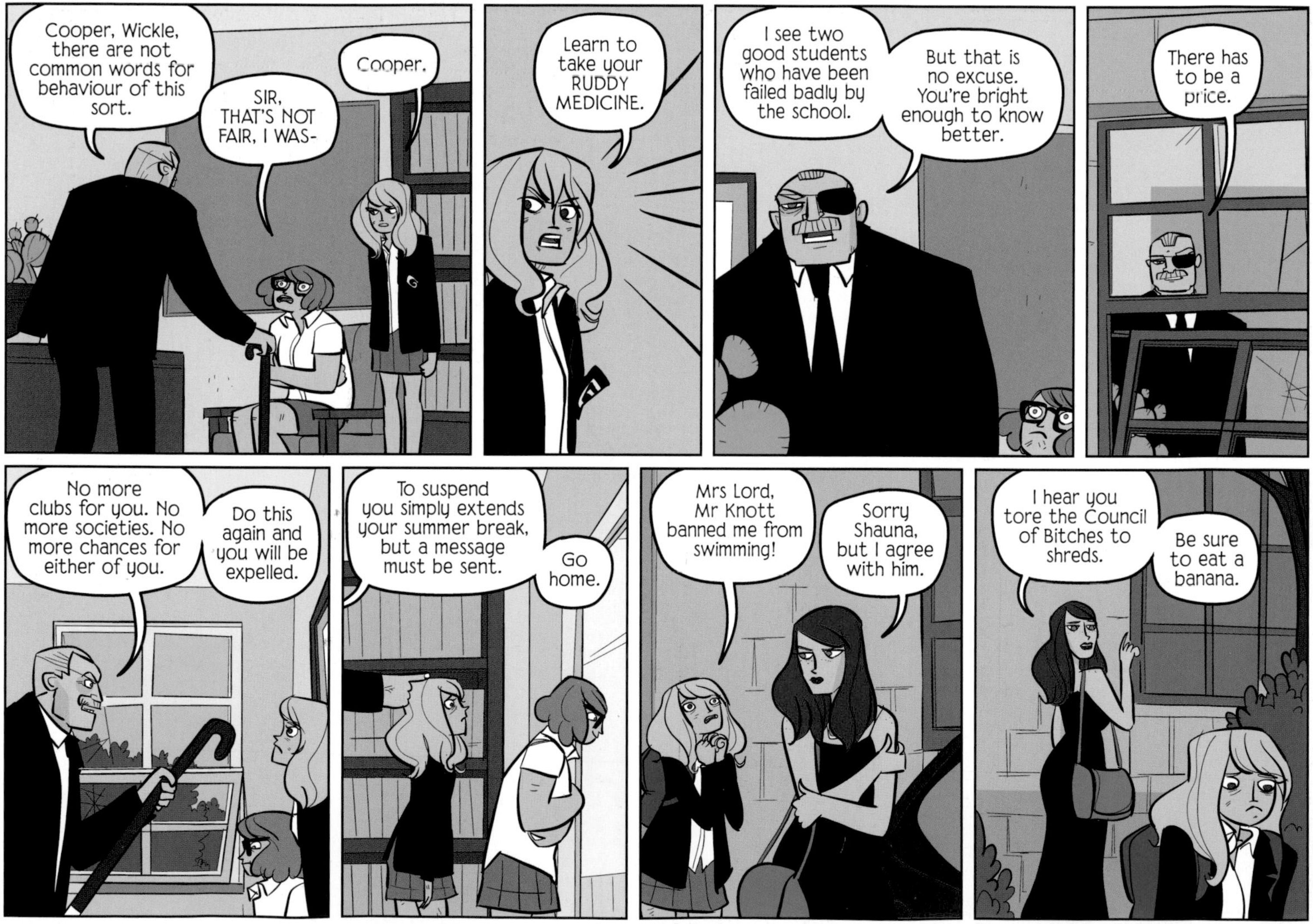
Cooper, Wickle, there are not common words for behaviour of this sort.
SIR, THAT'S NOT FAIR, I WAS-
Cooper.
Learn to take your RUDDY MEDICINE.
I see two good students who have been failed badly by the school.
But that is no excuse. You're bright enough to know better.
There has to be a price.
No more clubs for you. No more societies. No more chances for either of you.
Do this again and you will be expelled.
To suspend you simply extends your summer break, but a message must be sent.
Go home.
Mrs Lord, Mr Knott banned me from swimming!
Sorry Shauna, but I agree with him.
I hear you tore the Council of Bitches to shreds.
Be sure to eat a banana.

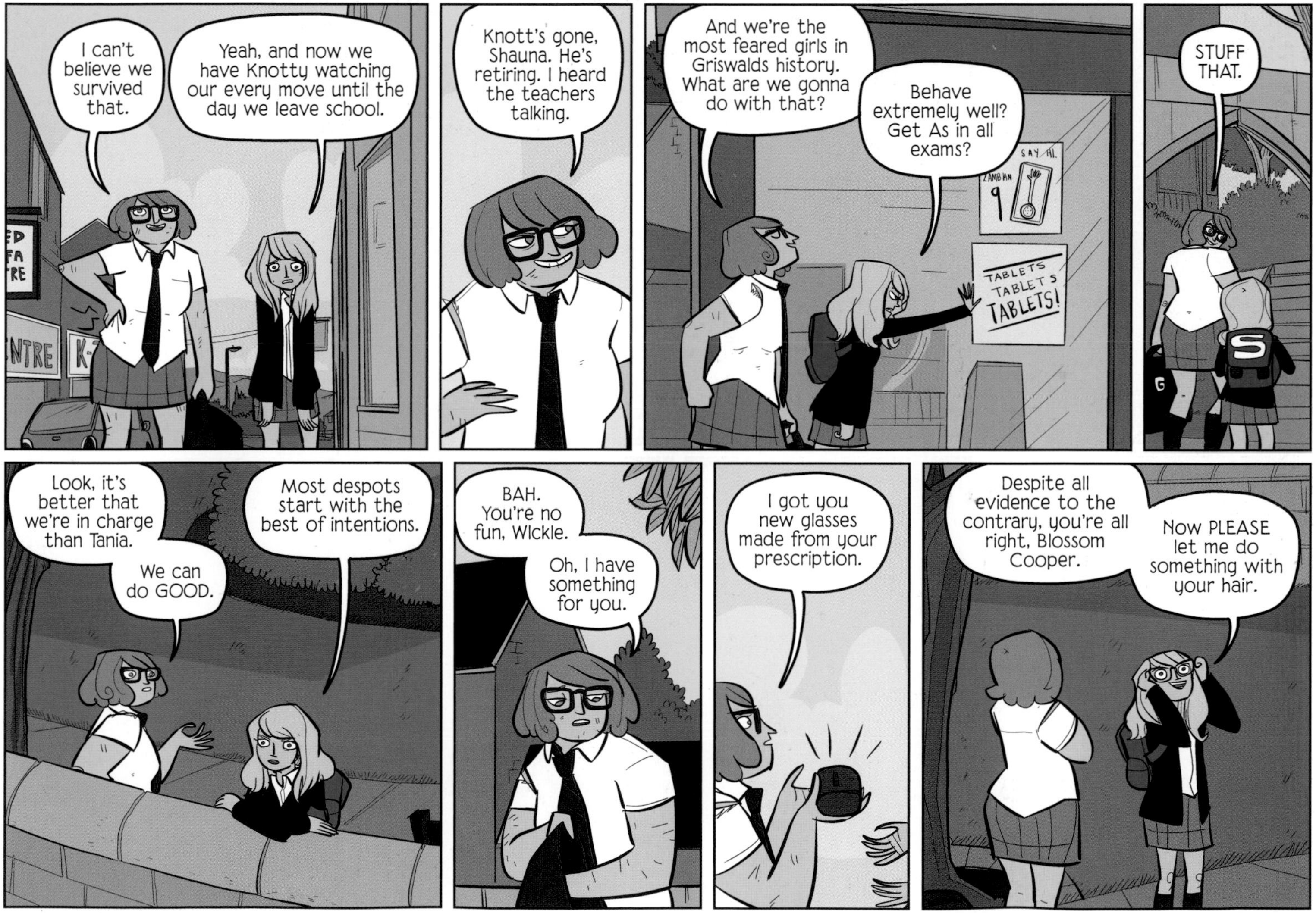
I can't believe we survived that.
Yeah, and now we have Knotty watching our every move until the day we leave school.
Knott's gone, Shauna. He's retiring. I heard the teachers talking.
And we're the most feared girls in Griswalds history. What are we gonna do with that?
Behave extremely well? Get As in all exams?
SAY HI.
ZAMBIAN
9
TABLETS
TABLETS
TABLETS!
STUFF THAT.
Look, it's better that we're in charge than Tania.
We can do GOOD.
Most despots start with the best of intentions.
BAH. You're no fun, Wickle.
Oh, I have something for you.
I got you new glasses made from your prescription.
Despite all evidence to the contrary, you're all right, Blossom Cooper.
Now PLEASE let me do something with your hair.

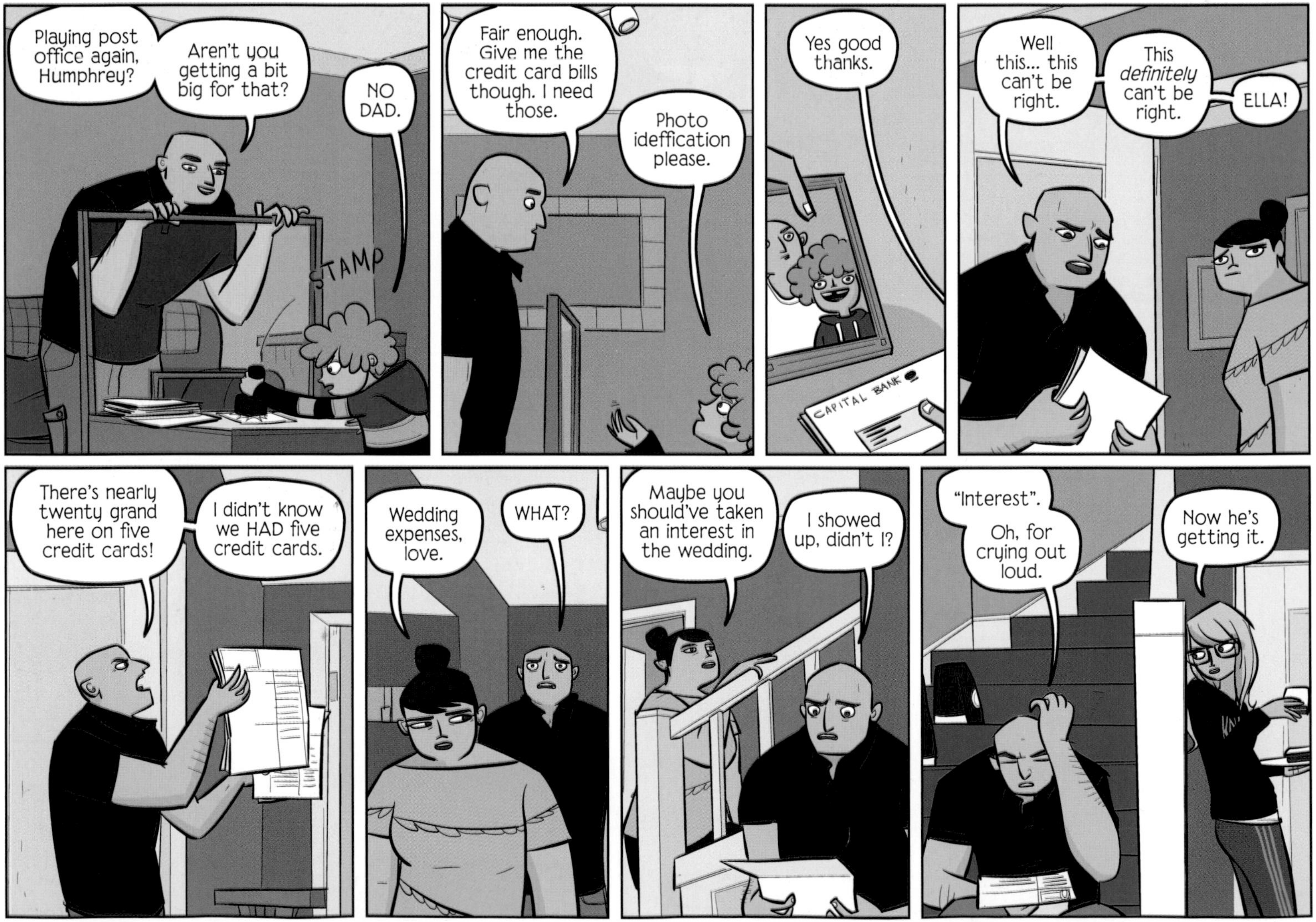
Playing post office again, Humphrey?
Aren't you getting a bit big for that?
NO DAD.
STAMP
Fair enough. Give me the credit card bills though. I need those.
Photo ideffication please.
Yes good thanks.
CAPITAL BANK
Well this... this can't be right.
This *definitely* can't be right.
ELLA!
There's nearly twenty grand here on five credit cards!
I didn't know we HAD five credit cards.
Wedding expenses, love.
WHAT?
Maybe you should've taken an interest in the wedding.
I showed up, didn't I?
"Interest".
Oh, for crying out loud.
Now he's getting it.

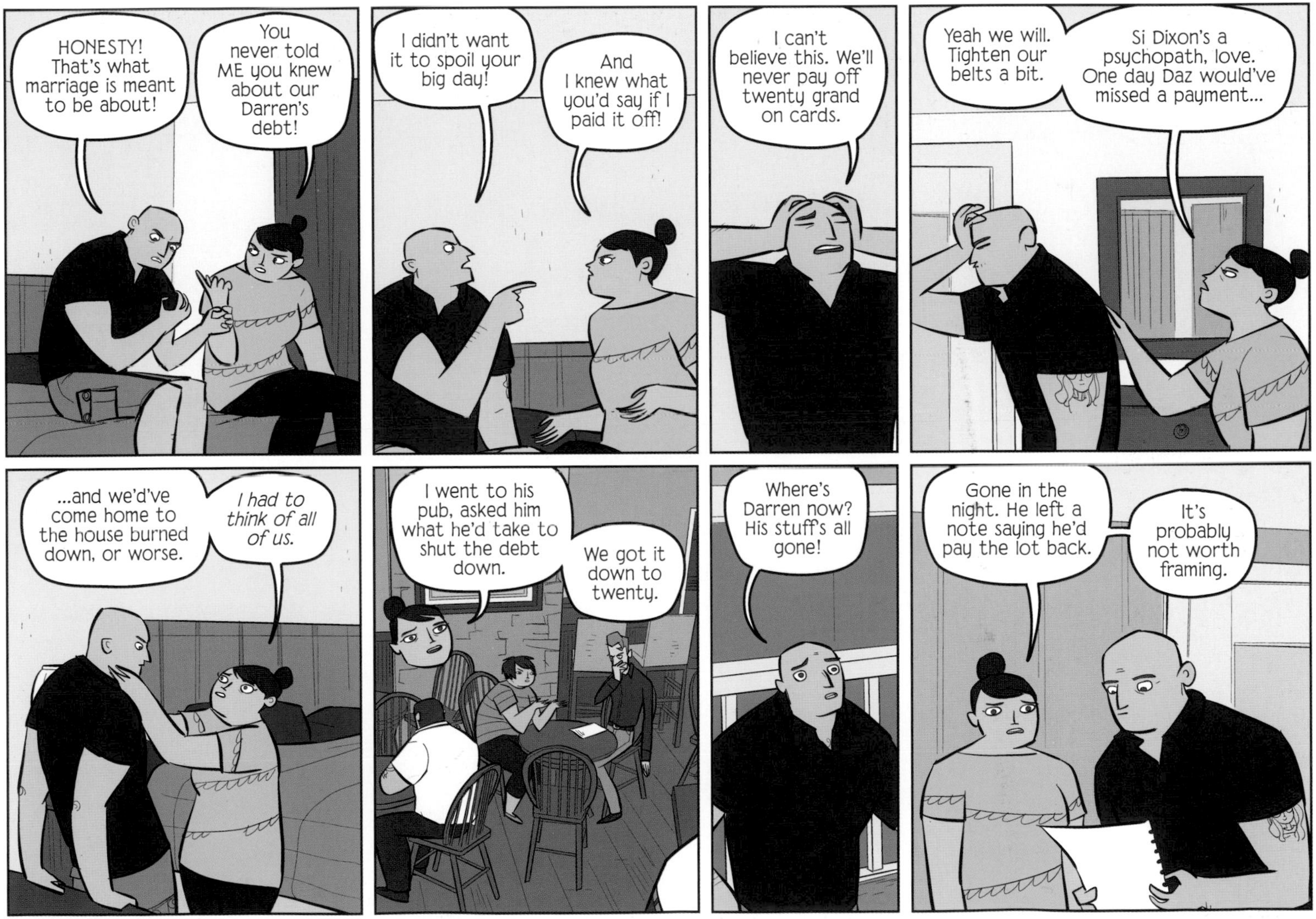

HONESTY! That's what marriage is meant to be about!
You never told ME you knew about our Darren's debt!
I didn't want it to spoil your big day!
And I knew what you'd say if I paid it off!
I can't believe this. We'll never pay off twenty grand on cards.
Yeah we will. Tighten our belts a bit.
Si Dixon's a psychopath, love. One day Daz would've missed a payment...
...and we'd've come home to the house burned down, or worse.
I had to think of all of us.
I went to his pub, asked him what he'd take to shut the debt down.
We got it down to twenty.
Where's Darren now? His stuff's all gone!
Gone in the night. He left a note saying he'd pay the lot back.
It's probably not worth framing.

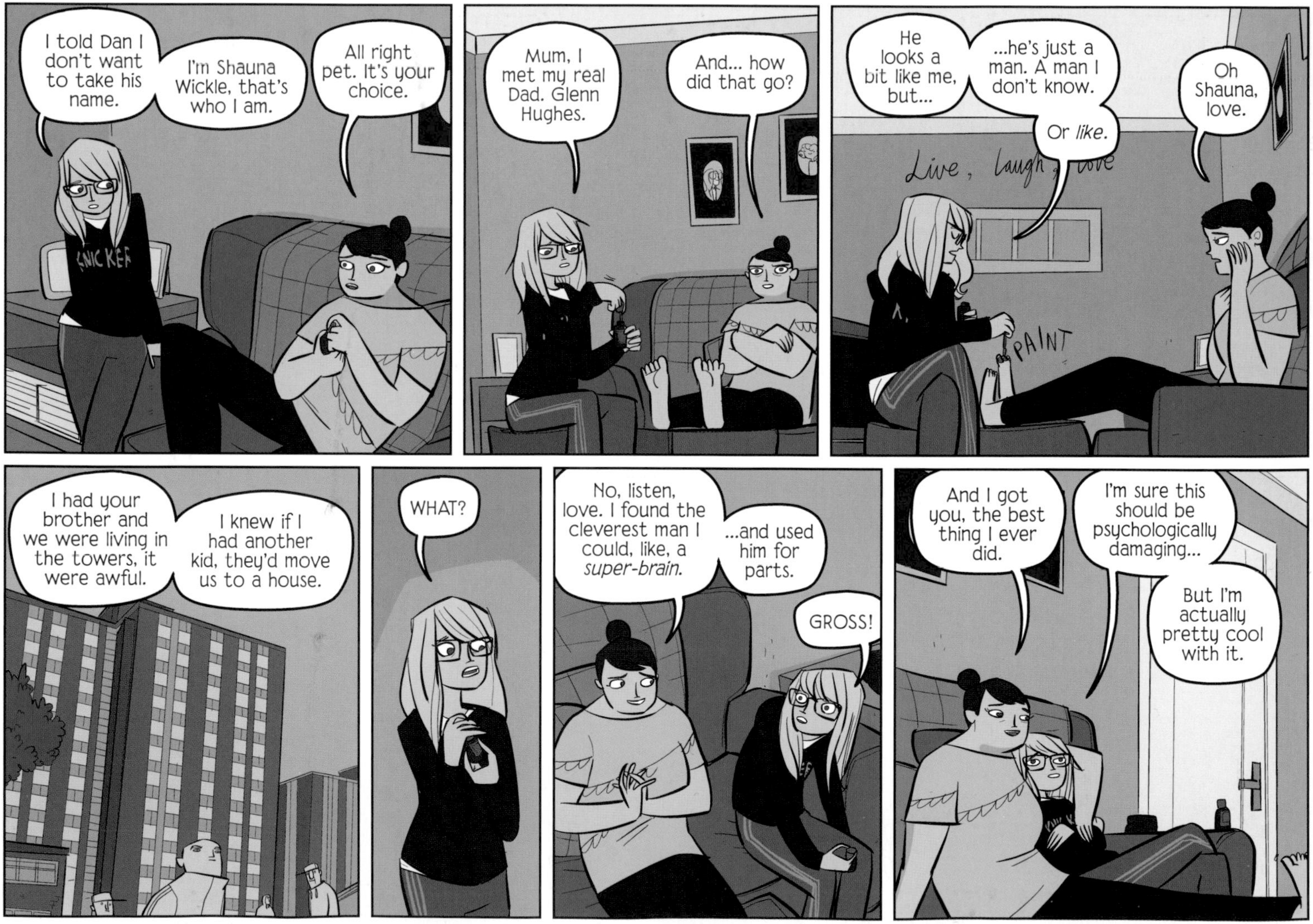
I told Dan I don't want to take his name.
I'm Shauna Wickle, that's who I am.
All right pet. It's your choice.
Mum, I met my real Dad. Glenn Hughes.
And... how did that go?
He looks a bit like me, but...
...he's just a man. A man I don't know.
Or *like*.
Oh Shauna, love.
PAINT
I had your brother and we were living in the towers, it were awful.
I knew if I had another kid, they'd move us to a house.
WHAT?
No, listen, love. I found the cleverest man I could, like, a *super-brain*.
...and used him for parts.
GROSS!
And I got you, the best thing I ever did.
I'm sure this should be psychologically damaging...
But I'm actually pretty cool with it.

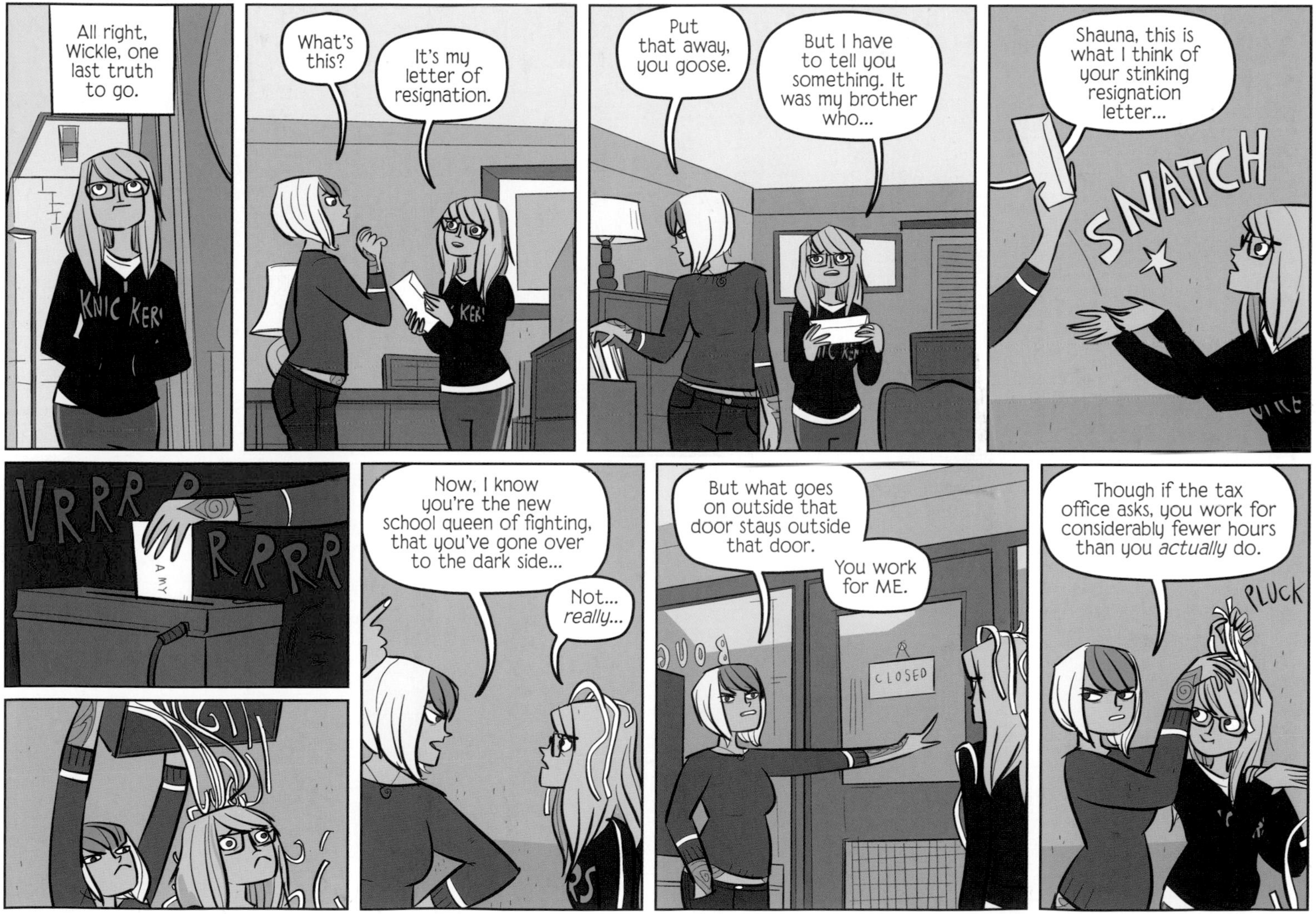
All right, Wickle, one last truth to go.
What's this?
It's my letter of resignation.
Put that away, you goose.
But I have to tell you something. It was my brother who...
Shauna, this is what I think of your stinking resignation letter...
SNATCH
VRRR
RRRRR
AMY
Now, I know you're the new school queen of fighting, that you've gone over to the dark side...
Not... *really*...
But what goes on outside that door stays outside that door.
You work for ME.
CLOSED
Though if the tax office asks, you work for considerably fewer hours than you *actually* do.
PLUCK

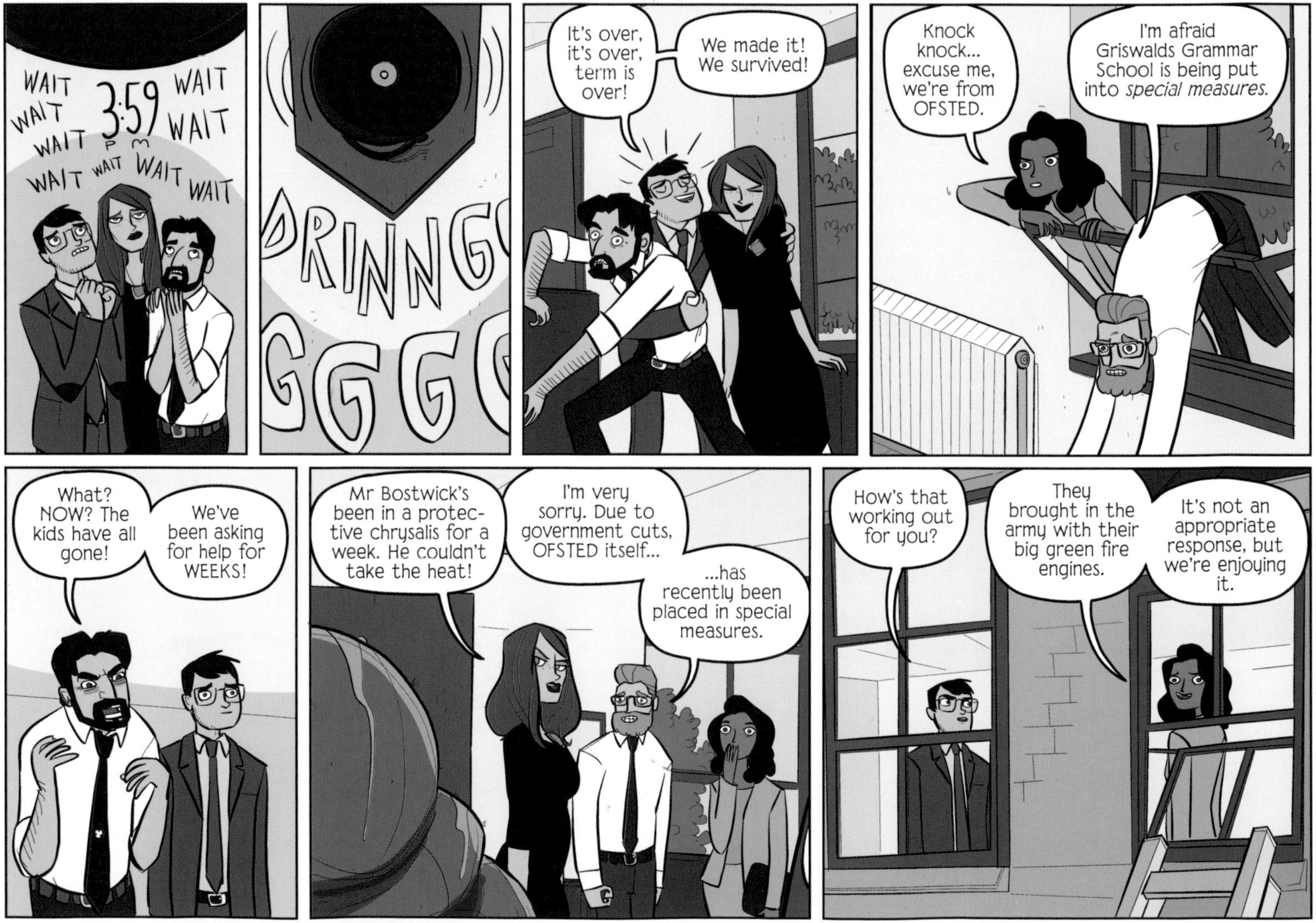
WAIT WAIT WAIT 3:59 PM WAIT WAIT WAIT WAIT WAIT WAIT WAIT
DRINNGGGGG
It's over, it's over, term is over!
We made it! We survived!
Knock knock... excuse me, we're from OFSTED.
I'm afraid Griswalds Grammar School is being put into *special measures.*
What? NOW? The kids have all gone!
We've been asking for help for WEEKS!
Mr Bostwick's been in a protective chrysalis for a week. He couldn't take the heat!
I'm very sorry. Due to government cuts, OFSTED itself...
...has recently been placed in special measures.
How's that working out for you?
They brought in the army with their big green fire engines.
It's not an appropriate response, but we're enjoying it.

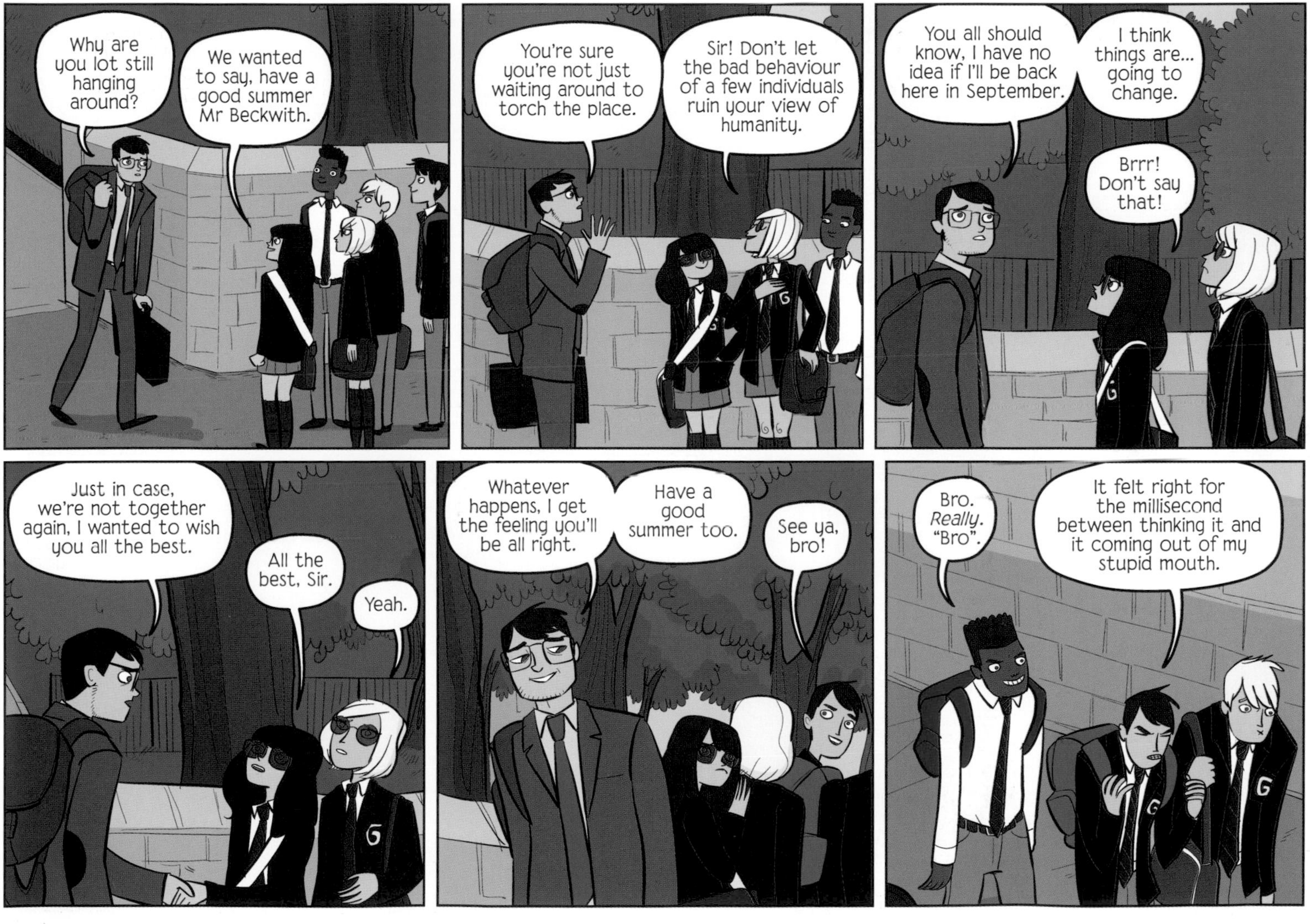
Why are you lot still hanging around?
We wanted to say, have a good summer Mr Beckwith.
You're sure you're not just waiting around to torch the place.
Sir! Don't let the bad behaviour of a few individuals ruin your view of humanity.
You all should know, I have no idea if I'll be back here in September.
I think things are... going to change.
Brrr! Don't say that!
Just in case, we're not together again, I wanted to wish you all the best.
All the best, Sir.
Yeah.
Whatever happens, I get the feeling you'll be all right.
Have a good summer too.
See ya, bro!
Bro. *Really*. "Bro".
It felt right for the millisecond between thinking it and it coming out of my stupid mouth.

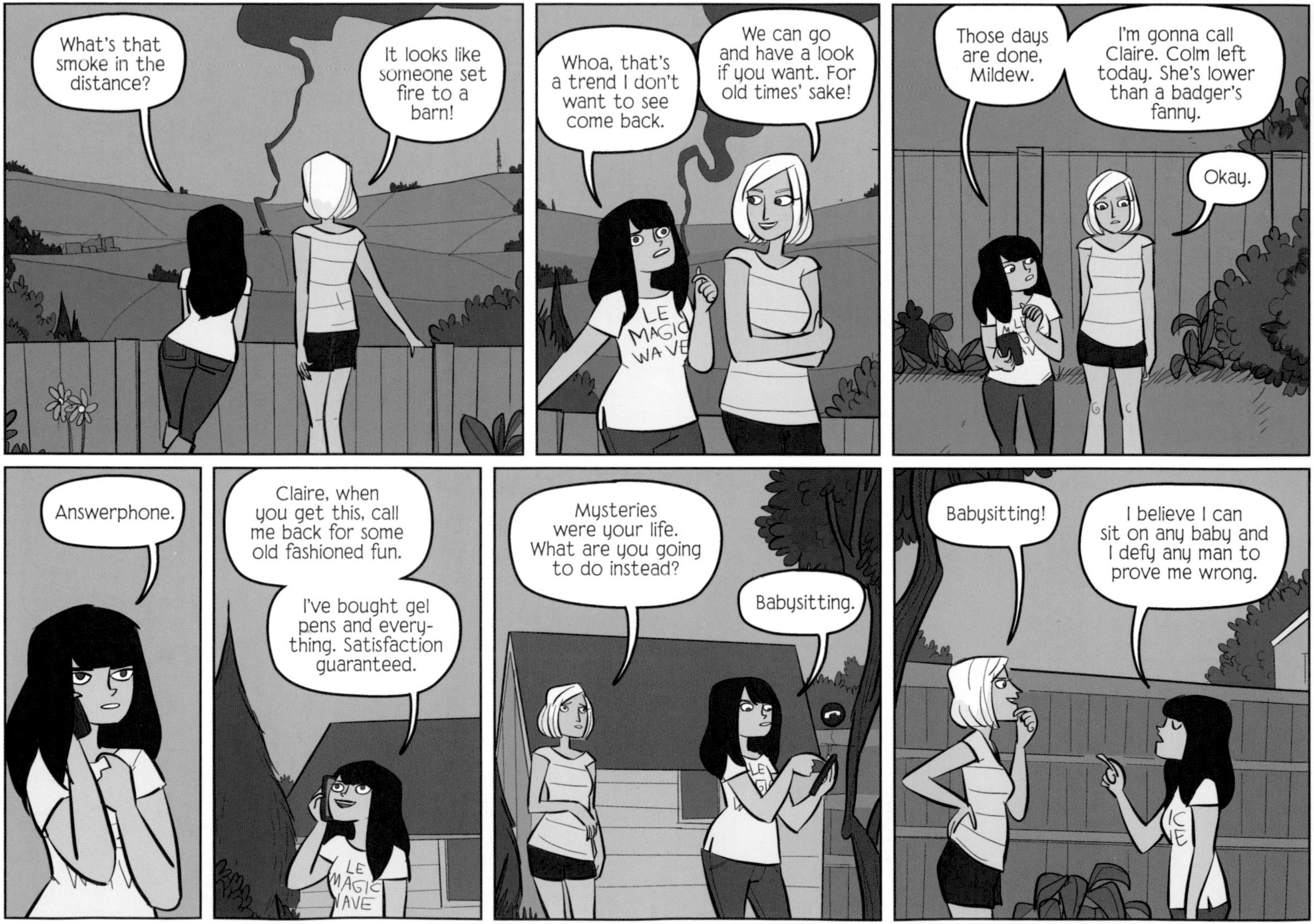
What's that smoke in the distance?
It looks like someone set fire to a barn!
Whoa, that's a trend I don't want to see come back.
We can go and have a look if you want. For old times' sake!
Those days are done, Mildew.
I'm gonna call Claire. Colm left today. She's lower than a badger's fanny.
Okay.
LE MAGIC WAVE
Answerphone.
Claire, when you get this, call me back for some old fashioned fun.
I've bought gel pens and every-thing. Satisfaction guaranteed.
LE MAGIC WAVE
Mysteries were your life. What are you going to do instead?
Babysitting.
Babysitting!
I believe I can sit on any baby and I defy any man to prove me wrong.

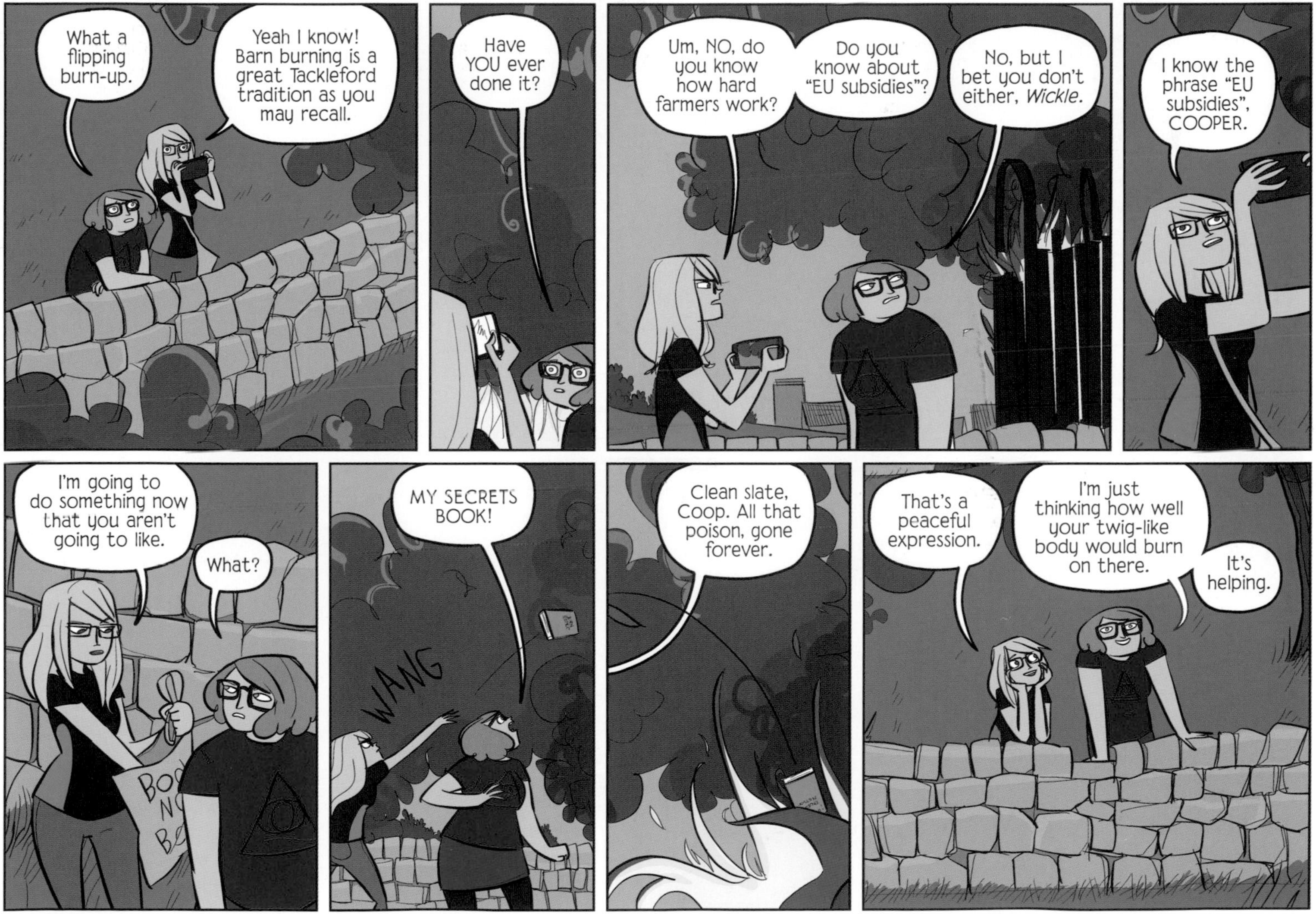
What a flipping burn-up.
Yeah I know! Barn burning is a great Tackleford tradition as you may recall.
Have YOU ever done it?
Um, NO, do you know how hard farmers work?
Do you know about "EU subsidies"?
No, but I bet you don't either, *Wickle.*
I know the phrase "EU subsidies", COOPER.
I'm going to do something now that you aren't going to like.
What?
MY SECRETS BOOK!
WANG
Clean slate, Coop. All that poison, gone forever.
That's a peaceful expression.
I'm just thinking how well your twig-like body would burn on there.
It's helping.

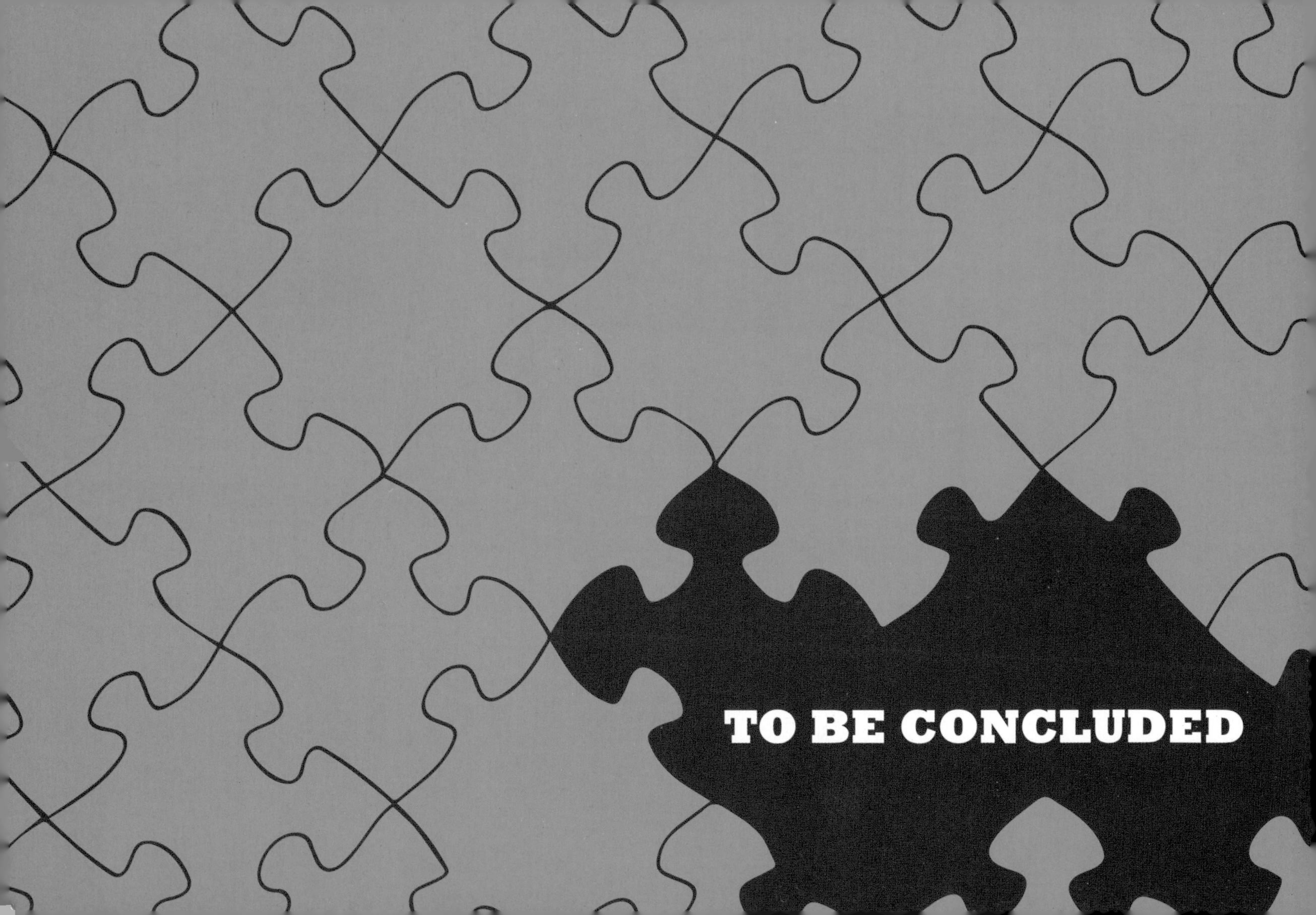
TO BE CONCLUDED

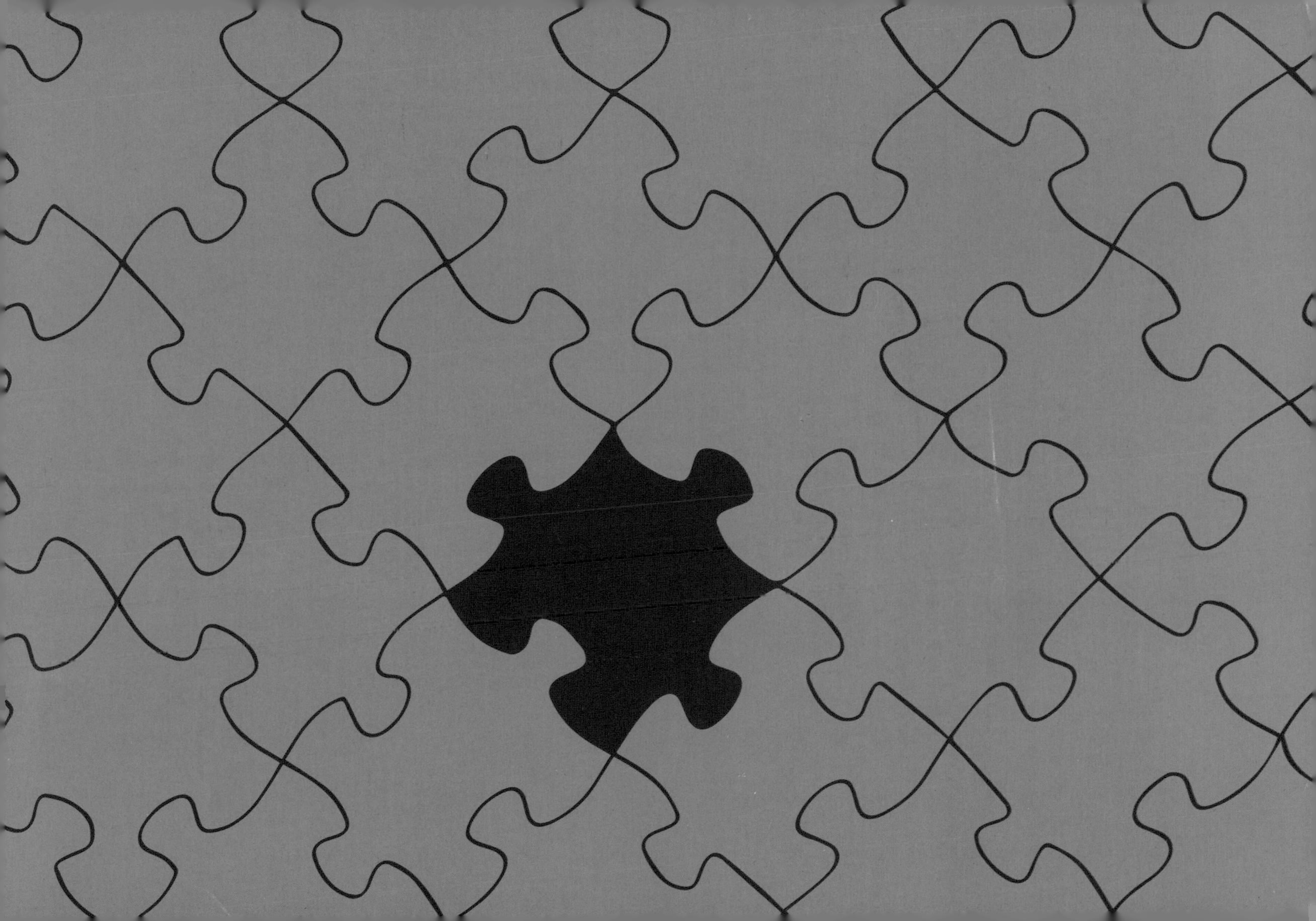

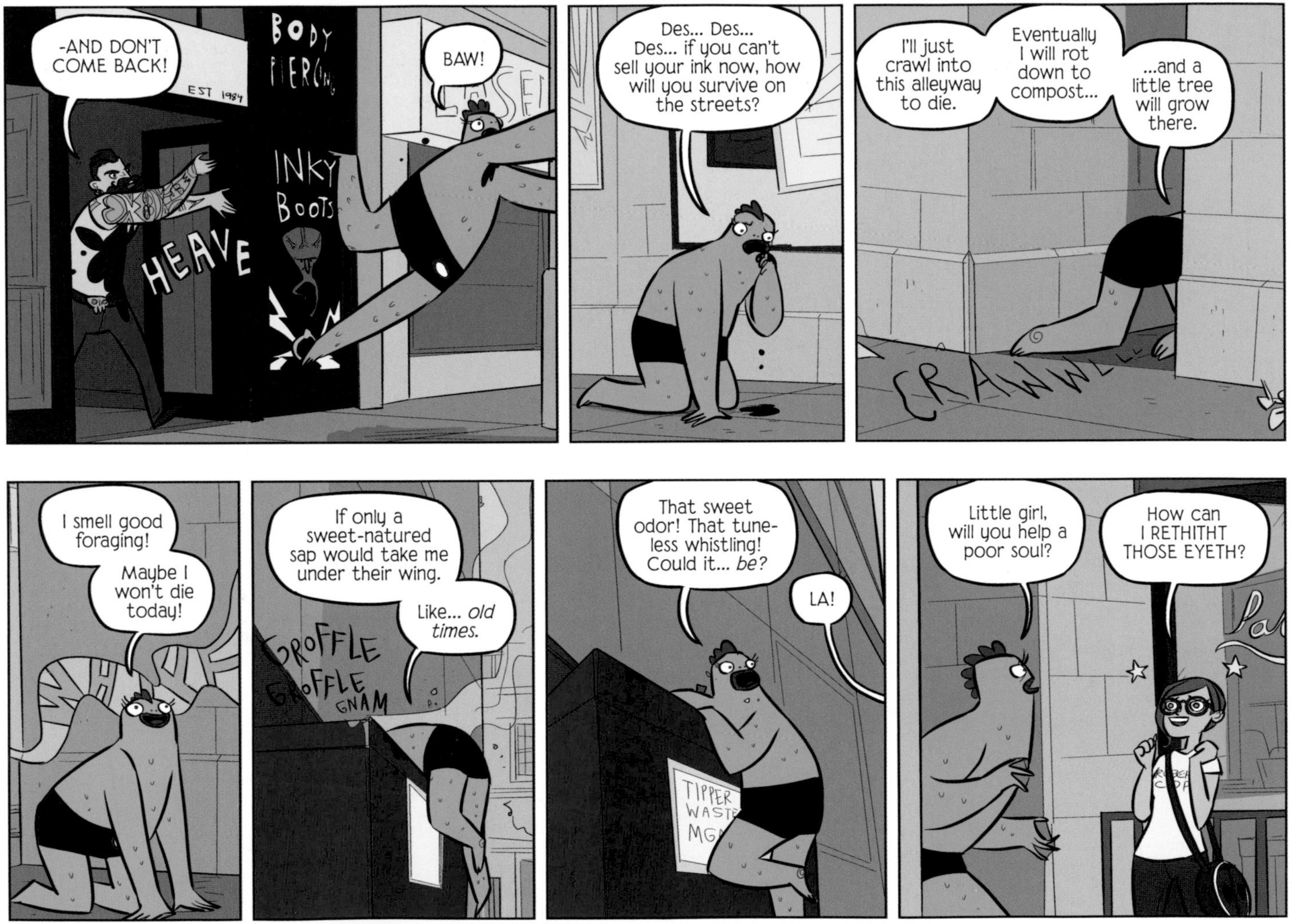
-AND DON'T COME BACK!
EST 1984
BODY PIERCING
INKY BOOTS
HEAVE
BAW!
Des... Des... Des... if you can't sell your ink now, how will you survive on the streets?
I'll just crawl into this alleyway to die.
Eventually I will rot down to compost...
...and a little tree will grow there.
CRAWWL
I smell good foraging!
Maybe I won't die today!
If only a sweet-natured sap would take me under their wing.
Like... *old times.*
GROFFLE GROFFLE GNAM
That sweet odor! That tuneless whistling! Could it... *be?*
LA!
Little girl, will you help a poor soul?
How can I RETHITHT THOSE EYETH?

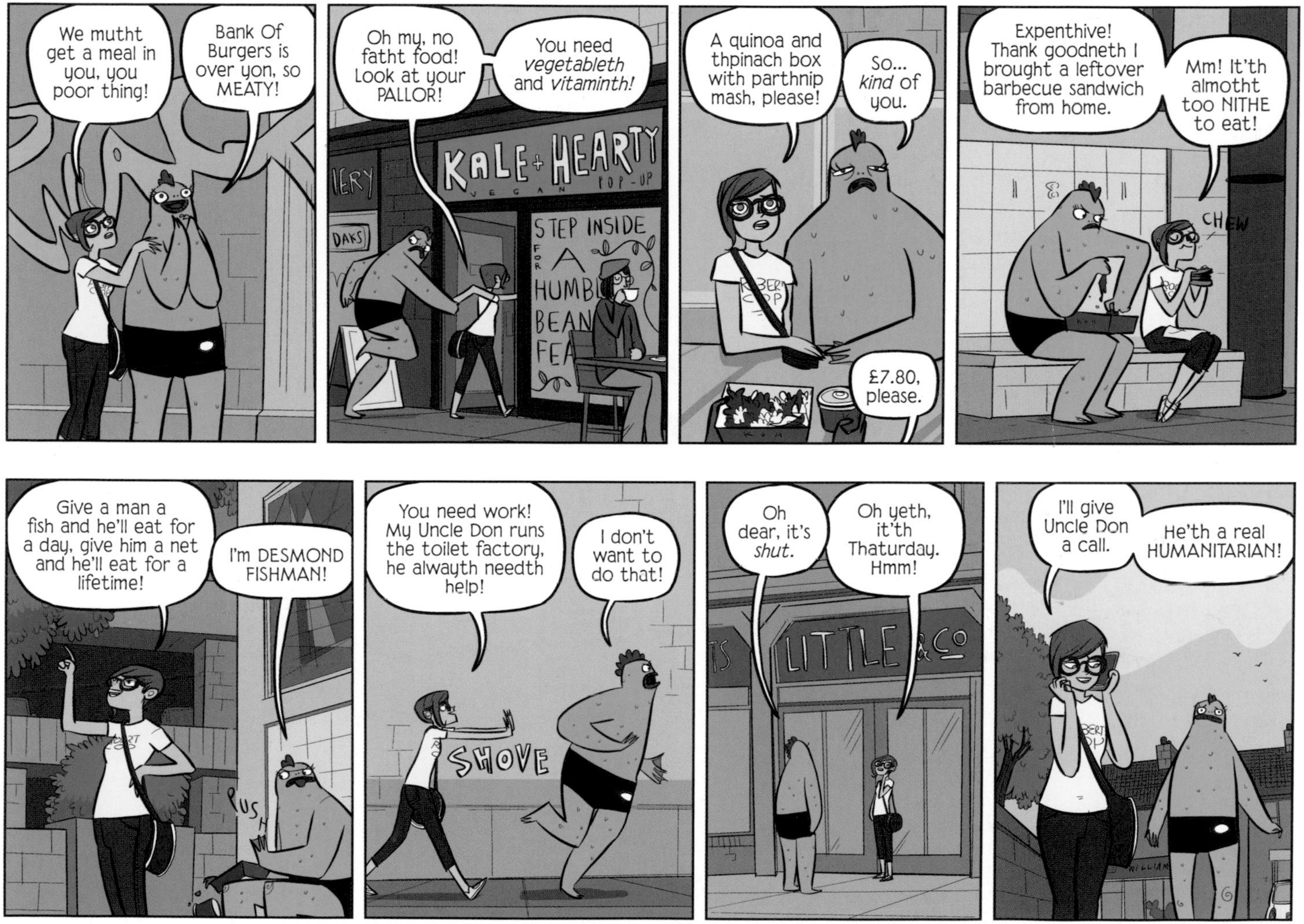

We mutht get a meal in you, you poor thing!
Bank Of Burgers is over yon, so MEATY!
Oh my, no fatht food! Look at your PALLOR!
You need *vegetableth* and *vitaminth!*
KALE + HEARTY
VEGAN POP-UP
STEP INSIDE FOR A
A quinoa and thpinach box with parthnip mash, please!
So... *kind* of you.
£7.80, please.
Expenthive! Thank goodneth I brought a leftover barbecue sandwich from home.
Mm! It'th almotht too NITHE to eat!
CHEW
Give a man a fish and he'll eat for a day, give him a net and he'll eat for a lifetime!
I'm DESMOND FISHMAN!
PUSH
You need work! My Uncle Don runs the toilet factory, he alwayth needth help!
I don't want to do that!
SHOVE
Oh dear, it's *shut*.
Oh yeth, it'th Thaturday. Hmm!
LITTLE &Co
I'll give Uncle Don a call.
He'th a real HUMANITARIAN!

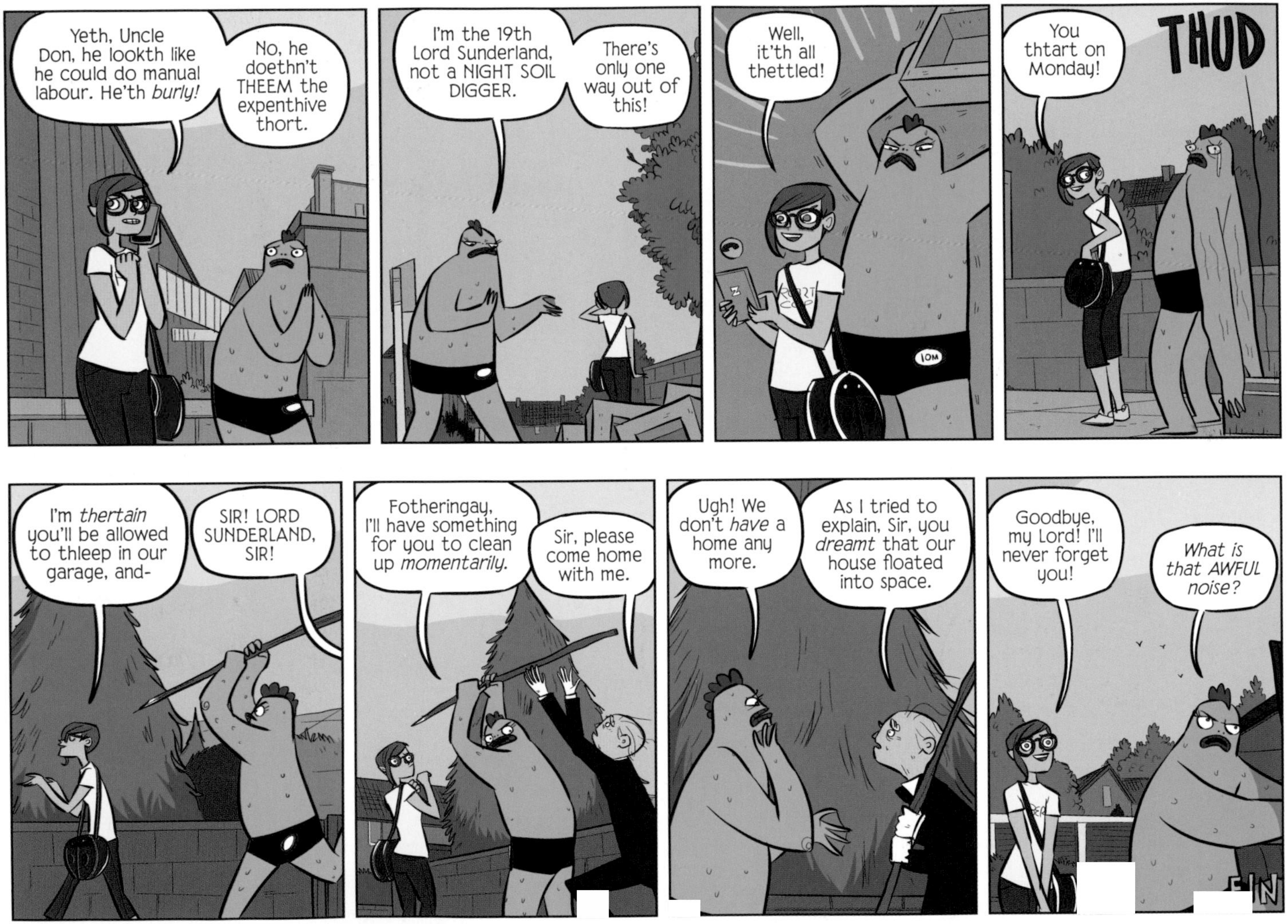

Yeth, Uncle Don, he lookth like he could do manual labour. He'th *burly!*
No, he doethn't THEEM the expenthive thort.
I'm the 19th Lord Sunderland, not a NIGHT SOIL DIGGER.
There's only one way out of this!
Well, it'th all thettled!
10M
You thtart on Monday!
THUD
I'm *thertain* you'll be allowed to thleep in our garage, and-
SIR! LORD SUNDERLAND, SIR!
Fotheringay, I'll have something for you to clean up *momentarily.*
Sir, please come home with me.
Ugh! We don't *have* a home any more.
As I tried to explain, Sir, you *dreamt* that our house floated into space.
Goodbye, my Lord! I'll never forget you!
What is that AWFUL noise?
FIN

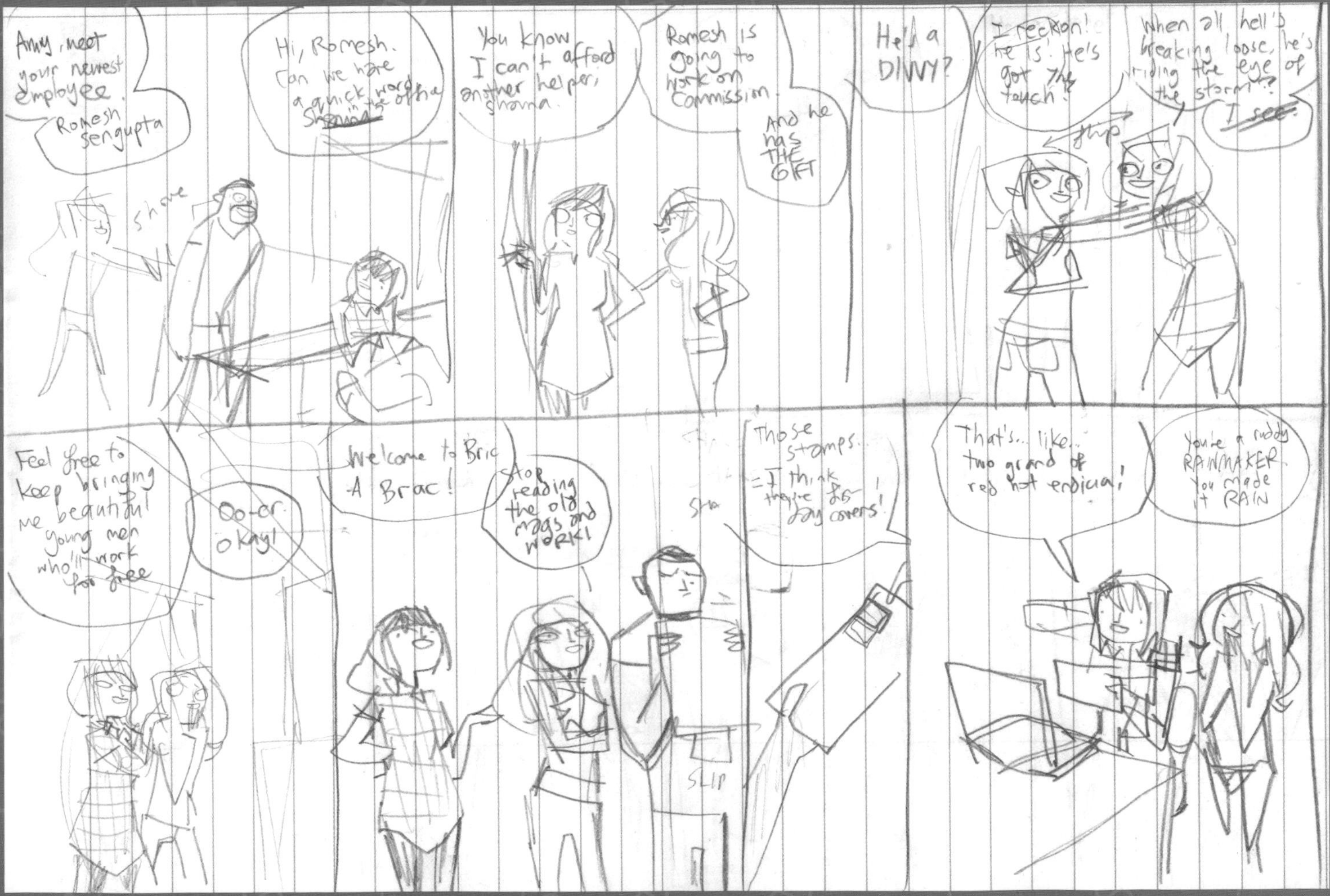

Amy, meet your newest employee.
Romesh Sengupta
shove
Hi, Romesh. Can we have a quick word
You know I can't afford another helper, Shauna.
Romesh is going to work on commission.
And he has THE GIFT
He's a DIVVY?
I reckon! he is! He's got the touch!
When all hell's breaking loose, he's riding the eye of the storm!
flip
Feel free to keep bringing me beautiful young men who'll work for free
Oo-er okay!
Welcome to Bric-A-Brac!
Stop reading the old mags and work!
Those stamps...
I think they're first day covers!
SLIP
That's... like... two grand of red hot
You're a ruddy RAINMAKER You made it RAIN

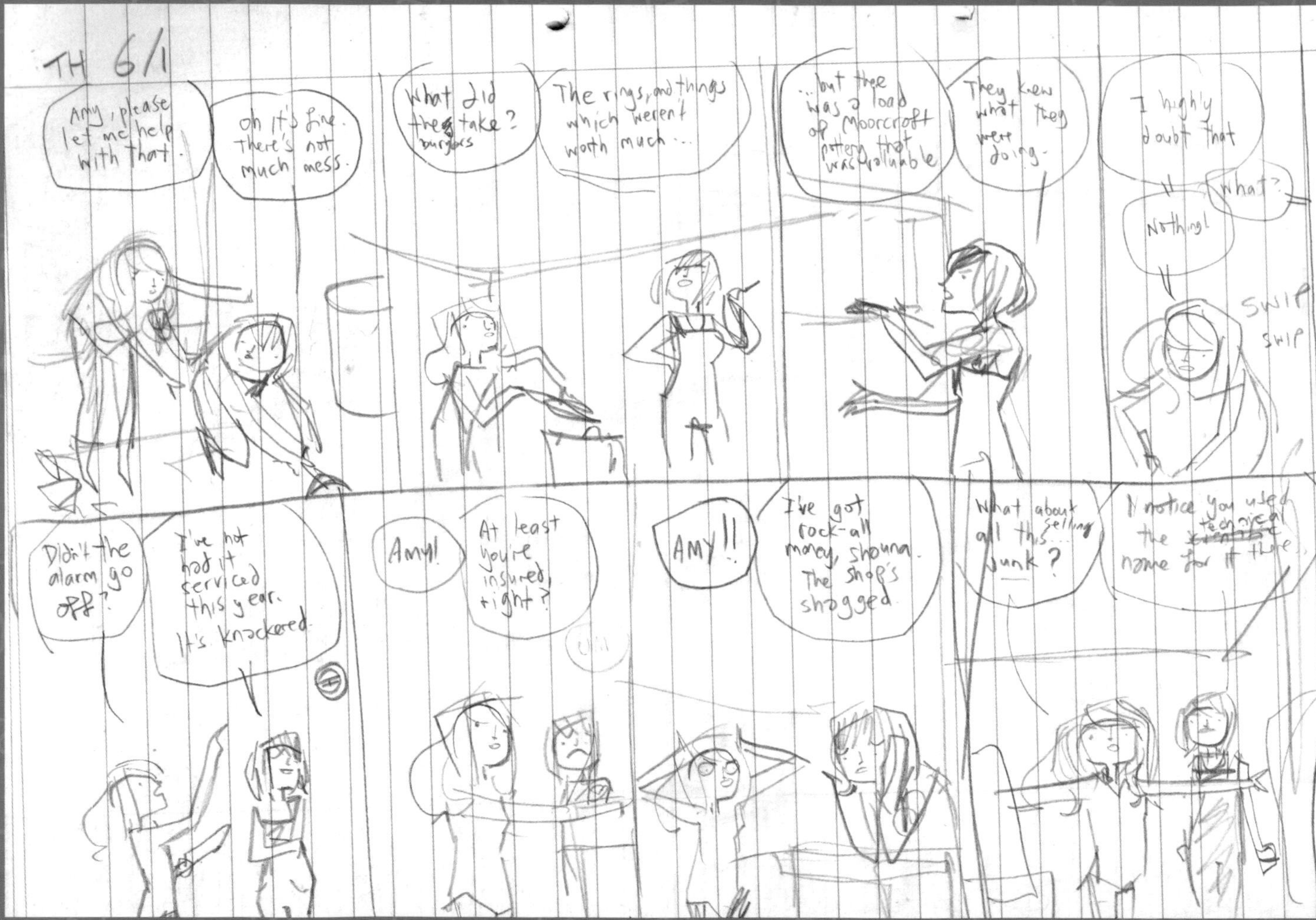
TH 6/1
Amy, please let me help with that.
Oh it's fine. There's not much mess.
What did the burglars take?
The rings, and things which weren't worth much...
...but there was a load of Moorcroft pottery that was valuable
They knew what they were doing.
I highly doubt that
What?
Nothing!
SWIP SWIP
Didn't the alarm go off?
I've not had it serviced this year. It's knackered.
Amy!
At least you're insured, right?
AMY!!
I've got rock-all money, Shouna. The shop's shagged.
What about selling all this... junk?
I notice you used the technical name for it there.

JOHN ALLISON

Born in a hidden village deep within the British Alps, John Allison came into this world a respectable baby with style and taste. Having been exposed to American comics at an early age, he spent decades honing his keen mind and his massive body in order to burn out this colonial cultural infection.

One of the longest continuously publishing independent web-based cartoonists, John has plied his trade since the late nineties moving from *Bobbins* to *Scary Go Round* to *Bad Machinery*, developing the deeply weird world of Tackleford long after many of his fellow artists were ground into dust and bones by Time Itself.

He has only once shed a single tear, but you only meet Sergio Aragonés for the first time once.

John resides in Letchworth Garden City, England and is known to his fellow villagers only as He Who Has Conquered.

—Contributed by Richard Stevens III

"THE TREASURE OF BRITANNIA"

READ MORE BAD MACHINERY!

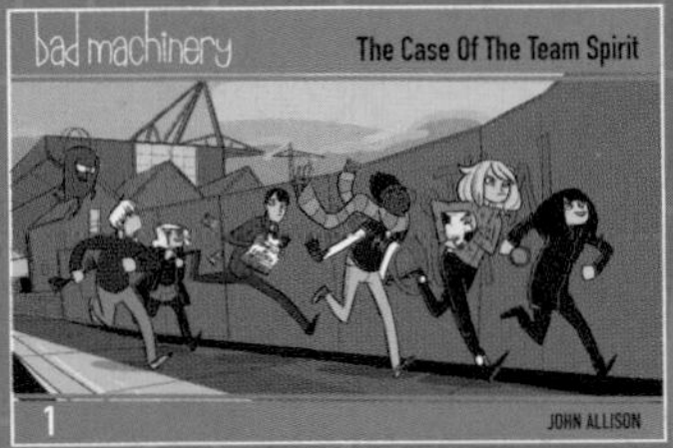

bad machinery
The Case Of The Team Spirit
1
JOHN ALLISON

BAD MACHINERY, VOLUME 1:
THE CASE OF THE TEAM SPIRIT
ISBN 978-1-62010-387-6
Pocket Edition In Stores Now!

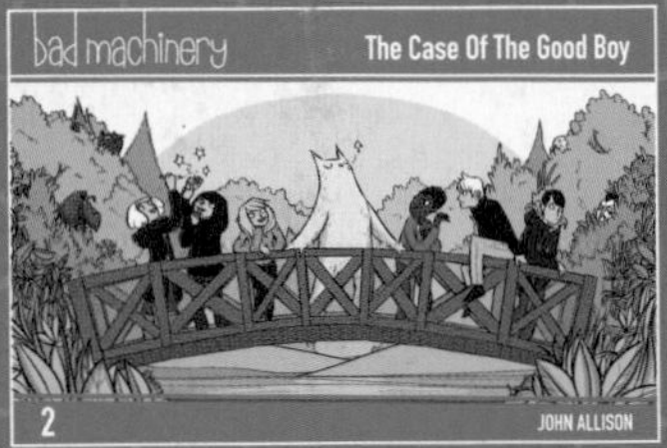

bad machinery
The Case Of The Good Boy
2
JOHN ALLISON

BAD MACHINERY, VOLUME 2:
THE CASE OF THE GOOD BOY
ISBN 978-1-62010-421-7
Pocket Edition In Stores Now!

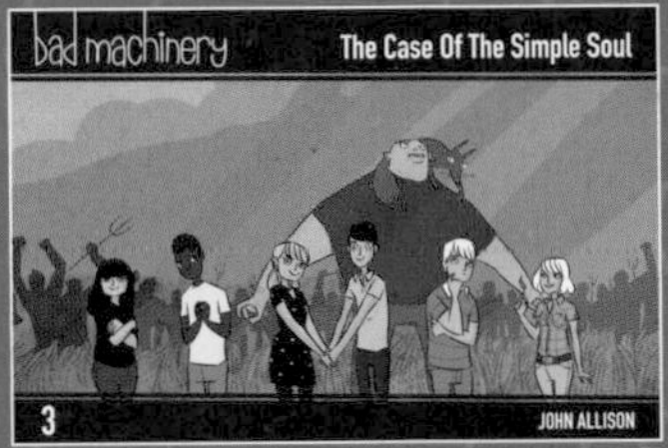

bad machinery
The Case Of The Simple Soul
3
JOHN ALLISON

BAD MACHINERY, VOLUME 3:
THE CASE OF THE SIMPLE SOUL
ISBN 978-1-62010-443-9
Pocket Edition In Stores Now!

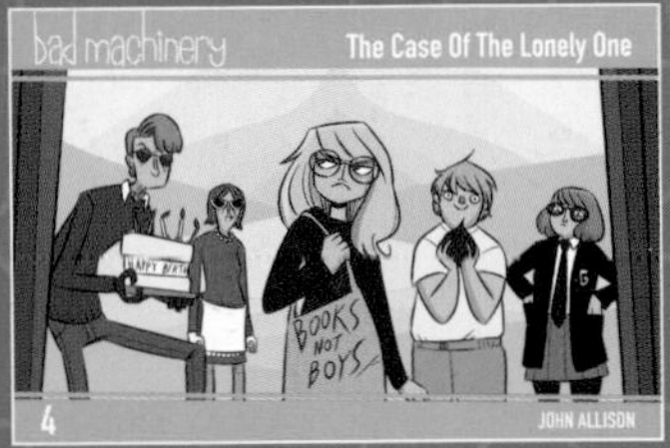

bad machinery
The Case Of The Lonely One
BOOKS NOT BOYS
4
JOHN ALLISON

BAD MACHINERY, VOLUME 4:
THE CASE OF THE LONELY ONE
ISBN 978-1-62010-457-6
Pocket Edition In Stores Now!

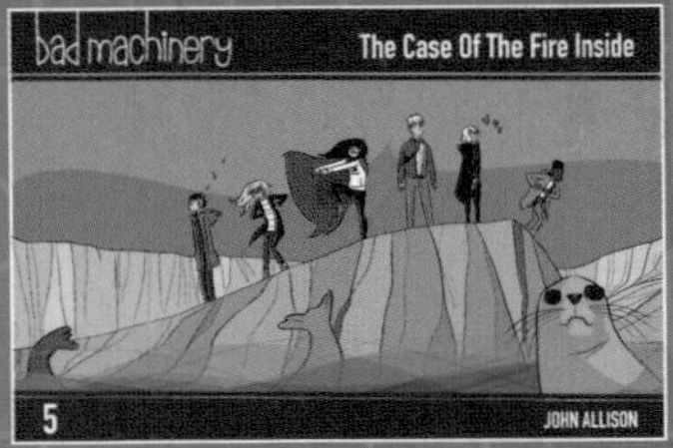

bad machinery
The Case Of The Fire Inside
5
JOHN ALLISON

BAD MACHINERY, VOLUME 5:
THE CASE OF THE FIRE INSIDE
ISBN 978-1-62010-504-7
Pocket Edition In Stores Now!

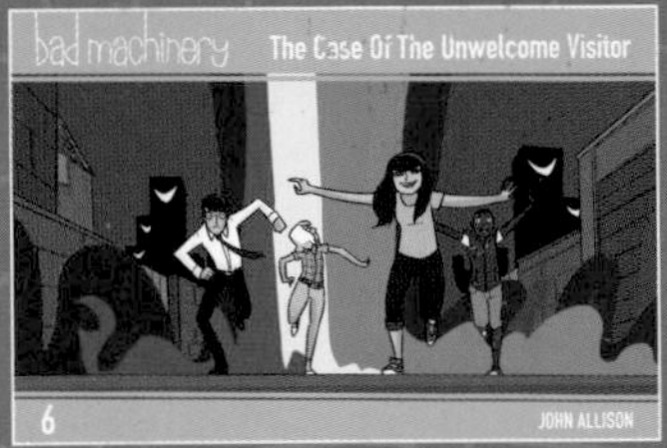

bad machinery
The Case Of The Unwelcome Visitor
6
JOHN ALLISON

BAD MACHINERY, VOLUME 6:
THE CASE OF THE UNWELCOME VISITOR
ISBN 978-1-62010-543-6
Pocket Edition In Stores Now!

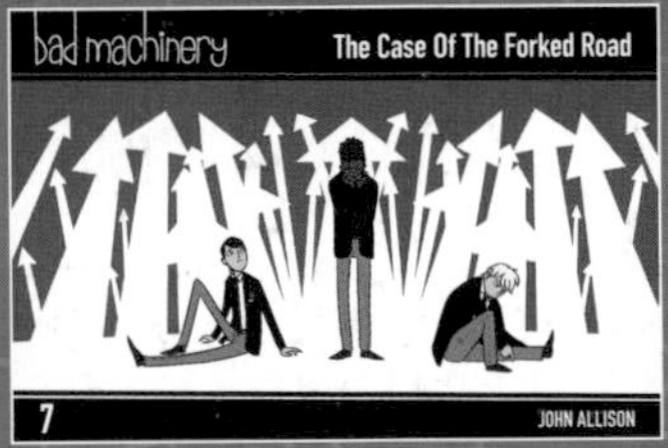

bad machinery
The Case Of The Forked Road
7
JOHN ALLISON

BAD MACHINERY, VOLUME 7:
THE CASE OF THE FORKED ROAD
ISBN 978-1-62010-562-7
Pocket Edition In Stores Now!

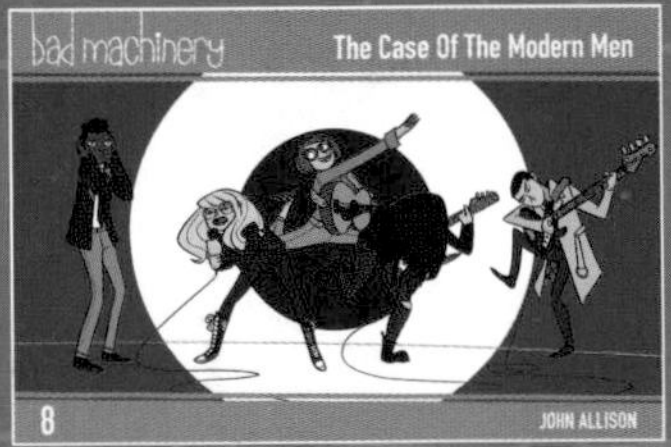

bad machinery
The Case Of The Modern Men
8
JOHN ALLISON

BAD MACHINERY, VOLUME 8:
THE CASE OF THE MODERN MEN
ISBN 978-1-62010-437-8
Pocket Edition In Stores Now!

ONI PRESS
www.onipress.com

bad machinery
THE CASE OF THE SEVERED ALLIANCE

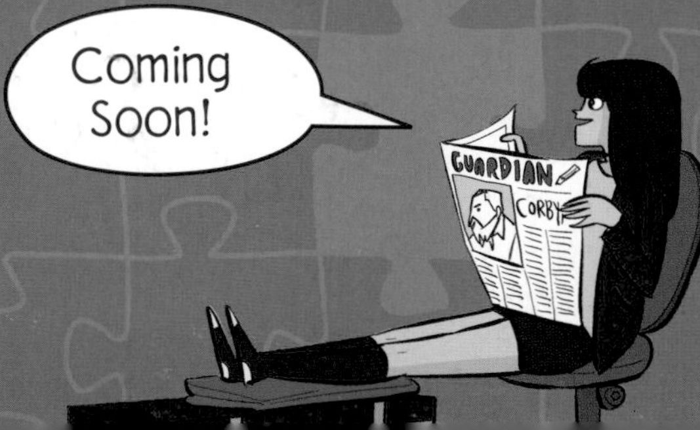

Coming Soon!
GUARDIAN
CORBY

FOR MORE INFORMATION ON THESE AND OTHER FINE ONI PRESS COMIC BOOKS AND GRAPHIC NOVELS VISIT WWW.ONIPRESS.COM.
TO FIND A COMIC SPECIALTY STORE IN YOUR AREA VISIT WWW.COMICSHOPS.US.